ary notables as Mark Twain, Bret Harte, Ambrose Bierce, Dan DeQuille and Eugene Field.

Mr. Myers paints lively portraits of all of them — and the book includes lavish selections from their writings, accompanied by sharp historical commentary and anecdote.

Mr. Myers, in effect, has given us a model anthology of a literature unique in and of its own times. And in doing so he has reaffirmed the Western journalist's lingering reputation as a hoaxer, fulminator, and all-purpose hell raiser — quick with the pistol as well as the composing stick — and verified his true position in American history: the clear-eyed, iconoclastic, trenchantly democratic observer who held up a mirror to his times, a vanished era that seems to have died laughing.

John Myers Myers, after giving up the idea of becoming a general at the age of 13 ("not being able to find any wars then"), went on to become one of the most experienced men in the field of Western history and biography. His other books include *The Harp and the Blade, The Alamo, Doc Holliday* and *San Francisco's Reign of Terror.* Mr. Myers lives with his family in Tempe, Arizona.

PRINT IN A WILD LAND

By John Myers Myers

THE HARP AND THE BLADE
OUT ON ANY LIMB
THE WILD YAZOO
THE ALAMO
SILVERLOCK
THE LAST CHANCE
DOC HOLLIDAY
DEAD WARRIOR
I, JACK SWILLING
MAVERICK ZONE:
Red Conner's Night in Ellsworth
The Sack of Calabasas
The Devil Paid in Angel's Camp
THE DEATHS OF THE BRAVOS
PIRATE, PAWNEE AND MOUNTAIN MAN
SAN FRANCISCO'S REIGN OF TERROR
PRINT IN A WILD LAND

PRINT IN A WILD LAND

by John Myers Myers

1967
DOUBLEDAY & COMPANY, INC.
Garden City, New York

To—
DICK LAUGHARN
Western man of print

ACKNOWLEDGMENTS

FOR HELPING ASSEMBLE the material on which this book is based, gratitude is especially owing:

Miss Llerena Friend, Barker Historical Library, University of Texas, Austin, Tex., for taking the trouble to copy and forward certain items, and to Miss Louise Kelly of Wichita Falls, Tex., for sharing the fruits of related researches.

Mrs. Thomas W. Streeter of Morristown, N.J., for sending me data concerning a unique imprint locked in the estate of her late husband.

John Barr Tompkins and his able assistants of the Bancroft Library, the University of California, Berkeley, Calif., for putting literary wealth at my disposal.

Alan D. Covey for furnishing the keys to the library of Arizona State University, Tempe, Ariz.; Donald Pady of the same institution for implementing inter-library loan service; and Mrs. Robert Muir for informational assists.

John Milton of the University of South Dakota, Vermillion, S.D., for his good offices in locating Dakota material, and J. Leonard Jennewein, of Dakota Wesleyan, Mitchell, S.D., for shipping a stranger a guide to same.

William A. Katz, of the University of Kentucky Library, Lexington, Ky., for pointing out some rare Western imprints.

Thanks for supplying valuable material and information are furthermore due:

Gilbert A. Cam of the New York, N.Y., Public Library; Miss Margaret J. Sparks and Andrew Wallace, Arizona Pioneers' Historical Society, Tucson, Ariz.; David W. Heron and Robert Armstrong, University of Nevada Library, Reno, Nev.; Miss Haydée Noya, Henry E. Huntington Library, San Marino, Calif.; Alan W. Farley, Kansas City, Kan.; Miss Lota M. Spell, Austin, Tex.; Richard Lyons, North Dakota State University, Fargo, N.D.; Mrs. Marguerite Cooley and Joseph Miller, Arizona State Department of Library and Archives, Phoenix, Ariz.; Fred Grove, Norman, Okla.; Mrs. Alys Freeze, Denver, Colorado, Public Library; Alwyn Barr and David B. Gracy II, Texas State

Historical Association, Austin, Tex.; Miss Ruth E. Rambo, Museum of New Mexico, Santa Fe, N.M.; Charles G. LaHood and Robert H. Land, Library of Congress, Washington, D.C.; Miss Margaret Rose, State Historical Society of North Dakota, Bismarck, N.D.; John Hames, Jr., Utah State Historical Society, Salt Lake City, Utah; Miss Mary K. Dempsey, Montana Historical Society, Helena, Mont.; Colton Storm, Newberry Library, Chicago, Ill.; Mrs. Barbara Elkins, Oregon Historical Society, Portland, Ore.; Jack I. Gardner, Nevada State Library, Carson City, Nev.; Mrs. Katherine Halverson, Wyoming State Archives and History Department, Cheyenne, Wyo.; A. M. Gibson, Phillips Collection, University of Oklahoma Library, Norman, Okla.; Mrs. Anna M. Ibbotson, Washington State Historical Society, Tacoma, Wash., Will G. Robinson and Richard Cropp, South Dakota Historical Society, Pierre, S.D.; Archibald Hanna, Coe Collection, Yale University Library, New Haven, Conn.; Marion Welliver, Nevada Historical Society, Reno, Nev.; Mrs. Anna Chiong, University of Washington Library, Seattle, Wash.; Warren J. Brier, University of Montana, Missoula, Mont.; Marcus A. McCorison, American Antiquarian Society, Worcester, Mass.; Donald F. Danker, Nebraska State Historical Society, Lincoln, Neb.; Mrs. Manon T. Bagg Atkins, Oklahoma Historical Society, Oklahoma City, Okla.; Merle W. Wells, Idaho Historical Society, Boise, Ida.; Mrs. Laura Allyn Ekstrom, State Historical Society of Colorado, Denver, Colo.; and Allan Ottley, California State Library, Sacramento, Calif.

CONTENTS

Acknowledgments   vii

A Foreword and Disclaimer   xi

Part I TRICKS OF A LIVELY TRADE

1   The Lettered Pattern Smashers   3
2   Raising Foreign Cain   15
3   Journalism without Schools   26
4   Ads à la Carte   37
5   Queen Cities and Quaint Subscription Lists   46
6   An Operational Composite   58
7   Problems and Sometimes Solutions   72
8   Slants from Cocked Eyes   85
9   The Sanctum No Sanctuary   95
10 Intra-Mural Sports   111

Part II SIDELIGHTS AND SPECIALTIES

11 The Press and the Sword   127
12 Impolitic Politicians   139
13 Bouts With Bacchus   150
14 Virginia Was a City   162
15 A Mess of Miscellanies   174
16 Criticism Unlimited   189
17 History and Its Cousins   202
18 A Literary Duke's Mixture   216
19 The Winged Bronco   234
20 Journalists in Other Guises   246

Ichabod: A Postscript   255

Bibliography   258

Index   265

A Foreword and Disclaimer

THIS IS NOT an attempt to offer, in one book of modest size, the history of a subject that would require a set of tomes to half cover in full. It is rather an effort to give an idea of how frontier men of print lived, together with some notion of what they achieved, or failed to, in the face of the problems posed by a newly settled region.

To that end chronological order has been largely junked; and so has the principle of separately reporting on developments in the seventeen Western states. Instead, an event of 1850 may rub paragraphs with one of 1890, and a California episode may be followed by one that took place in Texas or the Dakotas.

This is not, moreover, a report of the newspaper empires which had their roots in pioneer enterprise. The concern here is not with organizational fat cats but with individuals making chancy livings.

There were Western editors who became pillars of their respective communities, which owed much of their progress to enlightened guidance by men who held the same posts for decades. But such worthies had their opposite numbers in all corners of the United States, and this book is not about them. The editors and typesetters—in most cases one and the same—who responded to frontier rawness, and wrote or otherwise conducted themselves accordingly, are the subjects of PRINT IN A WILD LAND.

There has been no attempt to make this work as inclusive as possible by dragging in the names of as many wandering sons of the press as I could put a finger on. Those on this roster are the most interesting ones with which my researches acquainted me, and many of them reappear in chapter after chapter.

At the beginning I hoped to make this report more evenly

representative of the various states than has proved possible. The historians of some have taken a greater interest in home-grown journalism and literature than has been the case with others; hence I found plenty of guideposts in some instances and comparatively few in the remainder.

Some regions of the West, besides, weren't settled until the period covered by this chronicle was nearer its close than its beginning. There has been a great deal of debate as to when the West's frontier era actually ended. Here the concern is with the journalistic attitudes fostered by the pioneer epoch. In most parts of the West these had disappeared by the close of the nineteenth century, though in isolated sections—notably the Death Valley vicinity and the Staked Plains—they persisted for another decade.

But wherever and whenever the genuine frontier men of print held forth, they were the most interesting class of adventurers to invade the West, because as a group they were at once the most intelligent and variously gaited. They were also the best equipped to tell of how they made out in the new part of America they had come to.

In recognition of that fact, I have tried to interfere as little as seemed commensurate with my obligations of supplying background information, continuity, and narrative form. The meat of this book is the work of my singularly salty, and often rarely gifted, collaborators.

For one more word, the Eastern, Southern or Midwestern pasts of these men—save in the rare instances when points couldn't be clarified without referring to them—will not be noticed. If they started from different zones, they emerged with the unifying tie of being naturalized citizens of the only one considered here.

J.M.M.

Part I

TRICKS OF A LIVELY TRADE

1

THE LETTERED PATTERN SMASHERS

THERE WAS MORE than the dust—washed by prospectors, bitten by redskins and sent skyward by hoofs or wagon wheels—commonly ascribed to the West that used to be. On hand were others besides those who risked their necks for water holes, hole cards, whole cows, or demi-reps. More remarkable were the ones who pushed into a savage land with cultural chips on their shoulders.

In many cases they reached the frontier, printing presses in tow. In others they found them ready for use in their hours of need or moments for striking. In all cases they bucked the perils common to pioneers, plus the ones special to their callings.

Nor is it enough to state that they were journalists, and sometimes downright literary men, in a region where criticism might take the form of bullets. Even if they were admired by all, their words were set in type when and where almost any other line of work offered better promise of survival.

Although they knew it, the fascination of print snakeheld them. "When a child gets some printer's ink on his shirt," as Alfred Thomas said, when forced to shut down his Central City, Colorado *Miner*, "it is difficult to wash it out in less than three generations; and yet there is no occupation that yields such small returns. Yet such is the charm surrounding the art that they [meaning editors] would almost rather starve in a printing office than grow rich in other pursuits."

William J. Forbes, of the Virginia City *Daily Trespass*, among other Nevada papers, practiced what Thomas preached. As owner-editor of said journals, he wrote much that was reprinted by colleagues throughout the nation under the pseudonym *Semblens*, but kudos was all his pay. Temporarily disgusted when one of his sheets failed, he declared that "of twenty men, nineteen patronize the saloons and one the newspaper, and I am going with the crowd." Faithful to his word, Forbes opened a bar and prospered; but as soon as he'd accrued a sizable stake, he invested it in another mining-town rag.

But whether they stuck to the type stick, or came back to it after taking refuge in more practical frontier fields, the Western men of print were moved less by a desire to publish what would please others than by a yen to tell them what was what. For they strung with Sidney's Muse, when she urged Sir Philip to write what he found in his own heart. Don Biggers, of the Rotan, Texas, *Billy Goat, Always Buttin' In* was faithful to Sidney's ideal, although his choice of words differed. He described his paper as "a journal of such things as the editor takes a notion to write."

If for some reason given the format of a magazine, the Greenwater, California *Chuck-Walla* was in substance not one. For editors Curt E. Kunze and Carl B. Glasscock it was a venture in personal journalism, not differing in kind from many outright newspapers. One of the editors of the *Chuck-Walla* was more lyrical than Biggers, if not Sidney, yet he struck as positive a note in the first issue. To appreciate the initial line, it should be borne in mind that Greenwater was near neighbor to Death Valley.

> Ho, on the brink of hell, we've cooked for you
> This pot of dope, this mass of desert stew,
> This warm collation, hot with sulphurous fumes,
> And if it suits not, you know what to do.

It didn't matter to Western editors whether they owned a paper or not. If they were at the controls, they printed what they felt like writing; and the proprietors could find somebody else if they didn't like it.

That was the attitude of Junius E. Wharton—later to be mentioned in vastly different connections; and it led to his sacking by the group of men who had hired him to edit the Boulder County, Colorado *News*. "Instead of procuring items of local and general interest to the readers of the paper," these men complained, after Wharton had been replaced, "he converted it into a sewer through which a large amount of personal vituperation was ventilated . . . Thus the paper failed to accomplish any of the purposes for which it was designed by the proprietors of the press, and consequently was worse than none."

A rule of the trade was that colors were to be flown, and that's what Junius had done. But though he and the rest of the ink-slinging self-expressionists found the right climate on the frontier, they didn't get that way merely by stepping over the first meridian west of the Mississippi Valley. Behind them they left tracks which must be eyed, in order to see why it was natural for them to walk the way they did.

When the West and the nineteenth century were alike young, American journalism was not the duplex—with press wranglers living in one unit and writers in the other—which it has since become. It was mainly a house where the man who wrote copy for one paper might set type for the next he tied to. Yet whether he wound up in the composing room or the sanctum, he called himself a printer, and it was as an apprentice of that craft that he got his training in both fields.

Now it was by no accident that this amphibian played the lead in America's first picaresque novel. Henry J. Nott had looked the sorts over before writing *Novelettes of a Traveller; or Odds and Ends from the Knapsack of Thomas Singularity, Journeyman Printer.* And there were good reasons, too, why Tom's story was told by a fellow knockabout of type named Jerry.

To give an idea of the work's tenor, Tom had built a hot Scotch punch not long before being called from the composing room, and upon his return he accused his pal of watering it to hide the fact that he'd downed more than his share. "As I thought this imputation on my . . . honor was not to be borne," Jerry remembered, "I gave him a pretty solid clout on the side of the head; he returned it . . . and we commenced a regular battle. While we were fighting around the room, I got hold of one of the balls used for inking the type . . . Tommy, seeing me thus armed, seized another, and our faces and clothes were soon as well blackened as a form just ready for striking off. In making a violent blow, my weapon flew from my hand, and looking around for something to supply its place, I caught up a bottle. My an-

tagonist immediately dropped his ball and cried out with up-
raised hands, frightened looks and a doleful voice, 'For mercy's
sake, Jerry, don't break the whiskey bottle; it's more than half
full!'"

In addition to rows and drinking stints, Tom and Jerry were
given to throwing over jobs in order to see what life was like
elsewhere. That, too, was recognized as a nonfiction trait of
printers, as of the publication year of *Novelettes of a Traveller,*
which was 1834. Such freedom to come and go gained them the
envy of some spirits, as well as the disapproval of those who held
that grindstones were where noses belonged.

The footloose son of Gutenberg was more than Columbia's first
Bohemian. He was significant as the one who cracked the pattern into which life had been frozen by the end of nearly two
centuries of colonialism.

When Americans finally won their liberty, they weren't individually free to follow many paths. There were hardly more
occupations to choose among than were listed in the old counting-
out rhyme beginning, "Rich man, poor man, beggar man, thief."
A man could be "doctor, lawyer, merchant," or "chief" likewise,
if he was an Indian. He could also be "soldier, sailor, banker,
tailor," a practicer of a limited number of handicrafts, a combination minister and teacher, or, of course, a farmer.

But whatever the choice or inherited lot, an economy without
any fat on it meted a living wage mainly to those willing to work
their way up the pay scale by earning names for diligence and
the patience to stay put. Lads who didn't like glue on their moc-
casins might take to the woods, but they found little other lee-
way in a social order helpless to accommodate them.

Barring a few men with wealth enough to indulge non-
practical bents, there was no joker in the American pack until
the Industrial Revolution finally got around to turning out mass-
produced printing presses. Up until the end of the eighteenth
century print had been hatched by wooden contrivances which
differed little from the ones with which Gutenberg and his rivals
printed tickets in the 1400s. Made individually, they were expensive as well as cumbersome. But as the nineteenth century

neared, men began experimenting with metal and the application of the assembly line speed-up.

For a while they succeeded in reducing the cost of presses without much lessening the space needed for operation or the difficulty of rigging one for action. Like the hulking timber ones, the bijou iron devices bearing "Ramage" for brand name had to be supported by pillars of wood. Then to insure clear impressions, these had to be locked to the floor and ceiling of a solidly built structure.

Before something better suited to frontier needs was evolved, inventors on both sides of the Atlantic improved on the method of pressing the platen down on the form holding the type. For three centuries following Gutenberg's day it had been accomplished by a bar twisting a wooden screw. Snail speed was only one drawback. Balanced inking, or making a series of sheets uniform as to appearance, could only be gained by clamping the platen down, in every case, as tightly as the operator's weight and strength could force it; and to run off a sizable edition was too much for any but a multimanned plant to undertake. The substitution of metal allowed for the development of a toggle and lever combination, though. This device transferred much of the power to the machine, which supplied the uniform pressure which had to be struggled for in the past.

If not quite suitable for general frontier purposes, the cheap and easily moved Ramage presses found a fine market on the fast-growing Atlantic seaboard. There communities which had never been served by local newspapers, or known the advantages of a job printing shop, now began to bloom with them. Meanwhile, cities where presses had been comparative rarities turned into highly competitive publishing centers.

Prerequisite were enough trained hands to set the type, man the presses—and produce manuscripts for them to print. In those days men who wanted assistants caught them young and personally broke them to harness. Lads who aspired to be masters of a given craft, conversely, sold themselves down river into the quasi-slavery of the apprentice system.

All trades were party to that system, but America's burgeoning printing industry drew youngsters geared to work with their minds as well as their hands. Many became print-shop apprentices, because in a country where few could afford prep-school training, it was the best way to get more than a grade-school education.

They paid for it. Horace "Go-West-young-man" Greeley, who served his term at Poultney, Vermont, told what it was like in his reminiscences. The preferred age for new apprentices was early adolescence, and Greeley had just turned fifteen when he moved into the household of the man who was to be his de facto owner as well as his professional mentor for the period cited:

"I was to remain till twenty years of age, be allowed my board only for six months, and thereafter forty dollars per annum in addition for my clothing. . . . I had not been there a year before my hands were blistered and my back lamed by working off the very considerable edition of the paper on an old fashioned two-pull Ramage—a task beyond my boyish strength . . . While I lived at home I had always been allowed a day's fishing, and at least once a month in Spring and Summer, and I once went hunting; but I never fished or hunted, nor attended a dance, nor any sort of party or fandango in Poultney. I doubt that I even played a game of ball."

Before he was bailed out by his twentieth birthday, Horace put up with this serfdom for nearly five years, but he felt that he had got his money's worth. "They say," he wrote by way of comment, "that apprenticeship is distasteful to, and out of fashion with, the boys of our day; if so, I regret it for their sakes . . . I hold firmly that most boys may thus better acquire the knowledge they need than by spending four years in college."

Not taking his own advice about westing, Greeley hewed to the line of strict attention to business and followed it to success in New York City. Yet many of his fellow apprentices—including a lot who pioneered where he only went as a famous and wealthy visitor—were not of Horace's stripe.

Because print shops were recognized as schools where a general background, as well as particular skills, could be gained, they skimmed off much of the brightest and most ambitious youthful cream in the country. Still, cleverness and even a yearning for high goals are not always found in the same skin with Greeley's phlegm or clear eye for the main chance. As a tribe, men of better than average journalistic talent have not won a name for wisdom in the conduct of their lives. And the credit rating of those touched with genius is even lower in this respect.

Such indifferently balanced lads, bound to print because it was the only alternative to serving their fathers in shops or on farms, wore away their stripling years as Greeley related. When finally freed as journeymen, they had postponed youth to catch up with. Then as youngsters who had been weaned from their families, they were as rootless as West Point or Annapolis graduates.

The combined printing and journalism industry was this while growing in direct proportion to America's booming population. At this period printers could always get jobs, and as soon as they grew tired of one place, or curious about another, they shifted stakes.

Drifters of the Tom and Jerry sort, they had money in their pockets, barren years to compensate for, and no concern for the mores of towns they knew they could shuck at will. If vagabonds, they were better educated than most, and had standing on that account. Theirs was an era when superior mental training commanded a respect unknown to the age of perfunctory general schooling that was to come.

The passage birds of print often had politics, but the only altar of most was the imposing stone. Dave Day spoke for these when introducing the *Solid Muldoon*—a word he avouched to be "Zulu for virgin"—to Ouray, Colorado. "The *Solid Muldoon* is the boss, the only Fearless, Wide awake Red-hot newspaper published in San Juan [County]—Democratic in Politics, Independent in Development; and no religious convictions worth speaking of. She's a Daisy."

If without other faith, the men who'd got ink on their shirts as boys had a mystic trust in the power of print to meet all situations and carry them past all obstacles. That alone accounts for the zest with which they trundled presses into a wilderness where the problems of supplies, communications, and monetary returns seemed alike insurmountable. For if many came to have sad second thoughts about their chances of making publishing-house fortunes on the frontier, they joyously set forth to do so in incredible numbers.

They couldn't be as mobile as they eventually became until, during the first third of the nineteenth century, the Washington press was perfected. At once compact and solidly built, it needed no steadying wooden struts; in fact it called for no installation whatever. Unloaded from a wagon, it could be operated efficiently in a soddy, a rickety shanty, a tent—or in the open while some sort of shelter was being rigged for it.

Possessed of a Washington, the issuer of a Western paper might might be owner, publisher, editorial staff, and composing room crew all in one. Such was the versatility of Colonel E. A. Slack of the Laramie, Wyoming *Independent*. Of the colonel it was said that "he edited the paper, frequently made it up, did a large part of the job work, often took a turn at the hand press," and managed the business affairs connected with his sheet and his printing operation as a whole.

Slack wasn't well named; nor were he and his ilk paid in proportion to invested time and effort. "The average editor works eighteen hours a day," one of them mused in the Phoenix, Arizona *Gazette* in 1897, "sleeps the sleep of the just, pays for his paper in advance, pays help each week, lives on six-bits a week . . . and in constant dread of the inquisitorial grand jury that is composed chiefly of his delinquent subscribers."

On the other hand, not much in the way of capital investment was demanded of a commencing publisher. Aside from a press, all a man needed to be in business was a font or so of type, a composing stick in which to marshal the letters, galleys to hold columns pending arrangements in forms, an imposing stone to keep the type level while being readied for the press, wedges of various shapes to lock the forms in the master frame known as the chase, and the ink balls with which Tom and Jerry kept the type wet when not using them as weapons. Preferably of stuffed chamois, these capped the wooden shafts by which they were held while the type was being swiftly smeared between impressions.

As for supplies, the sole indispensable ones were ink powder and paper. If all went well, this last took the form of genuine newsprint, while more was stocked for other purposes. However dinky the plant, it offered job work services ranging from advertising throwaways to items entitled to be called books. Those who had been through the apprenticeship mill graduated as workmen versed in all departments of their craft.

Not so schooled as youths, a minority of the men dealt with here took up printing in maturity, because they wanted to join the fourth estate and found it necessary to be as ambidextrous as most of their competitors. A still smaller number were never at home in the composing room, being lawyers, doctors, or professors drawn into journalism because of either literary or political bents, after they reached the West.

Yet for the most part, and including most of those winged with great talent, they had come into the world of letters young, and through the door marked "printer." And though a good few of them eventually turned out work which appeared between book covers or in nationally distributed magazines, they were earlier glad to shine as authors of a few lines, published in the jerk-water journals for which they functioned as compositors.

However small, a frontier newspaper item was not expected to fall short of as much ginger as the writer could season it with. Before Western journalists could function as they did, though, a change as remarkable as the progress in press improvements overtook the American literary outlook.

Before the early 1830s such lightness as had leavened the country's books or periodicals had taken the form of mild whimsies, efforts to amuse "polite readers" by pillorying the impolite, and missed tries at writing in the manner of witty foreigners. With the honorable exception of Washington Irving's *History of New York*, the spirit of American comedy wasn't heard from until authors in the East's seaside cities quit trying to impress each other with their sophistication and began listening to the rowdy mirth begot in Columbia's back country.

The first to do so, as scholars now more or less agree, was one
Matthew St. Clair Clarke. After auditing the bravura chat of a
coon-hunting Congressman, Clarke anonymously published
Sketches and Eccentricities of Col. David Crockett of Tennessee.

That was in 1833. Probably getting off his marks in the same
year, for his was a two-volume effort, Henry Nott gave the market
his work a year later.

Not crammed with guffaws for modern readers, the novel, subtitled *Odds and Ends from the Knapsack of Thomas Singularity,
Journeyman Printer,* rocked the ribs of general readers and critics
alike. Because it exposed a large, exploitable vein, in place of
being *sui generis, Novelettes of a Traveller* was a more fruitful
book than Irving's delightful history of Manhattan, so far as the
early development of American literature was concerned. Together with Clarke's work on Davy Crockett, Nott's book showed
the possibilities of a native boisterousness which had no Old
World match. After Augustus Baldwin Longstreet scored a following hit with his still highly readable *Georgia Scenes* in 1835,
literary America was never the same again. Among the Reverend
Longstreet's sketches were brutally realistic ones as well as comic
portrayals. The American citizen with the bark on, and speaking
straight United States, had moved into Columbian reading matter
to stay.

The fact was not lost upon newspaper editors of the old, or
trans-Appalachian West. Either written by themselves or other
frontiersmen who knew which end of a pen was which, racy
items about local doings began to appear in sheets which had
formerly used as fillers only decorous matter culled from Eastern
papers. Nor were women spared, for some of the sketches sent
them down the line with no noticeable delicacy.

The once prim American book trade continued to lead this
cultural romp, courtesy of William Trotter Porter of New York.
In his *Spirit of the Times* his special delight was to publish items
by frontier correspondents dealing with brawlers, bragging hunters, horse traders, backwoods courtship, and the like lively matters. Then in 1845 he became the first anthologist of this school of
letters, publishing a collection called *The Big Bear of Arkansas.*

Short of 1845, it should be noted, there had been no American settlement of any part of America's West but newspaperless Oregon. While the printing press was being developed as described, and while New World attitudes and speechways were winning literary acceptance, Spain and then Mexico controlled better than a million of what are now considered Western square miles. And when Texans took over a bushel of them, in 1836, they didn't alter the area's status as non-Columbian soil.

Two years earlier a pair of presses had for the first time arrived in California and New Mexico respectively. Both importations from the United States, one reached Monterey by ship in June of 1834. Just when the other arrived in Santa Fe, via the trail named for that city, has nowhere been recorded.

Although the New Mexico number fitfully printed a newspaper called *El Crepúsculo de la Libertad,* neither of these presses comes within the scope of this narrative. Or at least they do not while issuing writings in Spanish. Both, as it chanced, earned later mention by falling into American hands.

The discrimination is not made for lack of awareness that the non-English men of print had interesting attitudes and professional habits reaching back into centuries of European tradition. An astonishingly large number of them—Germans principally— got around to publishing foreign-language items in the pioneer West. But though a special study is no doubt due them, this chronicle is no such thing, and does not keep them in mind.

Neither does it cover the efforts to give Indians the benefits of print, either through tribal papers or by translating hymns and tracts into native languages. There was a missionary press a few miles from the present Ottawa, Kansas, as early as 1834. There was another near Lewiston, Idaho, in 1839, giving Nez Percés printing service seven years before the palefaces of the Northwest enjoyed that advantage. But however worthy such ventures may have been, this work will take no further notice of them. Nor will it sidestep to praise some solid scholarly achievements that emerged from missionary printing plants.

If this chronicle has a limited beat, it is yet a sufficiently large one. Making history themselves as well as recording it, American printer-editors were involved in a mighty immigration surge which began to reach full proportions after the entire West— lacking only the Gadsden Purchase piece—became United States territory in 1846.

There was a preliminary era which cannot be overlooked, though. Not yet fully fledged with either the literary background or the mechanical equipment noted above, the joint wielders of the pen and the type stick had begun going into action thirty-three years earlier.

2

RAISING FOREIGN CAIN

THE STORY OF printing in the West begins, as any adventure tale profitably could, with a handful of men on a barge, riding the current of a great river toward parts they had never known before. They had, besides, a lofty mission which their numbers seemed wholly inadequate to compass. As much could be said for their equipment, save for one article. This was a small Ramage press.

Prefatory were the exploits of a young Cuban Creole called José Alvarez de Toledo y Dubois. Becoming a subaltern in the Spanish Army, he had at first won favor with the mother country's rulers by serving with the patriot forces supporting Sir John Moore, when that well-sung general was battling the army which Napoleon had sent to conquer Spain. Later representing Santo Domingo in some sort of imperial parliament, Toledo had to cut and run, when it was discovered that by mail he had been trying to promote independence for all Latin America.

By the time he reached the United States he had made himself a general. As a republican commander on the lam, he was well received in Washington. His declaration of intent to free Mexico won him money passed under the table, as well as other assists. In part these were due to a genuine democratic desire to free fellow men from autocratic sway, and in part in hopes of an unadvertised payoff. Its form was to be Texas, whose retention by Spain had rankled Americans ever since Napoleon had included it in the Louisiana Purchase.

Making his headquarters in Philadelphia, as of 1812, General Toledo there recruited a cadre which included a printer named Aaron Mower. Other members were a French chef, an American shoe merchant, what the Inquisition had left of a Spanish free thinker, and two chaps billed as the liberator's aides-de-camp.

Because one of these was Henry Adams Bullard, a young lawyer who became something of a historian, these and other details
were eventually published in the *North American Review* of July
1836. "Toledo, after visiting Washington City with a view of
propitiating the government," to quote the most pertinent paragraph, "set forward toward Pittsburgh with a few followers and
friends. They took with them among other things, a printing press
and a font of types, and the printer himself formed one of the
party . . . a man of singular versatility of talent, possessing a vast
amount of practical knowledge, and at the same time, brave,
enthusiastic and enterprising."

In December of 1812 the filibusters "embarked at Pittsburgh
for Natchez on a small flat boat." The little Ramage was the
expedition's largest implement of war. Otherwise, as Bullard
noted, "The material consisted of provisions, a few arms, baggage
and some books."

Even before this threat to the Spanish empire began drifting
down the Ohio and the Mississippi, America's federal government
had been working another finger into the pie of a nation with
which it was avowedly on peaceful terms. Fugitive in Louisiana,
in 1812, was a Latin of republican principles dubbed José
Bernardo Maximilian Guttierez de Lara. In cahoots with him was
William Shaler, a federal agent deputed to do all he could by
way of encouraging revolutionaries to break Spain's grip on
Mexico. Shaler earned his pay by mustering an expeditionary
force of which Guttierez was the titular head, though the real
war chief was an ex-U.S. Army officer called Augustus Magee.

Late in the summer of 1812, Colonel Magee took Nacogdoches,
Texas, with his following of some 300 borderers and Indians.
Having heard of that success before he left Philadelphia, Toledo
y Dubois had counted on throwing in with the vicariously
triumphant Guttierez de Lara. After the wonderfully laden flat-
boat reached Natchez in the spring of 1813, its crew, and such
volunteers as they could entice, fared westward overland.

Nacogdoches, meanwhile, was no longer occupied by an invading army, which had pressed deeper into Texas. Reaching the

town in May, Toledo et al readied the Ramage for action, and the first American printer to operate in the West began to set type for a paper designed to give Texas natives the itch to grab up revolutionary arms. It was therefore wholly in Spanish.

Datelined Nacogdoches, May 25, 1813, the one and only issue of the *Gaceta de Texas* carried an item about its compositor. "A citizen of the United States of America, A. Mower, living in Philadelphia and having a public press of considerable reputation . . . abandoned all his interests . . . in order to come and offer his services to the Mexican patriots."

It is possible that Mower was but the *Gaceta's* chief compositor. At some point Toledo gained a third aide-de-camp, in the person of Godwin B. Cotten. Later a noted frontier man of print, he may well have helped Aaron at Nacogdoches.

What can be certified, though, is that the *press* work for the *Gaceta de Texas* wasn't done on the Spanish side of the international boundary. Just as publication was about to begin, Toledo heard from the man of whom he had fancied himself an ally.

Through the prowess of Colonel Samuel Kemper—Magee having forfeited command by dying—Guttierez had become master of first LaBahia and then San Antonio. As these, together with Nacogdoches, were the only points of settlement in the province, José Bernardo was its head man. Not wishing to share his glory, he undertook to tell José Alvarez to keep his cotton-picking hands off Texas.

For this reason the type set in Nacogdoches wasn't inked and pressed on paper until after Toledo and the rest had withdrawn to the border town of Natchitoches, Louisiana. This was now the listening post of U.S. agent William Shaler, who had heard from José Bernardo, too. The man who had so profited by American aid said he wasn't about to recognize any rights to Texas claimed by the United States.

Shaler's wasn't the only throat Guttierez cut. He or those answerable to him slashed the jugulars of the entire surrendered garrison of San Antonio's then little celebrated fortress, the Alamo. By so doing they disgusted Kemper and many other Americans, a fact capitalized on by the bilingual Natchitoches *El Mexicano*.

Edited by the Cuban filibuster and the American secret service man, it was also printed by Mower, with Cotten perhaps assisting.

In the upshot Shaler was able to substitute Toledo for the straw man who had turned on him. William didn't profit by the maneuver, though. South of San Antonio, on the Medina River, the pickup army of José Alvarez was ruined by troops under a pro named General Joaquin de Arrendondo in 1813's August.

If Bullard and Cotten survived, the absence of any further word about him indicates that Mower was a casualty. The press so confidently loaded on the barge at Pittsburgh was presumably likewise destroyed.

The cause of literacy then lapsed in the West, pending the flight from Spain of another apostle of freedom. But after slanging a government which didn't take kindly to self-expression, Francisco Xavier Mina first took refuge in England. Already there, and for much the same reason, was Father José Servando Teresa de Mier.

Consulting this padre, Francisco was advised that the best way to get even with Spain's rulers was to stir up a revolution in Mexico, a project which Mier himself was game to abet. Perhaps he was also the man who raised the money to buy two ships and a printing press. At any rate General Mina was thus equipped when the expedition he commanded set forth in September of 1816.

By that time a young printer named Samuel Bangs was holding forth in Baltimore. Among Mina's lacks, when he made a way stop in that port, was a man of print; and as he belonged to the non-Greeley, or anti-caution division of the guild, Sam signed up to rescue Mexico from tyranny by slinging type.

Although supposedly on the same side, José Alvarez Toledo hadn't been able to make book with José Bernardo Guttierez. Francisco Xavier Mina also had trouble getting along with a fellow friend of liberty for Mexico. The doubtful ally in this case was Louis-Michel Aury, a French privateersman encountered in the West Indies. The difficulty was that both wished to lead, and neither to follow. When they finally agreed to be consuls—though one a general and the other an admiral—it was 1817. As they knew that veterans of Miguel Hidalgo's defeated rebellion of 1810 had holed up on the southern end of Galveston Island, they made that their own revolutionary base.

There, on February 22, Bangs and one John MacLaren not only set type but published a proclamation of Mina's announcing he had come to free Mexico and calling on all men of high purpose to find ploughshares they could beat into swords. A press had at length been worked in the West, but not on its mainland.

The situation didn't change, after Sam and John had published a second Mina manifesto near the mouth of the Rio Grande in 1817's April. For though then in continental North America, they were south of the river also known as the Bravo, and on soil never considered Western.

If Mina was ready to fight, Aury turned out to be only a coat holder. He ferried troops to the scene of battle, but didn't consider land warfare any of a sailor's business. Going it alone, Francisco scored a couple of minor successes, but was soon captured, backed against a wall, and shot.

Never heard of again, MacLaren seems to have been killed in battle. Bangs was captured, however, and as a POW he was forced to operate the also spared press in the service of Spain.

While he was still biting that bullet, the United States agreed to give up all claims to Texas, contingent upon the acquisition, through purchase from Spain, of Florida and the Gulf-bordering territory lying between it and Louisiana. As of 1819, that is to say, the federal government was on the opposite side of the fence from its position, when it had connived to assist first Guttierez and then Toledo in their efforts to free Texas from Spanish control.

But if Washington, D.C. had changed camps, Natchez, Mississippi, still clove to the line that Texas had been sold by Napoleon and bought fair and square with American dollars. Shocked at what they regarded as betrayal on the part of the government, citizens of the famous river town financed an expedition to right the wrong.

In command was James Long. His scheme of action called for organizing Texas as an independent nation which would so remain

until American voters should insist upon its incorporation in the
United States.

Among the founders of the first Republic of Texas were two
men of print. No information about the professional past of Horatio Bigelow has been handed down. Eli Harris, on the other
hand, left a trade trail extending across several Southern states.

He seems to have owned the press which was set up after
Nacogdoches had once more been taken by invaders from the
United States. Contemporary comment named him as the publisher and Bigelow as the editor of their joint productions. Being
printers of that day, they both probably wrote and set type in-
terchangeably.

Nothing they published has so far been found. Luckily, though,
they sent copies to the editors of still preserved journals which
printed excerpts. An 1819 issue of the Baltimore *Niles' Weekly
Register* published part of the Texas declaration of independence.
Its tenor that of the American one, this seems to have been the
first Western imprint cast in English, though trailing Mina's Spanish manifesto by two years. Then the second press to reach Nacogdoches was the first to operate anywhere on the West's mainland.

Harris and Bigelow also published the region's first newspaper,
properly speaking. Unlike the *Gaceta de Texas* and *El Mexicano,*
the *Texas Republican* went to press in the West; and while the
other two called it quits after one issue apiece, the organ of the
new republic made weekly appearances from 1819's August
through to October.

Its columns were of particular interest to the editor of the Nashville *Clarion.* No doubt this journalist had known Harris, who had
himself been a newspaperman in central Tennessee.

On October 5 the *Clarion* quoted the *Texas Republican* as fol-
lows: "It may not be improper here to remark, that the whole of
Texas, with the exception of two settled parts, is under the au-
thority of the patriots." At that time there were only four non-
Indian communities in the province. Spain still held LaBahia and
the metropolis of San Antonio. "The patriots" were in charge of
Nacogdoches and, nominally, of Campeachy on Galveston Island.
The man in command of a burg peopled by pirates and their

doxies was Jean Lafitte. Out of one side of his mouth Jean assured President James Long that he was as faithful to the cause of democracy as he had proved when aligning himself with Andy Jackson at the Battle of New Orleans in 1815. Out of the other corner the buccaneer kept Spain's colonial authorities posted as to the progress, or the lack of it, in the capital of republican Texas.

On October 12 its newspaper was again quoted by the *Clarion*. "As it is important to persons moving into the Republic, to know the terms on which lands are to be procured, we hasten to lay before them the following short sketch, showing the ease with which it [real estate] may be obtained and secured to them [immigrants] and their heirs for ever. . . . Six hundred and forty acres will be allowed to each actual settler, and as a further inducement, one hundred and sixty acres will be allowed to each child of his or her family . . . and three hundred and twenty acres to each member of his or her family over eighteen and under twenty-one years of age."

In a period when most people reckoned wealth mainly in terms of acreage, this generosity would undoubtedly have lured to Nacogdoches the recruits counted on by the republic's founding fathers. As earlier indicated, though, America's federal government was not the well-wisher of James Long that it had been of Josés Guttierez and Toledo. United States military and other agencies not only stopped would-be Texans at the border; they blocked the importation of critically needed supplies.

It thus happened that when Nashville newspaper subscribers were assured that each could have a square mile of Texas for the asking, doom was hovering over the infant nation. Because of the American food blockade, President Long was forced to send his electors afield to hunt game at the very time that a Spanish punitive force was closing in. James himself made a pilgrimage to Campeachy in an effort to get help from the man who had tipped Spanish agents off as to the republic's desperate situation.

Such of its defenders as could be located and recalled were defeated on the Trinity River on October 15. Harris and Bigelow were among the fleeing survivors, but Eli later learned that one of the first steps taken by the recapturers of Nacogdoches was to smash the *Texas Republican*'s press.

After Mexico finally won her independence in 1821, Stephen Austin and other *impresarios* were able to settle Americans in Texas peaceably. None of them thought to bring in a printer, although in 1823 a press was briefly operated in San Antonio, well west of American colonies.

Whatever the past of a man known only as Ashbridge, he was a craftsman who had good tools to work with. During an era not noted for typographical skill anywhere, he published a beautiful example in a scratch town, where missionaries had long given over trying to educate an isolated populace. How Ashbridge expected to rally subscribers where most people wouldn't have recognized the alphabet, if they'd found it in soup, is one of the West's mysteries. No copies of his proposed newspaper have been found, though a letter of Austin's indicates that San Antonians got to blink at an issue or so of the *Courier* at least. But the prospectus survives to show that its printer was as militantly cultured as he was deft at type arranging. Multiplying the history of San Antonio by two and some, the bilingual broadside barked at "the vicious policy of Spain, which for three hundred years has concealed from the world the rich and beneficial province of Texas, neglected education, stifled the arts and discouraged industry."

No son of print showed up to unstifle the arts in the American settlements for another six years. Then, within weeks of each other, two veterans of separate filibustering expeditions returned to Texas with journalism in mind.

Horatio Bigelow, editor of the *Texas Republican* ten years earlier, began writing and setting type in Nacogdoches again, when the *Mexican Advocate* was launched early in September of 1829. And during that same month Toledo's former aide-de-camp, Godwin B. Cotten, commenced publishing the *Texas Gazette* at San Felipe de Austin.

Ever a shadowy figure, Bigelow didn't leave a followable trail between his two Texas sojourns. Nor on the second of them did he carve much of a mark on the state's history. The case was different with Cotten on both scores.

After making his way out of Texas with Toledo and Bullard, the man who putatively helped Mower set type for the *Gaceta de Texas* did not step out of the limelight. Whatever his experiences before he became a filibuster, he later published newspapers in New Orleans and Mobile, then the two largest ports served by the Gulf of Mexico. And when he brought his press to Texas, he again set it up where the chances of doing business were favorable.

Now a dot on the map, best described as lying fifty miles west of Houston, San Felipe was for some years the liveliest town in a district where American frontiersmen were trying to convince themselves that they liked being Mexican citizens. As the since dropped "de Austin" suggests, it was the headquarters of the original *impresario*.

Prior to the Texas Revolution, Stephen Austin remained the most influential colonist, having much the status of an unofficial president. Operating in Stephen's town, Cotten ran a newspaper for which Austin himself supplied a great deal of the copy. Other matter was written by Robert Williamson, called "Three-legged Willie," because of an affliction which forced him to piece out a malshaped pin with a peg that reached the ground. A third filler of his paper's columns was Cotten himself.

In 1830 he alarmed Austin by writing an editorial in which he undertook not only to speak for some gamblers who had been convicted by Mexican authorities; he also lectured the authorities themselves. Stephen was welcome to his viewpoint that Americans in Mexico should play the game by Mexican rules, but Godwin was a frontier man of print, and he published whatever he felt like putting in his sheet.

"Several persons were arraigned before the Alcalde of this Jurisdiction, for having committed a breach of the ordinance for the suppression of gambling, and which had been but recently promulgated, and each of the delinquents were fined in the sum of fifty dollars. . . . This proceeding thoroughly evinces the potent arm with which the judiciary authorities are willing to wield the sword of justice, for the promotion of morals and the suppression of vice—— We would add, however, that . . . in consequence of

the recent publication of the ordinance, and their evident igno-
rance of its existence at the time of its infringement, should they
petition for relief . . . the Ayuntamiento will doubtless extend its
magnanimity and lenity toward them, for their first transgres-
sion."

Mild as that was, and comparatively trivial the bone it picked,
Cotten's editorial constituted the first statement of American dis-
satisfaction with arbitrary official conduct—eventually to make
porcupines of the colonists as a whole. Fearing just that, Austin
grumbled that the *Texas Gazette* was a dubious community asset.

Godwin nevertheless once suspended it, in order to undertake
a printing job which was by way of being a difficult public service
as well as a commercial venture. In the late fall and early winter
of 1829–30 he dropped his paper for nearly three months, so that
he could devote all the facilities of his small shop to the production of a work, important to men who were trying to adjust themselves to the requirements of a nation with a legal code at
variance with the one they had been accustomed to as citizens of
the United States.

What Cotten turned out was *Translation of the Laws, Orders
and Contracts on Colonization from January, 1821 up to This
Time, in Virtue of Which Col. Stephen Austin Has Introduced
and Settled Foreign Immigrants in Texas with an Explanatory
Introduction.* Aside from being a monument to the determination
of colonial leaders to get along with the rulers of their adopted
country, the pamphlet was notable because of being the first
Western imprint of greater scope than a broadside.

In the upshot, of course, the sincere intentions of Austin and
his like were defeated by the fundamental difference in the out-
looks and temperaments of the two nationalities involved. A mat-
ing that was never destined for permanence suffered stormy
divorce via the Texas Revolution in 1836. As American settlers of
the province now far outnumbered Mexican ones, they were able
to detach it from Mexico, and the second Republic of Texas came
into being.

The part played by newspapers in that assertion of independence will be dealt with in another chapter. Here it is only ap-

propriate to point out that while Texas more or less throve as a nation, Samuel Bangs returned and began publishing there.

For Sam the achievement of Mexican independence in 1821 had led to freedom from the bondage imposed on him, after he was captured with Francisco Mina in 1817. After meanwhile trying his hand at this and that both in Mexico and the United States, he brought a press to Galveston in 1839. The island on which he had printed Mina's proclamation twenty-two years earlier now supported a town which was the republic's largest. Scoring another beat, Bangs launched the West's first daily, its name, the *Galvestonian.*

3

JOURNALISM WITHOUT SCHOOLS

HAVING PAID SOME necessary attention to background and beginnings, this chronicle will proceed, as promised in the foreword, without reverence for the calendar. If history will incidentally be served, that will be a tagalong of the main purpose, which is to show what the journalistic epoch in question was like.

In the first place the word newspaper, in the pioneer West, did not necessarily live up to its dictionary billing. What was issued by a given pioneer man of print might not include news at all. The editor of the Canyon City, Oregon *Journal* opined that if any subscriber had a hankering for knowledge of what was going on elsewhere, he would do well to buy another sheet, too. "The latest news our readers will, in all probability, find in . . . *The New York Tribune* . . . or any other paper they are in the habit of picking up and reading." Neither did the *Journal's* director see a point in trying to compete with the town grapevine. "Local news, being of such a nature that everybody . . . knows every other person's business except their own, we shall publish such only as suits our purpose."

That was one governing point of view. Fred Hart, editor of the Austin, Nevada *Reese River Reveille,* thought it was up to a journalist to scour for home-grown bits and blow them up into epics. "One day, while out in search of an item," he reminisced, in the *Sazerac Lying Club,* "I asked a fellow citizen, 'What's the news?' 'Nothing startling,' he replied. Nothing startling! That man would never do for a newspaper reporter in a small interior town. Nothing startling indeed! Why, as he made that remark, two dogs were preparing articles for a prize fight right in front of his store; a wagon loaded with wood could be seen in the distance, which was sure to pass his way, if something didn't break down. Two women whom he knew to be mortal enemies, were approaching each other on a corner above; a doctor was hurrying across the street, and a man who always kicks up a fuss and gets arrested when drunk was just entering the door of a saloon a block below. If that fellow citizen had had the soul of a reporter within his bosom —or in any other part of his body where a reporter's expansive soul can find lodgment—he would have got out his jacknife, picked up a chip, and sitting down on the first convenient dry goods box, have whittled and waited for something startling."

Many editors conceived that, as publishers in communities barren of other fresh reading matter, anything of interest would be welcomed by their subscribers. Their papers were miscellanies of historical, descriptive, and literary items, clipped from magazine, obtained from correspondence in the East, or culled from their own memories.

On page one of the first issue of the Virginia City, Montana *Post*, Thomas Dimsdale saw fit to run Poe's *The Haunted Palace*. That was in 1864, and fine as the poem was it hadn't been news since its appearance in the Baltimore *Museum* in 1839.

After he started the Houston, Texas *Musquito* in 1840, Sam Bangs reached even farther back. He filled a column with a choice bit of invective borrowed from "Lord" Timothy Dexter, whose quaint literary career ended in 1806.

Some men of print were so carried away by the feeling that they were the only sluiceways by which culture could be poured into their wilderness-besieged towns that they aspired to make their rags complete universities. Nothing in the field of knowledge was left out of the reckoning of the Salt Lake City *Deseret News*. The prospectus of Willard Richards, issued when the paper was about to begin publication in 1850, assured Utah's pioneers that they wouldn't be cut off from the best civilization had to offer.

"We propose to publish a small, weekly sheet . . . to record the passing events of the State and in connexion, refer to the arts and sciences, embracing general education, medicine, law, divinity, domestic and political economy, and everything that may fall under our observation, which may tend to promote the best interests, welfare, pleasure and amusement of our fellow citizens."

At the other end of the gamut from Salt Lake City's all-embracing organ were journals which made no pretensions of running on more than one track. Ned McGowan published the Sacramento, California *Phoenix* for the purpose of scoring off his enemies. Bill Nye used the Laramie, Wyoming *Boomerang* to build up his reputation as a purveyor of comic anecdotes. Of his Colorado City, Texas *Josher*, Don Biggers noted that it was "A very weakly paper—Issued monthly—Devoted to Trouble."

Airier than any of these were the journals launched by Joseph Ellis Johnson. A lover of the outdoors, Joe had kept readers of the Wood River, Nebraska *Huntsman's Echo* better informed as to his field activities than anything else; and when his subscribers got serious about the Civil War, he cleared out rather than cater to their craving for partisan news about it. A York stater, Johnson wasn't pro-Southern, but he looked on the intersectional conflict as the work of the Devil; and he thought Old Cootie was a Republican.

"Friends and patrons—adieu," he wrote in his 1861 valedictory. "We have secessed, and tomorrow shall start westward and shall probably become a citizen of Utah. . . . This Republican reign of terror, blood, tyranny and oppression is too much for our Democratic style of free thought, free speech and freedom, where men who may chance to differ in opinion with wild, blood thirsty fanatics, are threatened and sometimes despoiled or murdered. . . . Should our life and abilities be spared, our friends may find our footmarks through the boundless west, and again hear the shrill, oracular notes of the Old Bugler, re-echoed from the vales of the mountain."

Settled in Utah, Joe still refused to take detailed notice of the big news of the day, when he launched *The Farmer's Oracle* at Spring Lake Villa in 1863. "Fate, or some well meaning power, places us again upon the tripod," his salutatory declared, "and so we submit with this our best bow and a flourish of our feather. . . . Our interests now will be to raise potatoes instead of armies . . . to count cabbages instead of votes, to stick and poll for beans instead of members of Congress. . . ."

Not yet known as Joaquin, C. H. Miller took the opposite stand, with respect to the War between the States, but not because it spoke to his sense of news values, if any. Knowing or caring nothing about the South, Miller espoused its cause while editing the Eugene City, Oregon *Register* in 1862, because about everybody else in that part of the timber was cheering for the North.

To leave special cases and take up the general run of those who tried to function as authorities on current events, there was no agreement among them as to the nature of sound news coverage. Examined in the light of today's needs, some of their sheets are richly informative, while others are more remarkable for what they don't tell than what they do.

To the exasperation of modern historians, the papers of some of the towns enlivened by famous Wild Western doings took little or no notice of these. But their editors might have reasoned, as did he of the Canyon City *Journal*, that his readers already knew all that was learnable about a local fracas, holdup, or lynching and would be bored by a printed rehash. They would therefore substitute reports of Atlantic seaboard or European events, which their readers couldn't learn all about by conferring with local barbers and bartenders.

On the other hand, local news, as Fred Hart made clear in his sketch of a Western reporter at work, wasn't always the easiest thing to come by, even when wanted. Frontier camps or not, many towns were no more the scenes of everyday excitement than small burgs in the East.

Willmont Frazee found that out, when he helped start the Ivanpah, California *Green-Eyed Monster* in 1894. Situated in high wilds, and peopled by men on the peck for gold, Ivanpah had the properties of a tough town, but it never made use of its opportunities. Hairy of puss but gentle of heart, the miners there did nothing with their waking hours but work and get peaceably potted. Desperate for items to feed his *Monster*, young Frazee earned the trade nickname of "Humbug Bill" by reporting what might have happened, if Ivanpah hadn't been the news dud that it was.

The one real conditioner of pioneer papers, outside of the whims and abilities of their respective editors, was the availability of

desired material and the extent to which it had to be supplemented. After the nation was spanned by telegraph wires, the
problem was eased somewhat, though most towns weren't so pack-
aged with the rest of the world until, in due course, railroads ran
in or near them.

Before the Morse code made rapid communication between
journalists possible, the best they could do to cooperate with each
other was an exchange system. On the understanding that he
would be credited with any item borrowed from him, a publisher
would agree to send his paper free to as many colleagues as would
accommodate him in the same way.

If the honor system more or less prevailed, when lifting material from each other, no such consideration was shown for magazine writers or the authors of books. Men who were strangers to
other forms of theft thought nothing of committing literary piracy.

Liking the novel but not seeing fit to reward Charles Dickens
for writing it, the editors of the San Francisco *Golden Era* cheerfully serialized *Bleak House*. They were also glad to report to
their readers that "Beautiful Evelyn Hope is dead," after finding
it and the lines that went with it in a book by uncompensated
Robert Browning. Chuck and Bob got by-lines, to be sure, but as
neither had been invited to exchange, they weren't so much as
sent copies of the *Era*.

Piracy in part made up for the lack of feature services. Correspondence, and not necessarily on the part of the men of print,
also helped. An editor in any given town made it a point to find
out what fellow residents were receiving informative letters from
various quarters of the country.

He also knew who were the magazine subscribers, and who had
friends in the East who would forward new books. And sometimes
the editor had the luck to find a competent amateur whose yen
to see his work in print would turn him into a regular free contributor.

From these sources, the pioneer journalist drew either the main
items of his paper—if his mind wasn't focused on the local scene—
or material to fill the holes left by local news. What he contributed himself might take any form, the only certainty being that

it would bear no resemblance to what is now considered proper newspaper style.

Dave Day of the Ouray, Colorado *Solid Muldoon* had the habit of turning his commentaries into medleys of prose and verse. Using an unorthodox term for Jacob's ladder, Dave thus reported the death of a fellow among God's creatures:

"A tenderfoot in the Animas Valley ascended the golden clothes pole last week; the ascension being occasioned by getting on the outside of the wrong brand of mushrooms.

> He loved not wisely but too well
> The mealy, spongy mush-a-roon,
> Now free from pain, he sleeps, poor kuss,
> In the land of the Solid Muldoon."

If an item was more or less cast in the mold of a news article rather than an editorial, it still owed nothing to the modern conventions of journalistic style. Nobody had then postulated that the first sentence should tell who did what where, and with such and such results.

The big story in Nebraska, as of September 1860, was the stringing of the telegraph wires that linked a once isolated territory with the Atlantic seaboard, and the nations connected with the East by trans-oceanic cable. Here's how Joe Johnson handled it in the Wood River *Huntsman's Echo:*

"Whoop! Hurrah! The poles—the wire—the telegraph—the lightning! The first are up, the second stretched, the third playing upon the line between St. Jo. and Omaha; and the people of Omaha are exulting in the enjoyment of direct communication with the balance of the earth and the rest of mankind. . . . . 'Thoughts that breathe and words that burn' will glide along the wires with lightning rapidity.

"Yesterday Messrs. Kountze and Porter called upon us whilst . . . providing for the distribution of the balance of the poles along the route. Come on with your forked lightning! Strike for the Great Western ocean, the land of gold and glittering stones and ore."

The differences between modern and frontier newspapers were

physical as well as stylistic. That was especially so where Ramage presses—cheaper than Washingtons and easier to transport because smaller and lighter—were the ones in use. Some models could print but rags which were dwarf, even as compared with tabloids. Cotten's San Felipe de Austin *Texas Gazette* was a three-column affair, the columns being less than ten inches deep. The Houston *Musquito* of Sam Bangs had only a pair of columns per page, though these were somewhat deeper than the *Gazette's* and were three inches wide instead of two.

The Canyon City, Oregon *Journal* had page dimensions of seven and three quarters by ten and a half inches, as compared with the eight and a half by eleven inches of today's standard typewriter sheets. At that the *Journal* could sniff at the Salt Lake City *Deseret News* with its seven and a quarter by nine and three quarters. And in most cases there were but four such pages.

A consequence of the small amount of room was a preference for pygmy type sizes, now only thought suitable for legal and want ads. A favorite size was a five-point type, as opposed to the eight point now commonly used for editorial matter. As type sizes were then known by names in place of numbers, the admired one was crowned with the title of "nonpareil." Despised, on the other hand, was "long primer," the ten-point size currently much in favor with book designers. Anybody who stooped to making his paper comfortably readable was thought of as stuffing his columns with big type in order to save himself work; and the prejudice against it persisted even when large presses—steam-powered jobs in some of the bigger towns and flush mining camps—removed all necessity for saving space at the expense of the reader's eyesight.

The above was spelled out, in order to bring out the values in an anecdote told of Alf Doten, editor-owner of the Gold Hill, Nevada *Daily News,* in Wells Drury's *An Editor of the Comstock.* After the camp began to slump, Doten hung on until, just as he was about to have a snort in a bar, he saw the owner post a sign which read, "At midnight all drinks in this saloon reduced to ten cents." That comedown was too much for Alf. "Not much use trying to run a nonpareil paper in a long primer town," he decided.

"I was willing to stick it out as long as there was a living chance, but now that there is nothing but ten-cent shebangs, the old *News* might as well suspend."

So much for typography. As to make-up, it was a matter of dealer's choice. The front page might be wholly or partially devoted to ads. Or it might be filled with a hodgepodge of items, none of them considered front-page naturals now.

That was the tack taken by the Missoula, Montana *Mountaineer* in 1889. In place of changeable headlines, there were hand-lettered and decorated department flags reading, "Poetry," "Scientific," "Humorous," "Correspondence," "Miscellaneous," and "Died."

Certain papers put local news in the front showcase, but it was more apt to be found on pages two and three. If not used for advertisements, in place of page one, number four could shape up as what would now be called a feature page.

If the editor felt the call of originality, unlooked-for compositions might nest among the features. J. L. Harris, of the Brownwood, Texas *County Banner*, evidently thought his readers were sufficiently versed in Latin to enjoy macaronic poetry. The year again being 1889, he accordingly served them a long ballad, dealing with a hunting expedition through the moonlit snow, of which these are three stanzas:

> Nox was lit by lux of luna
> And 'twas night most opportoona
> To catch a 'possum or a coona;
> For nix was scattered o'er the mundus,
> A shallow nix and not profundus.
>
> On sic a night with canis unus
> Two boys went out to hunt a coonus,
> The corpus of this bonus canis
> Was full as long as octo span is.
>
> Hic bonus dog had one bad habit,
> Amabat much to tree a rabbit;
> Amabat plus to tree a rattus,
> Amabat bene to chase a cattus. . . .

Nothing has been said about an editorial page, because no necessity was felt for such a thing at a time when the line between reporting and comment was so indistinctly drawn. Sometimes an editor would formally address his readers, but the ones who did so didn't necessarily make a regular practice of it. Leaving out borrowed items, the man of the masthead was all over his paper in person anyhow, so the whole sheet was an editorial.

That came to be true of headlines also. While papers were of typewriter page size or smaller, headlines were given no play to speak of. Often they consisted of no more than tag phrases placed at the beginning of items and not above them. When separate from the articles they referred to, they usually consisted of only one or two lines of type not markedly larger than that used in the columns below.

But when larger presses killed the need for huddling, Western editors reacted as they had not, in the case of type sizes for the reading matter proper. With the lid off, headlines expanded like the springs of a freed jack-in-the-box. Where there had formerly been one line or a couple, a structure divided into half a dozen banks might tower above a column.

A peculiarity was the practice of bunching sub-heads before the start of an article, rather than interlarding it with them, as has since become the practice. Then as nothing was done by the book, the head writer had leave to say whatever occurred to him. Because of those two factors, he was free to excite a reader's curiosity to a degree not possible via a two- or three-line epigram, worked out by a man who can't exceed today's stingy headline word count.

Proof of this pudding can be found in connection with a story run in an 1882 number of the *Carbonate Chronicle*. This was the weekly edition of Cad Davis's daily *Chronicle*, published at Leadville, Colorado.

"There is a gentleman in Leadville today who would given ten years of those he expects to live, if he had never learned to write. He never committed forgery, so far as is known; he never signed any one's name but his own to a letter, and 'There's the rub.'"

That was the lead. Now for the steps by which the reader's steadily brightening eye was conducted to this real-life romance.

DEMURE, BUT OH MY!

How a Coy Adventuress Played It
on a Rank Sucker

Market Quotations on Stiffs

A Possible Divorce Suit on the Best
of Grounds

The Letter Racket

How It Was Played on a Prominent
Citizen by an Innocent-eyed Little
Woman from the Effete East.

A complex headline might include a bit of verse, as when Ned
McGowan, of the Sacramento *Phoenix*, leveled off at the editor of
the San Francisco *Bulletin*, organ-in-chief of the Vigilante gang
that had pushed McGowan around. Said journalist had had other
careers, and Ned wished to make that clear in advance of the
biography he was offering in an 1857 number of his sheet.

The Life of Thomas S. King, Alias
Slippery Sim
From Earth's Centre to the Sea
Nature Stinks of Thine and Thee
The Fratricide! The Bawd's Pimp
Who Lives on the Bones of His Brother
and the Flesh of His Wife
Alias Slant-eyed Tom, the Nipper Kid,
alias Dead-House Cove.

But associated headlines didn't always refer to different phases
of one story; at times they dealt with an assortment of unrelated
items in the column beneath. In this example, borrowed from an
1889 issue of the Brady, Texas *Sentinel*, only the first two apply
to the same article.

A Train Robbery

Failing to Force the Express Car the "Agents"
Plunder the Passengers

The Sioux Reservation for the White Man

Pennsylvania Strikes

To Pay the Law's Requirements by Hanging

The Democrats of Kentucky Have an Increased
Plurality of Over 18,000

Wool Firm's Finances Shaky

With that all-embracing exhibit the subject of headlines will be considered covered. As advertising will be treated in another chapter, this sketch of how frontier newspapers were put together seems reasonably complete, except for one thing.

There were times when a Western editor used his sheet for a purpose other than to inform, amuse, uplift or aggravate citizens of the town where he held forth. Ignoring them entirely, he would use space to chat with some pal, living elsewhere, to whom he would send a copy of his rag in lieu of dropping him a line.

An instance, when Semblens Forbes so used his Unionville, Nevada *Humboldt Register* in 1863, is particularly interesting. For the person addressed has become imbedded in American literature, through the fact that he was twice celebrated in sketches by Mark Twain. Pete Hopkins was a Gargantuan saloon keeper, beloved of the writers who covered Nevada's capital for its various newspapers, when the legislature was in session. Nostalgic for Pete's oasis, Forbes hailed him in the *Register* by the elision that formed the boniface's nickname and asked to be remembered to lucky barflies who weren't in exile.

"PETOPKINS, of the Magnolia in Carson, is the one reliable and permanent feature giving a character of permanence to the Capital. Times change; Territories are torn down and States built up . . . legislatures convene, fret through their brief term and pass away. Hopkins alone is a fixture; immutable in the midst of change, his light still burns, a beacon to guide thirsty souls to where congenial spirits be.

"Hopkins, Lance, John C. and Morg., we greet you. It is not fitting that the outside world should know more of this."

4

ADS À LA CARTE

BECAUSE NEWSPAPERMEN GENERALLY wrote the promotional as well as editorial matter for frontier journals, and because ads were often captioned as though they were news items, telling one from the other at a glance wasn't easy. "Ruby's Linen" suggests promotional copy today, and probably did to readers of Leadville, Colorado's *Chronicle* in 1882. Meanwhile, fellow items titled "Stand from Under!" and "Chicken Fight!" are suggestive of an editorial and a news story respectively. Actually Ruby didn't want to pay for having her undies washed and made the police blotter by arranging for a boy friend to shoo her laundress away with a six-gun. The two other articles were both advertisements, albeit of a kind not found in tamer communities.

"Chicken Fight!" did not describe a bout between game cocks. It was a come-on, offering drinkers the lure of an entertainment feature, inserted in the paper by the proprietor of the sponsoring saloon: "There will be three Chicken Fights on Saturday Evening at Denver Beer Hall, on Pine Street, for fifty dollars a fight, between a Kentucky Party and a Colorado Party. All are invited."

"Stand from Under!" on the other hand, belonged to that category of printed matter known as a "card." This was paid-for space, in which the buyer got off his chest something he considered worth giving a public airing. Cards ushered a large percentage of the West's formal duels; and the sponsor, if probably not the writer, of the Leadville card in question wasn't peacefully inclined either.

"As there has been considerable talk in regard to the late glove fight between Mahoney and Morgan, the latter gentleman doing the talking, I make him a proposition to fight him a fair fight at 120 pounds in three weeks from date of first deposit for any sum from

$10 to $1,000. $100 is now deposited at Edward Monahan's, which he can take down when he likes. And as Jimmy Reed threatened to hammer me, when he got me down town, I also offer him the same as Mr. Morgan. Business I mean, so put up or shut up, gentlemen.

Denis McCarty"

Another source of revenue was paid-for political advertising that obliged the accepting editor to chime in with a proportional amount of puffing in the editorial columns. Harry Ellington Brook of the San Francisco *Wasp* and the Los Angeles *Times* made that clear in reminiscences which covered an in-between period, when he had edited such mining-camp rags as the Quijotoa, Arizona *Prospector*.

"An election was harvest time." After affirming that, Harry told how the reaping was done. "For the publication of a card announcing the candidacy, there was a graduated rate, running from $10 for a Coroner, to $250 or so for a Sheriff . . . the price charged including a commensurate amount of 'favorable mention.'"

Pioneer newspapers weren't above giving themselves favorable mention. In 1883 Colonel John W. Redington—the "W" stood for Watermelon, the colonel swore—was in the habit of promoting his sheet by emblazoning the rocks and buildings of Oregon with such plugs as "The Heppner Gazette—Hell on Horse Thieves and Hypocrites."

In the main, though, frontier publishers concentrated on persuading other types of businesses to advertise in their newspapers. It wasn't the easiest part of a nowhere soft way of making a living. One Oregon veteran of numerous Indian wars explained that he used to be a newspaper publisher, but that he found soliciting—and collecting for—ads on the frontier such a rough business that he'd asked the Army to let him play it safe and scout against the Sioux and whatnot instead.

Yet as those who stayed in the game had to have advertising, they worked for it as assiduously as do the steerers of modern metropolitan journals. The chief difference was that on pioneer sheets the editorial and advertising departments weren't separate. There was, above all, no lofty pretense that the sanctum wasn't interested in the countinghouse returns.

Sometimes an appeal for paying matter was woven into a bona fide editorial item; and such was the approach of the Oregon City *Spectator* in 1846. "The time has come," W. G. T'Vault wrote, in a passage which gives a glimpse of what a frontier universe-hub looked like, while in the throes of being curry combed, "for a thorough and complete organization of our City Corporation. Our mayor and trustees are doing business in the right way. Our advice to them is. . . . Gentlemen, dig up the stumps, grade the streets, tax dogs, prohibit hogs—and advertise in the Spectator."

But there was nothing roundabout in the cry for aid issued by H. L. Weston, when he commenced publishing the Como, Nevada *Sentinel* in 1864. In need of ads to make his rag a going concern, he burst into doggerel so inclusive that it didn't overlook the possibility that among the stampeders to the mining camp were scholars who would profit by a bit of promotion.

> Come, you who burn the midnight taper,
> Contribute something for the paper;
> Come all, support the enterprise
> And in the paper advertise.
> Merchants, tailors, doctors, lawyers,
> Landlords, blacksmiths, teamsters, sawyers,
> Bakers, too, of bread, cake, pies,
> Come one, come all, and advertise.

The Houston *Musquito* of Sam Bangs used a word-to-the-wise approach. "We never yet knew or heard of a person who advertised liberally in the newspapers that did not receive an ample equivalent in the increase of his business."

The tack taken by John P. Hyland, master of the Rincón, New Mexico *Weekly Shaft* in 1893 was to let the merchants of his town know that bankruptcy was the sure fate of those not promotion-minded. "As a warning to those men who attempt to run a business without advertising, the following verses are printed:

> He had traveled through Sahara,
> Braved the dangers of the Nile,

> Defeated enraged Musselmen
> And dined on crocodile;
> Knew everything of politics,
> Religion and the law,
> Could box and fence and scull and race
> And please his mother-in-law,
> In short had all accomplishments
> Of men both great and wise,
> But he couldn't run a business,
> For he wouldn't advertise."

There were other fashions of telling merchants they had better advertise, or else. When Will Porter was running the Austin, Texas *Rolling Stone* in 1894, he carried a regular feature called the *Plunkville Patriot*, which was a take-off on struggling frontier weeklies. In one issue of the *Patriot* appeared an item about Adams and Co., a grocery firm which had been unwise enough to withdraw its support of Plunkville's news organ. "No less than three children have been poisoned by eating their canned vegetables," the story wound up, "and J. O. Adams, senior member of the firm, was run out of Kansas City for adulterating cod fish balls. It pays to advertise."

Now Porter had lived in the West quite a few years, by the time of his *Rolling Stone* days, and he wasn't making fun of anything that didn't exist. Blackmail was practiced by needy editors, even if not in quite so blatant a fashion. A genial 1879 example was a front-page story in Legh Freeman's Glendale, Montana *Atlantis*.

"A Pike County man who was being shaved yesterday . . . jumped six feet out of his chair, and came near losing one of his ears by the razor, when a blast was fired [Glendale was a mining town] in the pit. He said he labored under the hallucination that he was the victim of an earthquake. . . . But then that fellow had been taking his drinks where they don't advertise to support their home town paper, and a few gulps more of such sheep dip as he had imbibed would have produced an effect on his nervous system tending to make him believe that judgment was at hand and 'Old Nick' lifting the roof of the infernal regions, with a pitchfork in one hand and a crucible of hot lead and brimstone in the other."

But the pioneer editor was as loyal to the businessmen who did the right thing by the local paper as he was critical of those who failed to. As in the case of politicians who inserted cards announcing their intentions to run for office, merchants who advertised could count on supplementary editorial boosts.

"Brewster is always getting something good," the Houston *Musquito* mused in an 1841 issue which chanced to carry an ad inserted by that grocery dealer. "He has just received ten barrels of first rate cider which he is selling mighty cheap. Go try it." Apparently the apple wine didn't move quite as fast as the purveyor thought it should, for the *Musquito* buzzed again not much later: "MULLED CIDER—This delightful beverage may now be made by calling at Andy Brewster's and buying some of his first rate cider and fresh eggs."

There was also washy for ticky in the Gallup, New Mexico *Gleam* in 1893. "A fine brand of imported whiskey called Marion County [Kentucky], Spring 1881, has just been tapped at Sawyer's Club Rooms. Try some of it for medicinal purposes."

In any given camp, saloons were apt to be the most dependable advertisers. They were also the business houses with whose products the men of print were most familiar; and they could show an enthusiasm that wasn't feigned, when they took off their editorial hats and turned advertising copy writers. Of particular interest are certain bar ads, for in them the hand of known journalists can be traced.

Anti-wool wash in his editorial columns, Legh Freeman took pains to point out that none need be feared by patrons of a good, newspaper-supporting bistro. The virtues of one of these was thus touted in the Glendale *Atlantis:*

"William Parker's Saloon
Blacktail, Near Watson, Montana
Travelers Invited to Drop In
No Sheep Dip Dispensed
A jovial party of hilarious fellows
May usually be found congregated at this shrine
of Bacchus."

And W. J. "Semblens" Forbes, of the *Humboldt Register*, practically wrote his autobiography when composing the following advertisement for a Unionville, Nevada saloon. It was headed, "What, Ah, What?"

"What's so enlivening, when a man is arousing from the lethean embrace of balmy sleep. . . . What so cheering, then, what so awakens the appetite and the mind's facilities as a delicious cocktail?

"What's so invigorating, when the burthen of the clay is heavy on you . . . as 'something straight' to stiffen up with?

"What's so appropriate in which to pledge the health of your new found German cousin, as a mug of foaming beer?

"What's so soothing, when the labors of the day are ended, and you are about to take yourself to your virtuous sheets, as a generous draught of something hot, and what's so agreeable and natural, after the draught, as another?"

Yet at least one ad for a bar can safely be credited to the authorship of its proprietor. He was a Mr. Reitze of Sonora, California, and to appreciate him it is first needful to scan a civic brag which appeared in that mining camp's *Union Democrat* in 1873.

"Ours is a decidedly musical town, music by day, music by night, music all the time. If the cultivation of one of the fine arts is an indication of civilization, and we believe it is, ours must be a highly civilized community. Few of our youthful belles but are cultivating this fine art. It is one of the best accomplishments that a young lady, or gent for that matter, can possess. . . . Let it be universally cultivated. Let its strains flow until the hills and valleys of Tuolumne [county] are filled with enchantment."

There must have been all the enchantment that the high and low spots of Tuolumne could stand two years later. For in 1875 the *Union Democrat* carried this plug for one of the fine arts.

HARMONIC SALOON AND SHOOTING GALLERY
J. K. Reitze, proprietor
The very best of Wines, Liquors and Cigars
Call and See for Yourselves
John K. Reitze will Furnish Brass and String Music
for balls, parties, picnics and parades

Lessons given on the piano, organ and melodeon
Pianos tuned on liberal terms.

A. M. Holter and Bro., of Helena, Montana Territory, was another firm which dealt in more than one product. It showed this
duality in an ad run in the 1870 number of the Bozeman *Pick
and Plow*. Distillers and rectifiers, the Holter boys led off with
the announcement that they were the makers of "Rocky Mountain Dew, Pure Liquor at Low Prices." But after thus gaining the
readers' confidence, the copy snaps the tongue it had hanging
out back in by the wood alcoholic reminder that the company is
"Also Manufacturer of Lumber, Laths and Shingles."

To get back to saloons; in at least one instance, an establishment's advertising hinged on the fact that a man of print had
been a patron. Already something of the celebrity he was to become, Charles Farrar Browne put in a stint as a staff member of
the Virginia City *Territorial Enterprise* in 1863. After his passing,
the same town's *Evening Bulletin* for long carried this memorial
to his standing as an *arbiter elegantiarum* "Artemus Ward, Who
is one of the Best Judges of Liquors and Cigars on the Great
American Continent, during his sojourn in our city, always took
his drinks at Winn and Center's New Saloon on C. Street . . .
where he says he was never better treated—nor oftener—in his
life."

Still pioneer ads dealt with other matters than drinks or the
places where they might be obtained, and the men of print did
the best they could with these uncongenialities. In 1856 some
writer for the San Francisco *Bulletin* came up with the ensuing
forced smile for a department store which was pushing a certain
line of boots.

> They're all my fancy painted them,
> They're lovely, they're sublime;
> I never saw a thing so sweet
> As these new shoes of mine.
> They make my feet look so genteel
> That I am quite surprised;
> They're surely gems in shape of shoe
> That should be immortalized

About the same period a scribbler for the *Golden Era* went to

promotional bat for Lyon's Flea Powder. Although a San Francisco journal, the *Era* was largely aimed at mining-camp subscribers in its early years. Such places were apt to be good
markets for Mr. Lyon's product, and many men of print had
found that out while prospecting. Whoever this one was, he injected in his copy a realism that suggests he was drawing on
personal experience.

> In summer when the sun is low
> Come forth in swarms the insect foe,
> And for our blood they bore, you know,
> And suck it in most rapidly. . . .
>
> But fleas, roaches, 'skeeters—black or white—
> In death's embrace are stiffened quite,
> If Lyon's powder chance to light
> In their obscure vicinity.

Sometimes, when forced to become panegyrists of dry goods,
editors cheered themselves up by finding literary connections
where they might least be expected. One instance was an ad in
an 1889 issue of the Bozeman, Montana *Chronicle*.

> "THE BUSTLE
>   Is not a modern invention, Bustles were worn at the end
> of the last century, and the following conundrum is credited to Sir
> Walter Scott: 'Why is the bustle like an historical novel? Because it
> is a fiction based on fact.' This statement is also based on fact, that we
> have the most popular bustles in the market, such as the Silver Crown,
> Tippecanoe [no fooling; that wasn't made up], Full Dress, Bridge-
> port, Pearl and Comfort at the same prices they are retailed in the
> East."

There was one non-booze ad, though, that fired up a man of
print. Love of the subject is written all over copy reproduced in
the Fresno, California *Expositor*.

> Attention! Sinners!
>
> Hot Stuff Coffins
>
> Asbestos! Asbestos!
>
> My factory . . . is turning out a line
> of Asbestos Coffins that are rapidly

going out of sight. No one need fear
the hereafter, as I guarantee to see a
corpse through without singeing a hair

W. Parker Lyon

Philanthropist and Furniture King

As has been true of later journals, notices of births, marriages,
and deaths were paid for by those who inserted them in pioneer
ones. The headings of this department were at times off standard,
however. In Fred Mariott's San Francisco *News Letter* these matters were lumped as "The Cradle, the Altar and the Grave." And
some pioneer journal, remissly not named in an American newspaper survey, was reported as using the caption, "Hatched,
Matched and Dispatched."

Other forms of classified advertising prevailed, of course, on
the Western frontier. More of it dealt with lost stock and located
land than was true of the rest of the country, but otherwise its
nature was much the same as that of such insertions elsewhere.
There were want ads, "For Sale" ones and personals, none of
them making for noteworthy reading matter. Yet here, too, the
picture brightened when men of print were the dealers.

In 1875, for example, William J. Berry inserted this classified
advertisement in his Yuma, Arizona *Sentinel.* "WANTED: A
nice, plump, healthy, good natured, good looking, domestic and
affectionate lady to correspond with. Object—Matrimony. Such a
lady can find a correspondent by addressing the editor of this
paper. . . . If anybody doesn't like our way of going about
this interesting business, we don't care. It's none of their business."

The best thought-out entry in this field, however, was run by
Judson A. Boyakin, associate editor of the Boise City, Idaho
Statesman. After somebody had sneaked into the paper's plant
and lifted his pistol, Jud advertised as follows: "STOLEN from
this office. A Revolver. The Person returning it will be given its
contents and no questions asked."

5

QUEEN CITIES AND QUAINT
SUBSCRIPTION LISTS

IN ADDITION TO local advertising, the pioneer newspaper publisher counted on cracking the national field. At least he did after the establishment of a stagecoach-line network made it possible for the government to offer much of the West something like regular mail service. Then newspapermen had a reliable means of communication with Eastern distributors, and these could count on getting proof that their ads had actually been run.

It is not the purpose here to discuss the nature of this imported advertising, as it was not originally printed, let alone written, in the West. Instead the subject will be an examination of what frontier papers had to offer Eastern industrialists in the way of circulations.

In this corner cozy dreams, in that one facts without a shirt. It is difficult to say which now seems more given to leaping before looking; the editor who saw in the wilderness a mass of subscribers or the man of commerce who invested promotional dollars in a journal, whose very site of publication might have been given back to the prairie dogs by the time he mailed payment for services rendered. But ever since Atlantic seaboard mercantile gents had cashed in on San Francisco as they had never believed possible, unreason had sneaked into the Rialto. So stay-at-home business johns were as ready to believe that any frontier spot was a treasury as were ink-slinging adventurers to find the map of a metropolis in intersecting wagon tracks.

This chronicle will leave the madness of Eastern industrialists to be inferred from a report of the circulations they saw as warranting the investment of money in distant periodicals. As for the men of print, the above remark about their state of mind was borrowed from Charles W. Brand of the Laramie, Wyoming *Sun*. Speaking of the typical frontier editor, Brand declared that, "Even in his sober moments—and he has 'em—he sees things. Given a country store at an isolated cross roads and he builds a city. . . . A forty dollar addition to your modest shack makes it a mansion, and his town is the only one and the best ever. He is always willing to fudge a little in handling cold fact, and as a prophet he simply skunks Elijah and all his ilk."

Some journalists did guess right, or more or less so, anyhow. Certain towns achieved economic stability and maintained steady growth during the nineteenth century. But not counting ports on the Pacific Coast, only Denver had taken on the dimensions of a capital city by the close of the pioneer period. Though showing some of the promise they have since kept, Houston, Dallas, and San Antonio were all well under 50,000. Smaller again but towering above the rest were Omaha, Lincoln, Topeka, Ft. Worth, Galveston, Pueblo, Salt Lake City, and Spokane.

Others that since have assumed metropolitan stature were showing no more signs of it, as of 1900, than the ruck of the slow-coach rural burgs which then made up the population centers of an area embracing over 1,800,000 square miles. Among these were many which were on the wane in place of waxing, while an uncomputed number lived only in the files of the papers which once had trumpeted their glories.

So in the vastness wedged between the Mississippi Valley and the Pacific Ocean less than a score of settlements had come anywhere near realizing the hopes vested in them, when they were apples in the eyes of editors looking for Romes to build. For the great fact about the West, in this connection, was that urban grandeur was the prevalent expectation of any seed huddle of huts. How many entries there actually were in this race for magnificence nobody has as yet undertaken to calculate, but there were many hundreds, including scores of which the very sites are now matters of speculation.

It was written of Merlin that he followed a gleam that none but he could see, while en route to some mystical but certain goal. The difference between the old wizard and most pioneer newspapermen was that the gleams in their eyes led them here and there but never to any but goldless rainbow ends. Many could never grasp the enormous odds stacked against them, because they were young and felt no facts of life were proof against the combination of their passion and the magic of the printed word. Fortunately for history, though, the scales fell from the glims of a sharp operative called John Hanson Beadle, who laid out the score, as seen in retrospect by a man who'd been one of the players.

"It is one of the 'curiosities of literature' with me, how these mountain towns can support the papers they do," he mused in a volume of reminiscence and comment. "Here is Denver with ten thousand people and three dailies. . . . Little Corinne, Utah, with some 1500 people, has kept up a vigorous daily for two years and a half."

Beadle rung in the Corinne *Reporter,* because he himself had been its editor in days when both its population and expectations were larger than they were by the time John began putting *The Undeveloped West* together. That work is notable for a passage which nutshells the story of the West's boom towns and their newspapers.

Corinne had come into being when the tracks of the Union Pacific reached Bear River in 1868. Although Bear River City was the terminal burg which erupted at the point of crossing, some son of opportunity had discovered that the stream's head of navigation was not far below. His reasoning then was that fleets of merchantmen, plying back and forth between Great Salt Lake and a river port served by a spur of the U.P., were bound to create a metropolis there.

"Sanguine real estate owners predicted a city of ten thousand people within two years," Beadle wrote of Corinne. "And they believed it, too. Let no man imagine that the citizens of new and lively Western towns are only talking to draw outsiders; they convince themselves long before they try to convince others—as witness the fact that very few of them sell out when the excitement is at their height. Corner lots in Corinne went up to fabulous prices. All seemed to be satisfied that the location of the

'Chicago of the Rocky Mountains' was definitely settled. Every morning the *Reporter* contained a new and encouraging scheme to insure commercial importance. Here was to be an enduring city, the entrepôt of all trade from the northern Territories; here was to be the Queen City of the Great Basin."

The *Reporter's* optimism got under the pelts of Salt Lake City's fathers, who feared their town would be overshadowed by the drumming cock grouse up the Bear River. "The Mormon papers," as John Hanson went on to note, "denounced Corinne as the home of devils. . . . They ransacked Scripture for precedents. . . . It was as wicked as Sodom, to perish under Heaven's wrath; it was Moab, and the Lord's washpot, it was Edom, over which he could cast his shoe.

"Vain denunciations and equally vain hopes. The railroad was completed, and all our floating population drifted to fresh fields; the 'dull times' of 1869 came on and Corinne subsided to a moral and quiet burg of perhaps 400 inhabitants. Better times came in 1870 . . . and the Queen City is now a thriving country village of perhaps 1200 people. My corner lots, which cost me $500, are on sale at a discount, and other real estate owners are in like case."

Towns which pinned their hopes on shipping were rare in the West, because rivers which could be depended on to be moist the year around were alike scarce. But other grounds for inspiring promoters with faith in future civic grandeur were frontier commonplaces. In the mountains there were the gold, silver, or copper strikes, drawing prospectors or mine workers and those who flocked to serve or prey upon them. On the prairie or plains the same function was performed by stampeders to grab up land claims. In both types of terrain railroads could bring the purchasing power of thousands of drilling terriers to terminal construction points. Or they could bolster towns which jumped for a while as the ends of cattle trails or the starts of those leading to gold fields.

But when the bright metals were gone—and frequently they were never present in better than short supply—the wonder towns they had brought into being withered to nothing much at best;

as often as not they dried up completely and blew away. Burgs of more permanence could and did emerge from the dust kicked up by land boomers; but what was found when it had settled was usually no more than an unglittering rural trading center. As for the fortunes of railhead towns, they can best be expressed by the law of gravity reading that whatever goes up must come down. Swollen by temporary conditions, they were deflated when these were removed.

Yet in spite of many collapses the belief that a fast beginning was prelude to future magnificence was *par excellence* the pioneer Western driving force. And what really marked the passing of the frontier was the dearth of more places conceived of as New Yorks to be.

Before that loss of innocence was arrived at, all hamlets were queen cities of the horizon; and it was the men of print who were their most ardent lovers. It wouldn't be fair to say they were fickle ones, merely because they perforce came to sing the praises of more than one. Their feelings were expressed by the lines of the ditty reading: "My love remains the same, the object only changes." When one town of royal promise died, or waxed too moribund for hope to stay planted there, a given editor would charge in quest of the veritable one he felt sure of finding somewhere. He might range but one state or territory, or he might make the entire West his queen city hunting ground. Arrived in a new Nineveh in embryo, he would pause only to change the dateline before going into glad promotional action once more.

Although there seems to have been but one paper which was actually so called—an editor in Dakota Territory put his love in the banner when he issued the Spearfish *Queen City Mail*—that's the star the roving men of print hitched their presses to. Remaining to be seen is what they had to buoy them in the way of evidence that prosperity was laying for them around the corner in any Western camp.

John Beadle got out of Corinne, when at length convinced that it would not become the Chicago of the Rocky Mountains. Yet, as he went on to say, the *Reporter* continued in business as a daily. The town it served slid further downhill, and at the turn of the century had only 231 inhabitants. But at the time John abandoned it, there was hope of steady, slow growth, even if ballooning was no longer seen as a possibility. Not as ambitious as Beadle, the men who carried on felt they had a pretty good thing, nor is there any reason why they should not have done so. By the standards of the pioneer West, their sheet had a healthy circulation.

The Undeveloped West, the work including John's account of the in-and-de-flation of Corinne, was published in 1873. N. W. Ayer's national newspaper directory for that year shows that the *Reporter* had a circulation of 960.

If that seems small, the figure will loom larger when compared with some to follow. All the given circulations, by the way, are based on Ayer's report of 1873. This was a median frontier year, for if the West had been spanned by rails, that had then been accomplished by only one line.

The daily Los Angeles *Star* had 500 subscribers. The Houston *Age* daily catered to but 325 buyers. At that it was doing better than the San Antonio *Express*. Having a subscription list which was exactly one fourth as long as the Corinne *Reporter*'s, the *Express* had 240 customers.

Still the voice of San Antonio was doing fine when its subscription income was measured against that of the Seattle *Dispatch*. The firm of Brown and Son, publishers of the paper, notified Ayer that it was daily sold to 144 people.

With an assist from a great utility, the Cheyenne *Leader* did better. Its publisher was so cheered by the state of his business that he told all about it in his report to the directory. According to him, the *Leader* was "the only newspaper in Wyoming sold on the cars of the Union Pacific Railway for over 500 miles." Because of that monopoly, the paper's daily circulation had escalated to 280, while there were 310 buyers of the sheet's weekly edition.

Most of the dailies put out a weekly, too. Commonly issued on Saturday, when out-of-towners rode in to do their marketing, it was made up of items culled from issues of the past five days. *The Rocky Mountain News* so supplemented its income, even though by 1873 it had attained the status described by Beadle. "Byers' Rocky Mountain News (the paper is scarcely heard of as dissociated with Byers) is *the* institution of Colorado. It has survived fires, flood, Indian blockades and Federal patronage . . . to tell us every morning at breakfast all of note that has transpired in any part of the world down to the midnight preceding." *The* institution of Denver, as well as all the rest of Colorado, boasted a daily circulation of 1475.

Before he read the writing on the wall, when the bars of a once high prancing town stooped to lowering the price of whiskey shots from two bits to a dime, Alf Doten had been scoring better than William Byers. In the years of its ascendance, of which 1873 was one, the Gold Hill *News* could count on 1500, able and willing to pay for it daily.

Considered a smashing success, Portland's daily *Oregonian* had an even thousand more subscribers than the Corinne *Reporter* for a total of 1960. Certain San Francisco papers had subscription lists running into five figures, to be sure, but from 1849 on the Golden Gate's city had been too much of a success to belong in competition with any other Western town of the nineteenth century. Leaving its dailies out of account, the best seller of frontier journalism was the *Territorial Enterprise* of Nevada's Virginia City. It was regularly reached for by 2100 patrons.

Although the number of pioneer diurnals was astounding, in view of the support available, most of the men of print settled for being masters of weeklies. These also reported their circulations to N. W. Ayer. Considering the modest figures quoted, it would seem that honesty prevailed, but a spokesman for the Beaumont, Texas *News Beacon* was not of that opinion. "Refuses to state circulation, because it gives rascals the advantage," the directory duly noted.

While some papers were a little better off, the Grasshopper Falls, Kansas *Grasshopper* was well above average in reporting 600 weekly subscribers. *The New Republic* of Bunker Hill, in the same state, turned in 400 as a circulation figure, but its publisher was careful to point out that this was but an estimate.

There were other guessers. Without bothering to say where old

Bogy was, some pioneer had undertaken to name an Idaho settlement New Bogy. With J. H. Moore at the helm, the New Bogy *Vindicator* served a public estimated as totaling 250.

It should be kept in mind that, then as now, the purpose of Ayer's annual directories was to post national advertisers as to what newspapers were available for promotional purposes. The reporting sheets were competing for advertising revenue, and some of them were not content to let figures speak unaided.

The Missoula, Montana *Missoulian* assured scanners of the directory that its 400 subscribers made it "the best advertising medium in the West." Claiming but 300 readers, the Blanco City *West Texas Republican* pointed out that it was the "only newspaper in the rapidly developing section northwest of San Antonio as far as El Paso, a distance of 700 miles."

Writing in from the then not separated Dakotas, L. D. F. Poore noted of the Springfield *Times* that its standing was that of "the frontier paper of the territory, circulates largely on the upper Missouri, at military posts and Indian agencies; official paper of the United States and Bon Hommie County." With all that help from the Indians, the Army, the united settlers of the high Missouri, and the federal and county governments, Poore couldn't have been blamed if he had yielded to the temptation of padding the returns. But he played it straight, just as he did when showing how Bon Homme was pronounced in Springfield, and wrote that there were 250 subscribers to the *Times*.

That was likewise the figure offered by the publisher of the Las Vegas, New Mexico *Gazette*. He pointed out, though, that his sheet could be depended on, whereas unnamed rivals could not. "The *Gazette*," he affirmed, "is the only regularly issued paper in San Miguel County."

Operating in Albuquerque, William McGuiness wasn't dismayed by his admission that the *Republican Review* had no more than an even 100 readers. For they were yet subscribers to "the only paper in Bernalillo County and one of the largest in the territory."

Incredibly, these rags did get national advertising, if not in fortune-making quantities. But that they got any at all testifies to

the gullibility of Eastern businessmen where the West was concerned. Like the pioneer editors themselves, they must have been
more swayed by excited claims on the futures of frontier towns
than by the cooler lessons of current arithmetic.

But the point worth heeding here is what the queen city hunts-
men realized in terms of local support of their papers. Nor did
subscription lists include only paying patrons. Many reported
subscriptions were partly based on hopes of what coming days
would shower down. Leaving men of print out of the count, the
camps with collapsible dreams of becoming Londons were peopled by more fortune questers than finders. But where all were
believed to have a chance at knocking over the red swan, all had
credit—until the boom began to sound hollow.

A burg's newspaper publishers—and there might be several
fighting for readers, where these didn't number more than 2000 or
3000—could not afford to turn down subscribers, so they extended
credit to any who asked for it. The *leitmotif* of pioneer journalism
consists, in fact, of alternate groans about free riders and appeals
to their perhaps non-existent better natures.

"If our employees were cannibals," the Marion, Kansas *Western
News* opined, "we'd feed 'em awhile on delinquent subscribers."

The Molson, Washington *Leader* tried the good-humored approach; and to render himself more appealingly human, its
spokesman dispensed with the Olympian "we" and wrote in the
first person. "Some women knead dough with gloves on; if [paid]
subscriptions don't come in faster, I will need dough without
anything on."

A wheedle based on the bird of time's discrimination was the
method tried by the Vermillion *Dakota Republican*. "The average
length of a farmer's life is sixty-five, while that of a printer is
thirty-three, hence the necessity of paying for your paper
promptly."

Payment, when forthcoming, didn't necessarily mean money.
The Salt Lake City *Deseret News* was but one sheet which
regularly published a list of the goods it would accept for subscriptions in lieu of cash. But perhaps the most comprehensive
statement was made by the Flagstaff, Arizona *Sun-Democrat*.

"We will take money, bonds, bills, cast off clothing, or anything else animate or inanimate in exchange for our newspaper efforts."

The *Sun-Democrat's* editor wasn't fooling, when he hinted that livestock would be acceptable. There was plenty of pioneer precedent. The owner of the Broken Bow, Nebraska *Republican,* for instance, got a bronco from a subscriber who had more cayuses than lettuce, though the mustang didn't stay hitched outside the sanctum. Owing a typesetter back wages, the publisher straightway turned the horse over to that worthy.

Buffalo tongues, shares of maybe-good mining claims—if it could now be accurately compiled, the list of items exchanged for subscriptions on the frontier would make bizarre reading. At stake here, though, are two different matters. The frontier man of print often did business by barter, which is another way of saying he was chronically undercapitalized.

That malaise, next to the failure of boom towns to stay prosperous, was the chief bane of the queen-city seekers. A publisher might be able to use a secondhand saddle himself; but he couldn't buy newsprint with it, or pay taxes in such coin either. The result was summed up by John Beadle, who had been there. Before launching a reasonably successful venture in Corinne, Beadle had fought a losing battle with the economics of pioneer newspaper publishing in Salt Lake City. After observing that a publisher was expected to pay his bills, whether or not his subscribers and advertisers did, John finished by stating, "My journal was now in the regular condition of half the Rocky Mountain papers: Struggle, debt and litigation make up their chronic condition and failure their normal end."

How editors kept able to move from the site of one bankrupt venture to the scene of the next one is a mystery in many cases. In others, there are accounts of their ways of raising a stake so they could try again. It has been told how Semblens Forbes made money on a saloon which he blew on a newspaper. Even farther removed from the expected pursuits of an editor was the second bow string of Orlando E. Jones. Between stints on such Nevada papers as the Virginia *Daily Union,* the Hawthorne *Oasis,* and

the Aurora *Star*, Orlando accrued the money to get back in
journalism by performing as a circus clown.

Of Edgar Rye, once of the Albany, Texas *News* and later of
the Los Angeles *Cactus*, Don Biggers wrote that he was by turns
"attorney, justice of the peace, poet, sign painter, builder,
decorator, vagabond and editor." There were other jacks-of-all-
trades who could easily find jobs when the journalistic going got
rough. There were also those who were able only at vagabondage
when away from the smell of ink. Living on nothing explained in
the dictionary, they would drift about until the wind blew open
some print shop door and set them back to work again.

Some were accustomed to moonlighting, drudging on the side
at this or that, so they could afford the luxury of putting out newspapers. Joe Ellis Johnson was a conspicuous example of such enslavement to the press. While he was publishing the *Huntsman's
Echo* at Wood River, Joe also ran a general store, a bakery, a
hotel, and a daguerreotype studio in that Nebraska town.

Now and then patronage would help a man of print solve his
problems for a while. Sam Bangs became the state printer of
Texas and James O'Meara—a rover from San Francisco Bay to the
Columbia River and back again—held the same post in California.
Cad Davis got to be the postmaster of Leadville, Colorado, as
well as editor of the *Chronicle;* John Clum headed Tombstone's
P.O. while functioning in the sanctum of the *Epitaph;* without
leaving the helm of the *Boomerang*, Bill Nye directed mail service at Laramie, Wyoming.

Poor health made Nye give up that bowl of gravy. It was badly
needed, too, for the *Boomerang*—named for Bill's pet mule—was
more enjoyable to others than it was a source of profit to him. In
place of sulking, though, he wrote the following letter to Chester
A. Arthur, then holding forth in Washington, D.C. as President
of the United States:

Postoffice Divan, Laramie City, W. T., Oct., 1883
Sir,
    I beg leave at this time to officially tender my resignation as post-
master of this place. If Deacon Hayford does not pay up his box rent,
you might as well put his mail in general delivery, and when Bob

Hurd gets drunk and insists on a letter from one of his wives every day of the week, you can salute him through the window of the box delivery with an old Queen Anne tomahawk, which you will find near the Etruscan wash pail. You will find the postal cards which have not been used under the distributing table, and the coal down in the cellar. If the stove draws too hard, close the damper in the pipe and shut the general delivery window. . . .

Although Nye didn't yet know it, he could afford to laugh about forfeited patronage; for he was about to join the frontier journalists who cashed in on their talents by going East, where they were well paid for. Some who stayed in the West, if they played it safe by sticking in one of the few solidly established towns, might also do better than get by. But the wandering queen-city lads repeatedly learned the truth of a quatrain published by the Laramie *Sentinel* when looking forward to the demise of the rival *Wyoming Morning News* in 1877:

> Leaf by leaf the roses fall,
> Dime by dime the purse runs dry;
> One by one beyond recall,
> Mushroom papers droop and die.

6

AN OPERATIONAL COMPOSITE

THERE WAS MORE going on in a pioneer printing plant than the publishing of a newspaper, of course. If that has earlier been little more than suggested in passing, it will be emphasized now by letting the Guthrie, Oklahoma *Getup* speak for the importance of job printing.

When writing of his career as a frontier editor in Arizona, Harry Brook declared that "none of the two-bit papers depended entirely on subscription and commercial layout for support." Seeing glim to glim professionally with Harry, the *Getup's* publisher flatly told his subscribers that he'd have to do other kinds of printing or go out of business.

The year was 1890, or the one following the Boomer Run of 50,000 paleface settlers, which had the effect of changing the Indian territory into a candidate for United Stateshood. "Praise God and all ye good people," the *Getup* intoned, "and let these prairies resound to the measured strokes of our job press. Ah, there is the rub, for if you do not give us job work, we will have to go back to our wife's folks. This would put us in a h—— of a fix, as we are not married."

But whether or not job work put more in the till than newspaper publishing—and that was no doubt a variable—the sheet issued at any town was the talisman counted on to bring such business in. For one thing, it was the plant's showpiece typographically. Then every time it appeared, it advertised the shop and reminded readers, usually by house ads as well as indirectly, that its facilities were available. It was also the means of making the printer-editor a citizen influential enough to render businessmen and politicians glad to keep on his good side by making use of his other facilities. It furthermore gave its name to the whole operation. For when a broadside or pamphlet was issued, there was commonly the notation that it was printed by the *Gazette*, *Star*, or what not.

Far from ignoring pioneer job work, this narrative will later devote chapters to productions of that kind. Here, however, it will merely be stressed that piece printing was about half the package in an editor's mind when he picked some point on the sunset side of old Westport, Missouri, as a publishing site.

By splicing together the statements of a variety of men, it is possible to fashion a continuity out of the story of the frontier newspaper. Undercapitalization has been declared as their standard condition. Yet it is an alias of necessity, when it comes to mothering inventions.

As corners had to be cut by printers in narrow circumstances, they bought what they had to and helped themselves to what they could. One item which could easily be obtained free, by a visitor to an unwatched cemetery, was the imposing stone. A slab of marble, face down, was none the worse for having *hic jacet* on the unused side; and that this was a view taken by some is demonstrated by a passage in the memoirs of one Jerry B. Graham. Billing himself as a tramp printer, Jerry noted of a roving colleague: "Old Ormsby's plant consisted of a couple of cases of 'long primer' head letters, an inverted gravestone and chases."

His equipment somehow assembled, the pioneer publisher was ready to find a queen city. Usually he looked for one where a settlement had already been started, but he by no means always waited for that formality.

William J. Osborn and William H. Adams, partners in founding the *Kansas Weekly Herald* at Leavenworth, were do-it-yourself pioneers. What they accomplished in 1854 was related by Henry King, editor of several Topeka papers, when addressing a gathering of Kansas newspapermen in 1877.

Of the *Herald*, King said, "It came even before our sins. The town-site folks found it when they were staking off lots and tossing coppers for choice building spots. It was under an elm tree down by the river, and the Indian summer sunshine gave a trace of gold to the printed sheets, and the absurd tympan, swaying to and fro in the open air. There was not a house within thirty miles, not so much as a cow path for a street, not a field of plowed land, near or far in all Kansas."

Osborn and Adams never told what had prompted them to choose a site which proved the seed of what was to be the state's metropolis for a good few years. They did print something about the publishing conditions imposed upon them, after the advent of subscribers had justified their move. "We have had to forego many of the luxuries of life, living and printing out of doors, writing editorials on a shingle and sleeping on the ground."

In retrospect, at least, the men of the *Herald* weren't lonely while bivouacked under their tree, or at all uncertain as to the outcome of their gamble. Of the elm selected as Leavenworth's cornerstone, the paper ran this 1855 rhapsody:

> Thy arms were kindly spread above
>   The Kansas Herald press
> No stronger evidence of love
>   Could move a human breast;
> And from beneath thy shade was sent
>   To every distant clime
> The sheet that first from Kansas went
>   To tell the march of time.

How many Vietnamese, Hottentots, or Laplanders found early issues of the *Herald* on local newsstands is something that hasn't been tabulated. But nothing could be a more complete expression of the queen-city attitude. Once a spot had been selected as the site of a metropolis, it was viewed as having the standing of one of the world's recognized population centers.

But there was one man, and in the same year, who went Adams and Osborn one better. Joe Ellis Johnson was so previous that he even outstripped his own equipment when undertaking to publish the Omaha *Arrow*. The metropolis of Nebraska was lucky to have Joe for its first citizen, for he saw to it that the town was appropriately named. As postmaster of the established burg on the Iowa side of the Missouri, Johnson had performed the service to poetry of having the name changed from Kanesville to Council Bluffs. When moving west of the river, such a man could be counted on not to deface the map with a clinker of nomenclature.

Leaving his press in Council Bluffs, Joe set up his Omaha office, not under a tree but on the stump of one. His desk was his beaver hat, as he began composing an editorial in praise of "this highly favored and beautiful Territory upon which we have now for the first time established a regularly weekly paper. . . . The pioneering squatter and the uncivilized red men are our constituents and neighbors. The wolves and deer are our traveling companions, and the wild birds and prairie winds our musicians. Surrounded by associations and scenes like these, what do you expect from us, anxious reader? Don't be disappointed if you do not always get that which is intelligible and polished from our pen. . . . Take therefore what you get with a kindly heart and no grumbling."

Joe himself didn't grumble even when the Missouri pitched a flood which forced him to cease publication for lack of supplies. "Well, friends," he wrote at the close of this interruption, "it has been some time since we last met, but here we are again. Providence and the BAD STATE OF NAVIGATION ON THE MISSOURI has played smash with our calculations, and we have not been able to 'come up to time' in the issuing of the Arrow, but expect before long to make it permanent at Omaha, or place it in hands that will do you justice and honor to themselves. In the mean time we send you the [Council Bluffs] *Bugle* in its place, which contains everything of stirring interest in Nebraska."

Later a journalist in Oregon, Addison Bennett wasn't so fortunate in his choice of a spot to promote as a town. Bennett, by the way, is credited with being the author of that piece of sardonic American balladry titled *The Little Old Sod Shanty on the Claim*. In this case the claim was not a mining one; it was composed of supposedly arable acres made available by the federal government under the Homestead Act.

Some that seized opportunity by the forelock got chapped hands in doing so. Nor did Addison overlook that fact when composing the following stanza:

> Oh, the hinges are of leather
> And the windows have no glass
> And the board roof lets the howling blizzard in.

> I can hear the hungry coyote
> As he sneaks up in the grass
> In my little old sod shanty on the claim.

In the spring of 1879, though, Bennett hadn't found out at first hand what winter could be like for pioneers pushing into a region where there was scant wood to build with, and where commonly the chips of gone buffalo furnished fuel for semi-dugouts, probed by the lancets of savage winters. Another thing that he hadn't learned was that for farm land to pay off it had to be harvestable as well as plantable.

There was only one house in the patch of Kansas sward that Bennett named Pearlette, when he hastened there to establish the *Call*. Yet it looked as though Addison had placed a sound bet. Pearlette had a far more promising beginning than Omaha, for 2500 homesteaders followed the editor into a section where the land was indeed arable. But in 1880 the reaping was done by grasshoppers, and Bennett was one of the 2400 who on that account left their little old sod shanties in an area they no longer claimed.

Precipitate and glad of it, on the other hand, were W. A. Laughlin and A. W. Merrick, founders, in 1876, of the Dakota Territory *Black Hills Pioneer*. Four months before this gold region was ceded by the reluctant Sioux, these Denver men of print put their scalps up for auction while wheeling a press to where the law said they couldn't yet operate. They kept their hair, but didn't avoid the next worse thing in a printer's *Articles of War*. Their type was pied, when their wagon tipped over, and they had to unscramble and resort it by letters before they could begin serving the settlement which became Deadwood.

What was true of most treasure towns, though, was that reports of magnificent finds drew editors, eager to be first to reach an already established camp. A case history of this sort was recited by Harry Brook, when recalling, in an item written for the Los Angeles *Times* in 1890, how he had started the Quijotoa, Arizona *Prospector* in 1881.

"In order to head off possible competition (as there was always a rush to establish a newspaper in any boom town), the first few numbers were set up in the office of a small weekly in Tucson, sixty-five miles distant, while awaiting the arrival of the first class outfit that had been ordered from San Francisco. The office in question had scarcely enough equipment to do its own work, and consequently the early numbers of the Quijotoa *Prospector* consisted of a little six-column, four page weekly presenting an astonishing array of types of all shapes and sizes, some of which had been knocking around the frontier for a quarter of a century."

There were, contrastively, mining towns whose stampeders decided that they were going to be queen cities before newspapermen got around to hailing them as such. Reasoning that they would have to have a journal to front for them, before the urban standing of their burgs would be elsewhere recognized, the citizens of such camps went shopping for editors.

That enterprise, on the part of the early residents of Boise, Idaho, changed the destiny of James Reynolds—and may well have accounted for the fact that their camp became the metropolis of the state in place of Idaho City. Having heard good things of that place, Reynolds was on the way there with a printing outfit in 1864, when a delegate from Boise City intercepted him. Authorized to find a publisher and pledge him a bonus of $1500, this fellow talked the kind of language a man of print didn't always hear. Instead of turning off toward Idaho City, Jim took the fork leading to Boise and there started the *Statesman*.

A mushrooming queen city hailed the actual founding of a newspaper as a coronation symbol. And whether or not the residents were able or eager to support one, they marked the arrival of editors by public rejoicing.

Such was the welcome given Semblens Forbes and Charles L. Perkins, when they came to Unionville, Nevada, in 1863, bent on publishing the *Humboldt Register*. In the absence of cannon, Westerners fired charges of gunpowder, compressed by being weighted down by blacksmith anvils. Consequent were salutes which were satisfactorily loud. There were thirty-one of such tributes for the *Register*, after which the townsmen held a mass parade, headed by Unionville's lone cornetist.

The reception given the founders of the *Sentinel* in Como,

Nevada, was even more ecstatic. Having taken the precaution of making sure they were wanted, via a visit in advance, the publishers-to-be had sent for their printing equipment. What happened when it arrived was jotted in the 1864 volume of his journal by Alf Doten.

"At various times during the day passers on the road arriving [in Como] reported the progress of the team with the press— preparation was made to receive them in posh style—P. M. the Como 'brass band' turned out—just a light spring wagon for band wagon—Alex's mule, and Hermit's big mule—both dressed out with plumes . . . Hermit and Jacobson rode also and supported pole with Cross's big flag—6 of us in all—played down through town and up—drove down to Palmyra . . . met team [the one drawing the press] just below town—stopped, treated teamsters to some cocktails we had along—gave them 3 cheers—escorted them up playing lively airs—all stopped at Arnhold's—he treated and we treated—drove on up—gave Dasye a time—stopped at Rappahammick shaft—got all the boys out—treated them—they gave us three cheers—all the miners on all sides left the diggins for Como to see the fun—as the plumes of our mules appeared over the divide—the anvils commenced firing—two batteries of them—1 at each end of town—firing just as fast as they possibly could. . . . Train preceded by band, playing 'Hail, Columbia' and 'Yankee Doodle,' passed gaily down Main St., past Cross's & up 5th Avenue to printing office—Citizens gave us lots of cheers —jolly time."

Whether he picked a publishing site, or was in one by invitation, the editor had to find a roof for his gear. Yet the sheltered plant could offer working conditions more dismaying than the open-air one of the *Kansas Weekly Herald*. Addison Bennett's authorship of the *Little Old Sod Shanty on the Claim* has been mentioned, but not the fact that his particular shanty was the office of the *Pearlette, Kansas Call*.

Pursuant to describing the difficulties of building a turf mansion, Bennett wrote of his professional duties. "And after we got in our little home, we found ourselves so cramped that things went very slow. Just think of a family of five living in a house 11 by 14 [feet]! Then in addition, put in a printing office, stamp factory, stencil shop, etc. . , and you will wonder why we can work at all—as we often do."

Ready, after some fashion, to start operating, the newspaper-man had to begin working for subscription support. In a Western town this process demanded a good head for liquor, witness Harry Brook, when telling how the Quijotoa, Arizona *Prospector* was floated. "In a canvassing trip for subscribers, through the embryo camp before the first number had been issued, I took in $315 within a couple of hours, at the rate of $5 a year, of which $30 went for 'hospitality,' as three fourths of the 'business houses' were saloons."

Advertising was secured in the same way in a world where most business conferences were held in bars, though at the outset there might be padding to make the paper look prosperous. Of the Prescott *Arizona Miner*, John H. Marion wrote that, as of 1867, "it contained about sixteen columns of advertising," but that "only one-half column was paid advertising, the remainder having been put in to fill up space."

Then there was the line taken by C. N. Harris in the first issue of his Carson City, Nevada *Index*. "We can't lose much on advertising," he cheered, "for we have started publication without any."

But with whatever assurances of support, or none at all, the paper was launched as quickly as it could be hustled off the press, either by a lone man of print, a pair of partners, or an editor well enough fixed to be able to hire somebody to set type. The ace led with was usually headed "Salutatory," a greeting which may or may not have contained a statement of purpose.

The above mentioned C. N. Harris chose to get the *Index* off to a whimsical start. "Religiously we are tolerant. Socially we are bland and accommodating. Our appreciation of the fine things of life is second only to that of a railroad president. Financially we are not a bonanza and commercially we acknowledge ourself a proper subject for the grand bounce."

When the Pueblo, Colorado *Chieftain* began life in 1868, the partner who wrote the salutatory chose to be diffident. "We make no windy promises of what we shall do to either increase or retard the earth's motion."

But when two men started the *Thomas County Cat* at Colby, Kansas, in 1885, the spokesman pointed to the chip on the editorial shoulder. Nor did he call his introductory remarks a salutatory. "Here's Yer Cat," was the heading. "The Cat will purr for Thomas County in what we deem the best interests of the people. The Cat will be located at the new town site on the Dog [River]. The Cat has velvet paws, but will not allow the fur to be stroked the wrong way."

This rag had a monopoly which no other paper was showing signs of coveting, but it was as bristling with fight as though it was in a city rank with competing journalists. No doubt these were instantly expected by the queen city's initial champions, but Colby grew so deliberately that it was a year and a half before another printer took the field.

The staff of the Wood River, Nebraska *Huntsman's Echo* wasn't crowded by other journalists either. Its members were subject to harassments of an unusual sort, though; and these were faithfully reported by Joe Ellis Johnson—well west of Omaha by 1859.

"Buffalo are again continually coming about our farm, ranch and office, bothering us by eating our vegetables, cropping the grass and kicking up dust generally. . . . We shan't try to stand it, and give timely notice that the *echo* of fire arms will be a common thing in this neck of the woods, unless these fearfully frightful looking creatures desist from peeking into our office and discomposing our printer."

The Huntsman's Echo couldn't have been located in a congested part of Wood River, for its editor didn't have to wander afield to study other forms of wild life than the American bison. "Last week, upon two occasions, we witnessed the playful pranks of several antelopes; and again a sprightly red fox came up near the enclosure, but cut and run when Towser came in sight; a nice race they had and both made time, but Reynard the best. A week ago three large white wolves hove in sight, and played around on the prairie at a safe distance—the same chaps probably, that made a tender meal from a good sized calf of ours that had been running out. The buffalo have taken our caution and for two weeks have not troubled us, or annoyed our printer."

As long as the bison behaved themselves, Joe had no quarrel with them, but they made the mistake of again rubbing close to the plant of the *Huntsman's Echo,* which in due course ran a story headed FATAL CASUALTY: "It will be recollected that . . . we gave out certain cautions and warnings against a large class of intruders upon personal property—viz: the trespassing of herds of buffalo upon our town site and arable lands. Unfortunately for the party concerned, no heed was given to our ominous warnings, and the result has been the fall of another aboriginal bovine—that fell a victim to curiosity. Walking leisurely to a point near our office he seemed to sniff an idea . . . and thus in a reflective, designing or calculating mood, and from under his long, shaggy lashes gazed toward us—stamped *our* ground, pawed up dust and earth, and then after sniffing the breeze lowered his head in a threatening mood; we could not stand it any longer, but started Sam [presumably the printer who didn't like having a buffalo look over his shoulder while he was working] who intercepted his progress before he had done much damage to our garden, and banging away—

'The well-aimed lead pursues the certain sight
And death in thunder overtook his flight.'

"The flesh being secured, our t'other half, little ones, self and the balance have been regaling upon roast, broil, fry and stew ever since."

Sam J. Allbright of the Sioux Falls *Dakota Democrat* wasn't as able to cope with the Yankton Sioux as was Johnson in the case of the aboriginal bovine. When the Yanktons raided Sioux Falls in 1862, they made off with the type found in the *Dakota Democrat*'s composing room.

Sam didn't get much, if any of it, back; but other palefaces eventually did. After order had been restored, the Yanktons resumed their practice of making articles for a frontier version of the tourist trade. Especially in demand were genuine Indian peace pipes, handsomely decorated after the immemorial fashion of the Sioux. Some that showed up after 1862, however, were improvements over their predecessors. Imbedded in the sandstone, after first being melted so that it could be refashioned into tasteful designs, was metal that had once spelled out the praises of Sioux Falls in the *Dakota Democrat*.

If trouble with redskins and buffalo could be regarded as uncommon, there was one prevailing professional difficulty. The one or more men who started a given sheet presumably brought along a fair amount of newsprint. But maintaining a regular supply of it was something else again in towns connected with the rest of the world only by seasonably unusable wagon trails. And even those located at coastal points might be in ports irregularly served by shipping.

"We have been compelled to use colored paper," Sam Bangs' Houston *Musquito* explained in 1841, "as we can get no white in the city, and that which we have ordered from New Orleans not having arrived. We hope that our friends will remember that variety is not only pleasing to the eyes, but according to the poet, is the spice of life."

The nature of his substitute for newsprint was defined by Frank Hall, when reminiscing about the difficulties of issuing the Pueblo, Colorado *Chieftain* in the late 1860s. "Supplies had to be brought out by ox team from St. Louis, and more than once was the stock of white paper exhausted, and the *Chieftain* compelled to come out on brown manilla wrapping paper."

Wallpaper was occasionally used, or paper might even be dispensed with entirely. It has been both affirmed and gainsaid that while John Overshiner was publishing the Calico, California *Print* in the 1880s that he once published an issue on strips torn from bed sheets. Whether true or not, the story doesn't stand outside possibility; for it is a matter of record that an 1885 number of the Blain, Washington *Journal* was printed on muslin, in default of paper of any sort.

The Salt Lake City *Deseret News* tried to beat the game by establishing its own paper manufacturing plant. But the journal's frequent pleas for rags to feed the hopper didn't meet with the desired response, as cloth was in such short supply on the frontier that any patch of it was commonly put to some use, until it was too frazzled to hold together. So the *News* never fully lived down the newsprint problem until the railroad linked it with distributors in the Mississippi Valley in 1869.

But whatever the substance it was printed on, a pioneer sheet had to be distributed to subscribers—dwelling not only in a town but the often extensive region of which it was the nucleus—in all weathers. That required the marshaling of rugged carriers. It also brought into being a special division of frontier literature.

Because Western newspaper distributors were asked to do so much more than they could be paid for, by giving them the customary newsboy's percentage, publishers sought to pass the hat for them among subscribers. The means of doing this was an annually issued broadside, or often quite elaborate brochure. Published on New Year's Day, it was written by a newspaper staff member bent on jollying patrons into a good humor on behalf of the petitioning delivery boys.

Sometimes these reminders that a handout was due were gracefully indirect. Such was the nature of the one which Matt Alderson of the Butte, Montana *Miner* composed for its carriers in 1887. A forty-four line poem, it deals with the plight of a woman married to an undemonstrative man.

> I met a lady friend to-day
> Who, as a maid, was ever gay;
> She smiled the while she passed me by,
> But smiles may rise above a sigh.
>
> She was a bride a year ago:
> To-day that face, once all aglow,
> A disappointed aspect wears
> And shows the lines of grief and cares
>
> No word she uttered when we met,
> To voice a longing heart's regret,
> And yet she plainly said to me:
> "I am not loved as I should be . . .
>
> His heart to me may still be true,
> I would not breathe a doubt to you,
> I think—Ah, could I only know!—
> If he would only tell me so." . . . .

The lesson in this parable was that the subscriber who wasn't appreciative of the faithful service rendered him by newsboys was a louse. And anybody who wanted to graduate from that class had better cough up tangible proof.

Alderson's work was billed, "Compliments of the Carriers of the Butte Daily Miner." More often, though, they were composed as though spoken by the distributors and were known as "news carrier addresses." A sample of the genre is the one published by Denver's *Rocky Mountain News* in 1860.

> King Patrons, good morning! a happy New Year
> To you all! May peace and prosperity cheer
> Your lives and your labors through all coming time:
> May you always be "flush," not lacking the dime——
> Or the quarter or more—to gladden and cheer
> The Carrier's heart at the dawn of each year.

The Rocky Mountain News is one paper which survived to print many carrier addresses, and to stay in business long after the practice of issuing them had followed other pioneer customs over the hill. Many sheets published but one, and perhaps not that. Sometimes less than a year elapsed between a man of print's salutatory at one town and the greeting he printed in the next.

Hear Thomas S. Harris, who started the Panamint, California *News* in 1874 and the Darwin, California *Coso Mining News* the following year. "After a hard eleven months struggle in Panamint, where we made a host of friends but no money . . . we packed up our office and after being on the road five days, we arrived here in Darwin and got out our first number . . . just twelve days from the day of starting. . . . It is no small job to pack up a printing office, fit it up again and issue a paper within two weeks. Some idea of the roads may be had when we state, for the benefit of those who have never traveled over them, that we were five days in traveling forty five miles."

Yet intervening between any two salutatories was the valedictory. Of this sphere of journalism a good entry is the one with which Edward Niles buried his Carson City, Nevada *Daily Times* in 1881. "Conscious of having ministered faithfully to a generous army of advertisers, a valued corps of subscribers and a cheerful

squad of deadheads, and also with the belief that the Times had
been lively, enterprising and moderately entertaining, its editor
and publisher extends sincere thanks to all who so generously
aided its vigorous career, and with malice toward none, and all
that sort of thing, will soon enter a new field of labor, trusting at
some further time, to profit by experience and with ample capital
again enter the editorial ranks."

The thought of returning to the newspaper battlefield was also
implicit in John Clum's valedictory in an 1882 number of the
Tombstone, Arizona *Epitaph*. Strictly speaking, the *Epitaph*
hadn't died; but after Clum's two partners had forced a sellout
to the opposition, the paper was about to perish as an entity in
the mind of the man who had shaped the sheet's policy up to
that time.

So feeling, he wrote, "On this bright spring evening, while the
birds are singing in the grease wood bush and Apaches are howling through the mountains, the Epitaph wraps itself in an American flag and dies like a son of a gun. Ta, Ta! We will meet again,
Clemantha."

7

PROBLEMS AND SOMETIMES SOLUTIONS

NOT ENOUGH STRESS has so far been laid on the fact that the processes of publishing, in frontier camps, were hand operations warred upon by conditions which often seemed to make their deft accomplishment impossible. The task was to bring inked type and paper together and emerge with a clean, unblurred product. Ranged against it as saboteurs there could be half the forces of nature.

A man setting type by hand in the pioneer era might be in a flimsy shack, infiltrated by wind that stiffened his fingers with the frost that laced it, or blinded him with the dust it flung through paneless windows. Then dust could get between the letters he was marshaling, or settle in the cases when they were opened, or on the ink balls applied to forms during the press run.

Wind could ruffle paper, just as a sheet was being slipped between type and the platen. And whether or not there were gusts to push it through windows, rain could infiltrate fissures in a poorly made roof. It didn't have to find much of an opening. A drop hitting paper just as it was being fed to the press, or pulled away from it, would mar the page with a puddle of ink.

If housing and weather conditions were problems for about all the journals launched in beginning burgs, a host of other occupational difficulties were reported by individual men of print. In the interest of sharpening the picture of what pioneer newspaper work was collectively like, a glance at some of these will ensue.

The earliest sheet to hold forth west of the Rockies, the Oregon City *Spectator*, had more than its share of troubles to shoot. When it was voted into being by the Pioneer Lyceum and Literary Club in 1845, the chief difficulty was that nobody in Oregon had thought to bring any printing equipment there. Getting off the dime in 1846, after a press and the trimmings had been shipped in, the *Spectator* found that it was one thing to have a newspaper plant and another to have novelties of information to offer the public.

As the Oregon Trail was only usable in the summer months and the *Spectator* had been launched in a winter one, the paper found itself a weak link between the rest of the world and readers anxious for news of it. The sheet had to depend on one of its subscribers, indeed, for word of an American development which was half a year old, as of February 1846. It was able to make that lame scoop because, although the Oregon Trail wasn't functioning, trading vessels turned up with occasional budgets of mail.

When giving its big story, the *Spectator* braced its own repute by vouching for the moral worth of its unnamed news source. "We are informed by a respectable gentleman who has just received a letter from the United States, dated Independence, Missouri, Aug. 12, 1845, that Texas has accepted the terms of annexation proposed by the congress of the United States."

Even more isolated, because no ships from other localities dropped anchor in Great Salt Lake, the *Deseret News* was a half year behind in reporting even California events. When it appeared in June of 1850, the *News* told its readers all about the fire which had half destroyed San Francisco the preceding Christmas Eve.

But months might pass before a subscriber turned in a letter containing items of general interest, or before a traveler showed up with stories worth printing; and most papers had a weekly deadline to reckon with. Even late in the century certain inland camps were tenuously connected with the rest of the globe, and so a journal's locale was often as much of the globe as was coverable.

Like stars and whiskeys, frontier towns were of different magnitudes. Some of them generated a lot of glitter and personality, while others wore the name without being a credit to it. And even the liveliest of them could let a newspaperman down. Calico, California, had the reputation of spitting fire as chronically as a Roman candle; but in an 1884 number of the *Calico Print*, John

Overshiner moaned that there was "not even a fight to chronicle
this week; verily ye reporter had a hard time finding news where
there was none to be found."

It was the absence of this staple commodity which was responsible for many of Western journalism's odd quirks, as well as some
of its shiniest features. If less gifted editors resorted to the unlimited use of shears, the brighter ones were spurred to creativity
by the need for supplementing the scant actualities of their burgs.

Among the favored substitutes for news were fictions, written
so artfully and served up with such a wealth of circumstantial
detail that they could pass for true reports. The newspaper hoax
had, of course, had practitioners in the East, the most famous instance being that of Poe's fake story of a transatlantic balloon
flight, published in the New York *Sun* in 1844. Yet in the East
playing tricks upon subscribers was not only a rarity, it was held
in general abhorrence by a profession with a tendency to take itself and its responsibilities seriously.

No such sense of journalistic dignity shortstopped Western editors, for they were in a raw region where no one had roots, and
where everybody was expected to look after himself as best he
could. It was a land where the only universal was living by wits,
and the man most admired was the one deftest at making something out of the scratch of nothing in any walk of life. So when
newspapermen took to the wings of invention, in preference to
having nothing to report, they were as true to the spirit of the
world in which they moved as journalists have in general forever
been.

But what started as necessity became an admired trade practice, spreading from the isolated camps where little went on to
bustling cities that enjoyed the advantage of telegraphic communication with other parts. Where it was not needed, in fact, it
came to be best used, and the prince of Western journalism was
not the skilled assembler of facts, but the juggler who could ram
fiction down the public throat and have it digested as news.

The most outrageous example was the sell fashioned by Arthur
McEwen for the San Francisco *Daily Mail* in 1876. The *Mail* came
into being because Mark McDonald had run out of other things

to buy with the boodle he'd surrounded in the marts of trade, and so began panting for a seat in the U.S. Senate. Finding that none of the existing journals would bark for him, Mark tossed money to a previously unwell-heeled newspaperman named Davison Dalziel, and told him to begin making noise.

Not about McDonald himself at first, though. Mark was shrewd enough to see that the *Mail* had to be established as a well-known and apparently independent paper first. That achieved, it could discover his political virtues as though by happy accident.

Dalziel was a Bohemian in a town which preened itself on its stud of loosely anchored literati. To get a staff he wrenched a number of these from their saloon hangouts, but among them was one ace newspaperman in the person of McEwen. Before coming to San Francisco, Arthur had been with Alf Doten's *Gold Hill Daily News,* and time was to see him in New York as Hearst's chief editorial writer when the great battle with Pulitzer was in full career. Told to help put out a paper which would gain public notice, McEwen went about it as only a tophand Western writer would have thought of doing.

As the fake news scoop he startled the city with is too long for quotation, only a summary can be offered here. Complete with all the usual circumstantial data, Arthur reported the remarkable fate of a named young man, moved to commit suicide because of disappointment in love. A thorough lad, he equipped himself with a pistol, a rope, and a bottle of poison before going to a cliff overlooking the Golden Gate. There he hitched one end of the rope to a rock, tied the other around his neck, swallowed the bane, and plunged toward the sea. But to make trebly sure, he tried to shoot himself while in mid-air, only to have the bullet go awry. Instead of hitting his head, it severed the rope just above it, letting him drop into the ocean below. Falling from such a height, he sank so far that before he could surface he had swallowed water whose salt content made it an emetic. The poison was therefore coughed up before it could be absorbed into his system. While in the depths and afraid he would never breathe again, he had lost all appetite for despair. Swearing off suicide, he paddled toward shore and an eventual meeting with the *Mail's* alert representative.

This romance with a moral did get the paper talked about in San Francisco. It also caused the reporters of rival sheets to be hauled on the carpet for missing the best news story the city had had in years. Investigation then showed it to be a hoax of hoaxes; but as it had been bought by everybody, Dalziel was delighted. He treated the whole staff to a champagne-flavored dinner, held in McEwen's honor.

Yet that wasn't as far as the practice of printing fiction in the guise of news was carried in the West. By the close of the nineteenth century, storytelling had become such an accepted part of a skilled journalist's equipment that the genuine hoax was supplanted by the fake news story in which no one was expected to believe, although it was written with all the care that once had been lavished on the real thing.

An instance of this was furnished by the later famous Dick Wick Hall in a number of the Wickenburg, Arizona *News-Herald* in 1903. "Frank Midlon who has been prospecting in the Harqua-Halar and Harcuvar mountains for the past two years, came here Saturday afternoon after provisions, as he is in the habit of doing every three months. Instead of bringing his five pack burros as usual, Mr. Midlon came sauntering into town leading a monster Terrapin. . . ."

This is the tall story brought home to roost, though told in crisp repertorial style. What the editor was doing here was to ring his subscribers in as sharers of a joke rather than victims of a hoax. By writing nonsense about actual personalities, Hall could generate almost as much interest, in a community where all were known to one another, as he could have, had news been ready to hand.

For the Rotan, Texas *Billy Goat, Always Buttin' In,* Don Biggers devised a continuous feature in which named townsmen participated. Haunting the wilds that surrounded Rotan was the Wampus Cat, "a ferocious beast—a cross between a wild cat, a badger and a lobo wolf, with fangs two inches long and claws that could peel the bark off a mesquite tree." When needing to fill a big hole in his paper, Don would tell of epic pursuits, from which, however, the dread feline emerged as a still extant local menace.

Up in Wyoming, meanwhile, Grant Jones was engaged in telling of his discoveries in the realm of natural history. At the turn of the century, that is to say, he was composing for readers of the Dillon *Doublejack* a Western version of the medieval bestiary. It included such fauna as the one-eyed, screaming Emu, a bird capable of swallowing itself when wishing to get away from it all. There was also the Cogly Woo, a six-legged varmint which could foil pursuit by using its tail to bore itself into Mother Earth's protecting clutches.

Thus much for the absence of news and what might be done about it. Next to something to print, the essential need of a newspaper is a printer. In 1848 the Oregon City *Spectator* lost John Fleming, the only type jockey in town, because of circumstances over which it had no control. What happened was later explained by the *Spectator* in an apology for having let its readers down for some weeks.

"The *Spectator* after a temporary sickness, greets its patrons and hopes to serve them faithfully, and as heretofore, regularly. 'The gold fever' which has swept about three thousand of the officers, lawyers, physicians, farmers and mechanics of Oregon from the plains of Oregon into the mines of California, took away our printer."

The typesetter who did only that was apt to be even more of a floater than the knockabout editor, for he didn't have the burden of equipment to condition his comings and goings. One look at this hummingbird should suffice to demonstrate how it could dip and dart away.

As avouched in the memoirs of Fremont Older, the ranking tramp printer of the nineteenth century's last third was one Harry Babbitt. As a typesetter, Harry was so skilled as to always be given a job, and so gaited that he would soon shag from wherever he was, leaving a host of non-negotiable IOUs.

Not yet on the editorial side of the fence, Older was a printer for the *Territorial Enterprise*, when Babbitt left a freight car in

Virginia City—oozing grime, charm, booze fumes, and encyclo-
pedic wisdom—in 1874. In the course of one of his many swings
back and forth across the continent, Harry had come to give Nevada the benefit of his personality for a while.

Although never functioning else than as a setter of other people's words, Babbitt was, according to Older, superbly equipped
to have gilded pages with his own. "Apparently he had read
everything and knew everything," to use Fremont's words, "and
spoke and wrote fluently both French and German."

But Harry was possessed of other attributes. Of these the most
original was that he was so used to being spifflicated that he
yawed in his gait even when sober, and would whack into a wall
a yard to port or starboard of a doorway he'd marked for entry
or exit. In spite of having lost his compass and being too tight
to work half the time, he kept his job on the *Territorial Enterprise*
for as long as he wanted it. When he no longer did, he blew.

An effortless con man, Harry had meanwhile lived up the in-
comes of colleagues with less expensive tastes than his own, but
he was not one to let friendship go unrewarded. Older recorded
that when Babbitt left Virginia City he feasted twelve pals, courtesy of a German restaurateur whom he'd snake charmed into
supplying the best wines in his cellar.

Harry was at Reno, when Fremont came there to work for the
Crescent somewhat later. Ready to raid the East again, Babbitt
soon entrained for that direction, yet not without first indulging
in a bit of printing finesse.

Having come out the hard way, riding the rods, he took steps
to insure better conditions for the return trip. To this end he set
up a letterhead purporting to be that of the Chicago, Milwaukee
and St. Paul Railroad—a line which did not run through Reno,
and thus one with whose stationery local railway officials would
not be familiar. Neither were they familiar with the signature of
the C., M. and St. P.'s president, whose name the printer penned
below a letter asking railway men, wherever found, to lavish hos-
pitality on that esteemed employee of the Chicago, etc., H. Babbitt.

Having meanwhile talked a Reno tailor into sewing brass but-

tons on a blue serge suit which he had inveigled from the best
outfitter of gents in Virginia City, Harry boarded an eastbound
train with a confidence which proved justified. Older—to whom
the fake conductor owed politeness, as Fremont was one of the
Nevadans left clutching empty IOUs—received several cards,
mailed en route, reporting that the service couldn't have been
better.

If Harry was a national institution, and without a peer, he was
yet representative. Not all printers were either crooks or super-
men, but most of them—and that was especially true on the frontier—were flitters with no sense of attachment to any paper they
worked for. Older himself was of this stripe; and it wasn't until
he began writing for rags that his foot stopped itching.

A printer could be as hard to hold on to as a leprechaun, but
assuming that a paper had one staked out in the composing room,
its next need was people to read what he set in type. Subscribers
weren't always nailed down either. For in the same year that its
compositor left the Oregon City *Spectator* looking sad and foolish,
the readers of both San Francisco's sheets walked out on them en
masse.

Originally founded at Monterey in 1846, and brought to the
Golden Gate's city a year later by Robert Semple, one was the
Californian. The other was the *California Star*, founded in 1847
by a printer called Sam Brannan. As of the middle of 1848 they
both had paid-up subscription lists; and still they died of loneli-
ness.

The cause was the same stampede which siphoned off the *Spectator's* John Fleming. Actually James Marshall's nation-shaking
gold discovery had been made in February of 1848; but it was
some while before it was widely known in California, and general
belief lagged even farther behind.

Extant is an April 1848 number of Sam Brannan's *Star*, a special issue devoted to appraising the current assets and future possibilities of California. It mentions local discoveries of silver,
mercury, and copper, but says nothing about gold.

A couple of months later, though, Californians at large became
convinced of what editors were slow to credit. So many San Fran-

ciscans left to join the gold rush that the *Californian* stopped publishing, for lack of a public, as of June 2. The *Star* held on a little longer, but then its-at-length-persuaded owner called it quits with the June 14 issue.

This was Elba, and not St. Helena, for both, however. The gold that editorial Thomases had doubted turned San Francisco from a semi-ghost town into a booming market city. Revived, the once rival papers were combined in 1849, forming Eldorado's first daily, the *Alta California.*

Sheets that thus prospered required the services of a fellow to which little attention has so far been given here. This is the editorial opposite number of the hired composing-room specialist. He might be referred to as an associate editor, a reporter, or a "local" —meaning that it was his business to deal with vicinity affairs, as opposed to news from other sources—but he had no stake in the paper other than his salary.

If not quite to the same extent as free-lance printers, these hirelings of the sanctum had much the make-up of thistledown. And when not drifting, frontier reporters could be problems, too.

While Alf Doten was steering the Gold Hill *Daily News,* he sent an operative to cover a story at Winnemucca, Nevada, 150 railroad miles away. In place of returning on time, the reporter wired the collect confession that he had blown his expense funds on booze and had to have more money, in order to be able to buy a ticket back to Gold Hill. Young once himself, Doten sped the requested cash north, only to learn that this had likewise been passed across bars.

Alf was equal to the occasion, though. According to Wells Drury, who unfortunately didn't name the delinquent, the editor wired the stationmaster at Winnemucca to corral his vagrant news gatherer and send him south by freight, Cash on Delivery. As this deal was consummated, the reporter, not to mention his increment of hangover, was in due course restored to the *News.*

The self-styled hotshot from the East was also an occasional affliction suffered by journalists of a region with few facilities for tracing bold assertions back to the nurturing Cave of the Winds. Although Eugene Field used verse when telling of the man who

had claimed the revered Charles Dana as his mentor, there can
be no doubt that he based his work on something that had be-
fallen him, or had been told him by victimized colleagues. The
years 1881 and 1883, incidentally, spanned Gene's stint as editor
of the Denver *Tribune*.

> Thar showed up out in Denver in the spring of '81
> A man who worked with Dana on the Noo York Sun,
> His name was Cantell Whoppers, 'nd he was a sight to view
> Ez he walked into the orfice and enquired for work to do.
> Thar wa'nt no places vacant then—fer, be it understood
> That was the time when talent flourished at that altitood;
> But yet the stranger lingered, tellin' Raymond and the rest
> Uv what prodigious wonders he could do when at his best—
> 'Til finally he stated (quite by chance) that he had done
> A heap of work with Dana on the Noo York Sun.

After name-dropping got him a job, Cantell had a free ride to
match the one enjoyed by Harry Babbitt at the expense of the
Union Pacific.

> This fellow, Cantell Whoppers, never brought an item in—
> He spent his time at Perrier's shakin' poker dice for gin;
> Whatever the assignment, he was allus sure to shirk—
> He was very long on liquor and all-fired short on work!
> If any other cuss had played the tricks he dared to play,
> The daisies would be blooming over his remains to-day;
> But somehow folks respected him and stood him to the last,
> Considerin' his superior connections in the past;
> So when he bilked at poker, not a sucker drew his gun
> On the man who'd worked with Dana on the Noo York Sun.

In the next chapter of the episode Dana himself figured. After
referring to the great editor's tour of the West, Field continued:

> But when he came to Denver in the fall uv '83
> His old friend, Cantell Whoppers, disappeared upon a spree;
> The very thought of seein' Dana worked upon him so
> (They hadn't been together for a year or two, you know)
> That he borrowed all the stuff he could and started on a bat,
> And strange as it may seem, we didn't see him after that. . . .

On the frontier even management wasn't safe from invasion
by impostors. In the summer of 1852 Judson Ames trekked to the

Atlantic side of the nation, leaving his San Diego, California *Herald* in charge of some nameless assistant. When Jud had been gone for some days, a man called William N. Walton hove into San Diego. Whether he had read about the departure of Ames while elsewhere or had picked up word of it after his arrival, Walton was not long in town before he made his way to the *Herald's* office. Gazing upon Jud's rightful stand-in and finding him gosling, Bill announced that he had been appointed by the publisher as interim director of that sheet. When the pigeon meekly surrendered it, Walton relaxed into Ames' chair, enjoying a paid vacation which didn't end until Jud showed up in the spring of 1853.

More common than usurpation by crooks was legal besiegement. John Beadle was but one who attested that civil actions to collect money from shoestring publishers caused the demise of countless newspaper enterprises. There were, however, two ways of beating this.

The one which took longest was sparring for time in court, while struggling toward eventual solvency. Although San Francisco's *Golden Era* got to be a handsome money-maker, the threat of foreclosure hung over it for nearly twenty-four months. Between 1852 and 1854, as J. Macdonough Foard recalled, he and his partner, Rollin M. Daggett, had "many a bout with the Sheriff to prevent him from putting his lock on the door."

The short cut was taking it on the lam. William Jernegan only got to be the father of Nevada journalism as a whole, and the sire of the *Territorial Enterprise* in particular, because he hurried to put the mighty Sierras between his press and officers on the verge of seizing it in Cacheville, California, where he had been publishing the *Yolo Democrat*.

Next to dunners with sheriffs as seconds, the chief enemies of pioneer publishers were other men of print. J. H. Bradley of the Ventura, California *Signal* wrote cogently on that subject in 1876.

"The newspaper business is sadly overdone in Los Angeles County. We tried to get an accurate estimate of the number, but was unable to do so. There is probably one paper to each thousand inhabitants. It is hardly necessary to add there are too many, and that the day is not far distant when some of them will turn their toes daisyward."

Still a monopoly wasn't always prized by the man who owned it either. Hear John R. Curry, who wasn't crowded by anything but snowflakes while issuing the Silverton, Colorado *La Plata Miner* in the 1880s.

"Items are scarce and the life of an editor in the Rocky Mountains is as dry as a charity festival, and his efforts at collecting items are as barren of results as the browsing of a calf on a sand bank. Just think of a high, barren range of mountains covered 40 fathoms deep in snow, stretching between you and all the rest of the world, and all the news you get comes 40 miles over these mountains on men's backs."

John Curry at least got to see the town he was covering in the *Miner*, but Theodore L. Kerr had to dispense with even this newspaper nicety when publishing the Stafford, Kansas *Citizen*. "For thirty-one weeks," he chirped in 1878, "we have been amusing ourselves at journalism, during which time we have acted in the capacity of editor, reporter, business manager, book keeper, compositor, proof reader, press man and devil; and must confess that it's a little the liveliest amusement we were ever engaged in. On account of our limited finances, we were obliged to do our printing at Sterling, which being thirty-three or four miles from our town of publication prevented us from making a flying visit to the beautiful little city we have had so much to say about, oftener than once in three or four weeks. During the last thirty-one weeks, however, our bump of imagination has increased to such an enormous size that we feel perfectly competent to write *all* the local news, notwithstanding the many miles of prairie that hides from our view our county and our people."

There was one other challenge for publishers peculiar to the West. This was the problem of delivering papers to subscribers living in outlying settlements whose names were matters of debate. As often as not, the confusion was due to a feud between the partisans of poetry and commerce. Fronting for the first, a prospector or whatnot would squat somewhere and draw from his spirit a name as fitting as suds on ale. But some later settler

might wish a name more suggestive of a sober trading center—
and persuade postal authorities to impose a label not at all acceptable to the region's old timers.

  This is obviously what happened in the vicinity of Greenwater,
California, where one of the editors of the *Chuck-Walla* was
moved to write, "If you want to send a letter to Skidoo, address
it to Hovie, California. It is wise, however, to place the name
Skidoo somewhere on the address, so that the stage driver will
know where Hovie is."

8

SLANTS FROM COCKED EYES

ONCE SOMEHOW IN business, pioneer editors had other pursuits than the crowning of queen cities. Chief among these was shying stones at traditional objects of veneration or awe.

The stones weren't invariably smooth. The concept of the family newspaper, laundered so as not to dismay the chaste guardians of the modern U.S. Postal Department, was not a star that was followed. Neither were Western editors hamstrung by libel laws to any crippling extent.

It is true that T. W. Eckert, of the Arkansas City, Kansas *Traveler,* was fined for observing that a rival newspaperman was a "eunuch . . . snorting around the basement but unable to do anything," but that seems to have been because Eckert had impugned a fellow's manhood. Almost anything else could be, and was, said without drawing remonstrance from the law.

As for the pressures normally exerted by religionists and the backers of conventions, they were of no force until the frontier began to fade. Not since or before has liberty of the press been an American reality; but it was in the pioneer West, and J. C. Martin caroled his joy of it in the salutatory he wrote for the Kingman, Kansas *Mercury* in 1878.

> Here's freedom to him that would read,
> Here's freedom to him that would write!
> There's none ever feared that the truth should be heard
> But they whom the truth would indict.

Indictment certainly wasn't a worry of John Wasson of the Tucson, Arizona *Citizen.* Because of remarks he had published about Judge Isham Reavis, this territorial magistrate had undertaken to wave the threat of contempt proceedings. That attempt to muzzle the press was disposed of by John in one paragraph.

"Reavis, a few words to you and your court. In common with
the mass of people of the Territory, we hold you and your court
in the utmost contempt. We dare you to send along your contemptible warrant for our arrest for contempt of your contemptible court; but bear in mind if you do, you will not be practicing
upon any such as you have in your district, who will submit
through fear of your tyranny and disregard of personal rights and
liberty."

Taboos? The Western men of print didn't speak Polynesian. In
1879 the twenty-fifth of December got to Glendale, Montana, on
time; and in recognition of the anniversary, bottles were opened
and emptied. In mentioning as much in the *Atlantis,* Legh Freeman cited a man as "celebrating the birthday of Mr. J. Christ."

Nor did classical wise men meet with more respect than current divinity. No figure in the history of Greek philosophy has
seemed as armored with unassailable dignity as Diogenes. Solving
the housing problem by moving into a disused tub, he cut all his
other living expenses down to the minimum, the better to con-
centrate on his forlorn quest for but one exemplar of human honesty. Although he invoked the aid of a lantern by day as well as
by night, his search was fruitless until it at length occurred to the
master cynic to join the gold rush to the Death Valley area in
1907. Finding that the sage had made this move, either Carl B.
Glasscock or his associate, Curt E. Kunze, thus reported the event
in the Greenwater, California *Chuck-Walla:*

> Poor old Diogenes, the bum,
> Out to the West at last has come,
>   The bum
>   Has come.
>
> With lantern and his famous tub
> Has looked long for some honest dub;
>   Some dub,
>   Some cub.
>
> The sagebrush catches on his togo,
> He swears and curses like a hobo,
>   A hobo
>   In a togo.

He's looked far for that honest man,
He's searched around with many a damn,
  Oh, damn
  The man!

Out in the Western mining towns
Promoters meet him with dark frowns,
  With frowns,
  The clowns!

These annoyed promoters couldn't understand the philosopher's viewpoint, accustomed as they were to take uprightness for granted. And Diogenes himself was quick to see that his quest could have ended sooner, had he but thought to join an earlier gold stampede.

The honest man he's followed far;
Now finds one standing by each bar,
  Not far
  Each bar.

He's searched in vain 'mong babes and nurses,
He's looked with many oaths and curses;
  He curses
  The nurses,

For on the desert he has found
That honest men, and true abound,
  Abound
  Around . . .

He finds that none of them will lie;
He's nothing left to do but die,
  To die,
  O my!

It is pleasing to note, though, that before qualifying for burial in Greenwater, Diogenes celebrated his triumph with a never-before-indulged-in spree.

The search of ages now is past,
The world-old trouble ends at last,
  At last
  Is past.

So with a happy smile he goes
From bars to dancehalls with hoboes,
He goes
With 'boes.

Christian tenets could expect no more support than the notions of a pagan epoch. After he'd succeeded Harry Brook as editor of the San Francisco *Wasp* in 1881, Ambrose Bierce dismissed both Catholicism and the Reformation with one whisk of his editorial brush. "A French priest has abandoned the errors of the Romish for those of the Protestant Church."

William Cowper Brann, of the Waco, Texas *Iconoclast,* was another who flipped ink at organized religion. "Waco, like other places, has it drawbacks," he wrote in the course of striking at the town's odd batch of blue laws in the 1890s, "but taken by and large there is no better. While it is true that you can't secure a bath, shave or clean shirt here on Sunday, the saloons and churches are open and the Reservation [red-light district] hath all seasons for its own."

Reverence for the cloth could be a minus quantity, witness an 1859 editorial of the Sioux Falls *Dakota Democrat.* "Ministers are not more addicted to dissipation than the men of other professions," it cautioned against prejudice. "The great majority of them are as good as lawyers and doctors. If you want a true Christian, marry an editor."

The man of culture might not fare any better than the man of God. If music, as has been elsewhere shown, was the ruling passion of Sonora, California, during the 1870s, all in Austin, Texas, weren't hypnotized by it in 1894–95. That was the life cycle of the *Rolling Stone*, a period in which Austin's maestro of the baton was a thirsty Teuton.

It can be gathered that he cashed in on his celebrity, considering his company a fair exchange for the drinks he mooched. In any case he caught the eye of Will Porter, who was the *Rolling Stone's* cartoonist, as well as its editor. It thus chanced that the sheet featured a rear view of the conductor, caught in the act of drawing musical strains from the members of his orchestra. Below the sketch was this legend:

With his baton the professor beats the bars,
'Tis said he also beats them when he treats,
But it made the German gentleman see stars
When the bouncer got the cue to bar the beats.

Martyrs passing the hat for homage weren't apt to collect much. Certainly they didn't at Boulder, Colorado, while Lucius C. Paddock was directing the *Daily Camera*. And when pulling Honest Abe from the pedestal on which he customarily perched, Lucius gave pedagogy a nudge in the ribs for good measure.

"A Lincoln story which wasn't revived this year, so far as we have noticed, was told us by a school teacher in the middle '70s. Susan B. Anthony was arguing with Mr. Lincoln over woman's rights, for the establishment of which she was a pioneer.

"In an intense moment Miss Anthony exclaimed: 'Why, Mr. President, what is the difference between you and me?'

"Immediately . . . Lincoln replied, 'Madam, I cannot conceive.' "

If national heroes could be joshed by Western editors, those generally out of favor might find champions among men of print. In 1869 the *Weekly Republican* of Montana's Virginia City was edited by Hez. (presumably short for Hezekiah) L. Hosmer. Because of the fury generated at the time by the issue of polygamy, no man was as generally execrated as was the then head of the Mormon Church; and some of the boss execrators were in Washington as representatives of their respective states. But Hez. ran a column called "Grasshoppers," and in it he broke this piece of news:

"Brigham Young agrees to confine himself to one woman, if every member of Congress will do the same."

If national prejudices could be hoorahed by pioneer editors, so could Western fetishes. Of these one of the most widespread, as of the last quarter of the nineteenth century, was the concept of the cowboy as a chevalier of the chaparral.

Edgar Rye, editor of such Texas papers as the Albany *News*, the Rockport *New Era*, and the Graham *Radiator*, offered the usual view of the steer drovers in his fine book of reminiscences, *The Quirt and the Spur*. Although admitting they had shagbark aspects, Rye devoted a chapter to them written in the key of the summing couplet.

> Behind careless sang froid and beneath rough exterior,
> God enthroned a true man who will bow to no superior.

J. S. Martin, of the Prescott, Arizona *Journal-Miner,* also employed verse when giving a different appraisal of the same American specimen in 1886. In *The Song of the Cowboy,* there is no inkling that the boy has time for any pursuit as orderly as the chivvying of bovines.

> Oh, I am the cowboy of legend and story,
> Whom the back eastern youngster all so admire,
> The slaughter of pilgrims is ever my glory,
> And few have escaped when they drew out my fire.
>
> On the deck of my bronco, I skim o'er the prairie,
> A terror to all who my daring behold;
> I defy any civilized constabulary
> And all vigilantes the country can hold.
>
> As proud as the proud soaring birds of the ocean,
> I speed on my way over valley and plain,
> And no man dares make the least treacherous motion,
> That lives for a moment to do it again.
>
> The joys of existence I don't claim for ever;
> Some day I must missle [succumb] like other galoots,
> But the Old Boy will have to be devilish clever
> If he gets me laid out while I stand in my boots.
>
> When I'm roped at the roundup of judgment eternal,
> And corraled in a furnace forever to dwell,
> I'll be able to teach them some capers infernal;
> I won't be a tenderfoot, even in hell.

Pioneer men of print were likewise prone to eye social institutions through knotholes that most people didn't know were in the fence. The Houston *Musquito* of Sam Bangs decided that a bigamist expended double the effort necessary to gain the results he came up with. "A negro fellow the other day got himself into trouble by marrying two wives. A great many white men do the same by marrying one."

The nineteenth-century institution of chaperonage was with-

out an advocate in Ouray, Colorado. In 1879 some conspiracy of
the elements blocked communications with the outside world so
effectively that the town ran out of all means of lighting houses.
Another newspaper might have expressed regret at this civic
calamity. There was no such bleat from the *Solid Muldoon,*
though, for Dave Day was philosopher enough to perceive that
there was a bright side to even universal darkness.

"No people, young people, ever enjoyed such a season of un-
disturbed courtship as the belles and beaux of Ouray are now ex-
periencing," he mused. "Not a drop of coal oil or a candle in the
village."

> Backward, turn backward
> Oh, time in your flight
> And make me a boy again
> Just for two nights.

The Los Angeles *Star* not only gave Victorianism the horse
guffaw but compounded the insult by accusing its local backers of
not being on the square about their moral outlook. George Washington Barter was the *Star's* editor at the time, and he got to rib
the professionally virtuous in 1878.

During that year a local artist with no further call on fame
served up a bowl of water in the foreground of one of his can-
vases. Behind it was a comely lass in the buff and presumably
scheming to get together with the aqua. Jumping to that con-
clusion himself, the painter had dubbed his study of the F.F.D.
"The Morning Bath."

After the dauber got a drugstore-owning patron of the arts to
parade his picture behind a plate-glass window, Los Angeles became a divided camp. Aligned on one side were frank admirers
of the external feminine. In the opposing faction were cits pro-
fessing shock at a public display of winsome nudity.

But in order to be properly dismayed, they had to study the
subject thoroughly first, and it was while doing their homework
that they came to the attention of G. Washington Barter. To his
finding some of "The Morning Bath's" loudest denouncers had
come back for second and third helpings of shock. After observing

as much, he made it public knowledge, and further rubbed blue
noses the wrong way by pointing out that he himself had been
virtuously busy while they were sight-seeing.

"In passing the display window several times this morning
(note the fact that we were merely passing), we saw some of the
most staid and pious burghers of the place greedily drinking in
the beauties of the occasion."

Yet casting doubt as to the integrity of moralists was not the
most disquieting finger pointed at the social structure by a
frontier man of print. However such journalists as John Wasson,
of the Tucson *Citizen*, might feel about individual dispensers of
justice, there was no general disposition—even in the West—to
quarrel with the dictum that law is the one factor which makes
civil organization possible. A dissenter was writing for the San
Francisco *Californian* in 1865, though.

To Mark Twain it was apparent that the cement holding society together was of a questionable quality, and he proceeded to
demonstrate as much in the agony column which was one of his
journalistic dodges. Signing himself "Discarded Lover," one of
Mark's straw men had braced Twain with this problem: "I loved
and still love, the beautiful Edwitha Howard, and intended to
marry her. Yet during my temporary absence at Benicia last
week, alas! she married Jones. Is my happiness to be thus blasted
for life? Have I no redress?"

"Of course, you have," the columnist assured his querier. "All
the law written, and unwritten, is on your side. The *intention* and
not the *act* constitutes the crime. . . . If you call your bosom
friend a fool and *intend* it for an insult, it *is* an insult. If you
discharge a pistol accidentally and kill a man, you can go free,
for you have done no murder; but if you try to kill a man, and
manifestly *intend* to kill him, but fail utterly to do so, the law
still holds that the *intention* constitutes a crime. . . . Ergo, if you
had married Edwitha accidentally, and without really *intending*
to do it, you would not actually be married to her at all, because
the *act* of marriage could not be complete without the *intention*.
And ergo, in the strict spirit of the law, if you deliberately intended to marry Edwitha, and didn't do it, you are married to

her all the same—because, as I said before, the *intention* constitutes the crime. It is as clear as day that Edwitha is your wife, and your redress lies in taking a club and mutilating Jones with it, as much as you can. But you have another alternative—you were married to Edwitha *first*, because of your deliberate intention, and now you can prosecute her for bigamy in subsequently marrying Jones. But there is another phase of this complicated case. You *intended* to marry Edwitha and consequently, according to law, she is your wife—there is no getting around that but she didn't marry you, and if she never intended to marry you, you are not her husband, of course. . . ."

If the majesty of the law was so reduced to the court clown by Mark Twain, Semblens Forbes found nothing more than the source of professional jokes in the hollow eyes of the Grim Reaper. "Death cannot be a matter of much moment to an editor," Forbes remarked in an 1865 number of the Unionville, Nevada *Humboldt Register*. "No thirty days' notice required by law—it is the local incident of the moment [a matter of] a few days as advertised on the fourth page, a few calls by subscribers not in arrears. A short, quick breath—then the subscription paper for burial expenses."

Where others were concerned, there was none of the mealy-mouthed "*De mortuis nil nisi bonum*" spirit; John Overshiner, at any rate, was no man to take his hat off just because somebody had been demoted to a corpse. Writing of an anonymous stiff that turned up in a Calico, California, dance hall in 1884, John dismissed him with two of the *Print's* lines. "John Doe was killed at the Pastime. Good riddance."

If traditionally deprecated in most American parts and eras, even suicide had one smiling frontier commentator, too. When self murder was achieved by a San Francisco vigilante in 1857, Ned McGowan was moved to sing, in the Sacramento *Phoenix*, a stanza in which he employed a term for hanging borrowed from vintaged English thieves' cant.

> We know he has perished, but why shed a tear?
> The generous bowl all our sorrows can cheer;
> The Strangler is gone, whom we knew in his day
> Delighted in banishing and scragging post lay.

The editorial approach to vital statistics was not always satiric or cynical, however. When Como, Nevada, had an 1864 population explosion of one—a little girl and the only child ever born in that now-you-see-it, now-you-don't camp—H. L. Weston was pleased. Sighting down the Como generations, of which she would putatively be the matriarch, he felt that prose wasn't a warm-enough medium in which to honor the new arrival. Putting on his poet's hat, after first perhaps imping his wings via a nip of Castaly or Hippocrene, Weston took this lyric flight:

"Welcome, little stranger, we're glad to see you here;
We'll drink your future happiness in a glass of lager beer."

9

THE SANCTUM NO SANCTUARY

AS NEWSPAPERMEN WERE not the only headstrong people who took their dispositions west of the Mississippi Valley, a conflict of interests often resulted. And not every editor had Eugene Field's famous, or infamous, device for quieting objectors.

While editor of the Denver *Tribune*, Gene had his office—on the wall of which hung a sign reading, "God bless our proof reader, He can't call for him too soon"—equipped with but one chair other than his own. Reserved for the chance guest was a capacious piece of furniture, well constructed save for the detail that its cane bottom was missing. To cover up this defect, Field made a practice of placing a newspaper or so between the abyss and the eyes of incoming stormy petrels.

Although the *Tribune*'s maestro never waved any angry visitor to this pitfall, a man bent on unburdening himself of wrath was not likely to shuffle his feet until asked to be seated. Instead, he would flounce upon the sole perch available—and have only himself to blame when he ended with his stern on the floor and his nose jammed against his knees.

A keen student of human nature, Gene had figured that hauteur, and even righteous indignation, couldn't hold their own in this position. His entrance thus spoiled, the visitor was better geared for an exchange of ideas, while Field on his part was all apologetic solicitude. When he had seated the deflated complainant in his own chair, he would be as winning as few besides himself knew how to be; and a meeting of minds would follow.

But men with Gene's genius at public relations have been at all times rare, and his peer wasn't to be found in the pioneer West's fourth estate. When other editors rubbed readers the wrong way, they had to stand up to the consequences, if they felt able, or dodge them in some fashion when they didn't.

Although often deliberate aggressors and on the *qui vive* accordingly, the men of print at times found rattlesnakes they didn't know they had riled. Such was the case with Richard Weightman, of the Albuquerque, New Mexico *Amigo del Paiz* in 1854.

A great wrangle of the moment hinged on the best route through the West of the projected transcontinental railway. In New Mexico a southerly course was naturally favored. For a while there was only one possible southern path for iron horses. This was the route along the thirty-fifth parallel—eventually used by the Atchison, Topeka and Santa Fe Railroad—which had been discovered by Francis X. Aubry.

But by 1854 the picture had been changed and unity in New Mexico shattered. The year saw the ceding of the Gadsden Purchase, a territorial addition which opened the possibility of laying tracks along the thirty-second parallel. The feasibility of doing so had been more or less demonstrated by Colonel Philip St. George Cooke, when laying out a military wagon road during the Mexican War of 1846–48.

Once for Aubry's route, Weightman threw the influence of the *Amigo del Paiz* behind Cooke's and thereby made an enemy he hadn't counted on, in as much as he hadn't thought of the issue as a personal one. Neither did Richard expect to meet Francis X. in Santa Fe, when some business brought the editor to the capital in 1854's summer.

Aubry wasn't there when Weightman arrived, as a matter of fact. The explorer was still eating dust, while completing a journey which his eventually published journal described as unsatisfactory. Apaches had dogged him much of the way, for one thing, and as a sedative for nerves the outing had been a bust.

Hot and parched, as well as in a bad humor, Francis X. made for a cantina when he at length hit town. Had he been able to profit by its soothing lotions before seeing Richard, the outcome would doubtless have been different; but he never got to be ministered to by a bartender, for he saw the man of the *Amigo del Paiz* first.

To Weightman's astonishment, Aubry pronounced statements made against the thirty-fifth parallel as attacks on his character and asked why the voice of Albuquerque had published such lies. It was an unfortunate choice of words, addressed to a poorly chosen auditor. Having a glass of some sort of schnapps in his hand, the editor flung it in the explorer's face.

Aubry's second mistake was to go for his gun and work its trigger without waiting to clear his eyes of hot spirits. He didn't have time to commit a third error. As a youth, Richard had been let out of West Point on the technicality that he had blooded a fellow cadet with a bowie. It was with this same weapon, as tradition has it, that Weightman opened up the explorer's midriff.

The editor of the *Amigo del Paiz* was equipped to deal with balky readers as he of the *Rocky Mountain News* at first was not. When William Newton Byers came to a town not yet certainly known as Denver, he was a man of peace. That remained true in spite of one bad experience as a pacifist. In the course of trying to persuade two drunks not to have at each other with shotguns, William had emerged as the only one of the three with a charge of lead in him.

A surveyor in Nebraska at the time, he found one arm so crippled that he couldn't carry on as a mapper any more. And about the day he realized that, he was given a printing press as a substitute for money owed him.

With this asset Byers joined the "Pike's Peak or Bust" gold rush in 1859. In the spring of that year there were only two settlements in what was then not known as Colorado, because it was still a part of Kansas. Glaring across Cherry Creek at each other were the rival communities of Denver and Auraria.

As of April, each had a man of print racing to corner the subscription market. Located in Denver, Jack Merrick was hoping to be first with the *Cherry Creek Pioneer*. Not wanting to commit himself, Byers didn't say where the *Rocky Mountain News* was being published. He put Cherry Creek in his dateline and let it go at that.

On the twenty-third of April the *News* and the *Pioneer* were both born. Byers got his sheet on sale a few hours ahead of Merrick, though, and claimed a monopoly which Jack didn't again challenge.

Still a man of peace a year later, William felt that he ought to mend the ways of a town full of prospectors and those bent on taking gold away from them by means not favored by the Chamber of Commerce. Strong in his righteousness, the *News* began saying harsh things about named gamblers.

Its editor was evidently of the opinion that men he described as ruffians wouldn't think of getting tough with a letter-press crusader. In due course, though, Byers lost that part of his faith in the goodness of mankind. For a gamester named Carl Wood entered William's sanctum, without first bothering to knock with the hand that wasn't holding a cocked derringer.

By means of this instrument, Byers was marched to a saloon crammed with unrepentant victims of his editorial lash. He had a bad time of it before he was rescued by a noted frontiersman named Charlie Harrison, and before he got back to his sanctum William had switched philosophies. In brief, he had decided that pacifism was for the birds; and he didn't mean doves.

From then on the *Rocky Mountain News* was staffed by men who worked with their shooting irons handy. They proved they were ready to use them that very day, too. Sore about the editor's escape, some of his foes garrisoned a building across the street from the newspaper and sent one George Steeles to find out what the men of print were up to.

Having posted watchmen, these were all stretched out on the floor, each with a rifle or shotgun aimed at the head of the stairs up which George was creeping. It was curtains for the spy, even though he got nervous and fled without taking a look. After he had first been winged by Byers, Steeles was followed and shot dead.

As most of Denver's cits made it clear that they were on the *News'* side, that war was over. But William wouldn't have won it if he hadn't turned his office into a fortress.

The pistol in the drawer or the shotgun in the corner were as

THE SANCTUM NO SANCTUARY

much a part of the standard equipment for Western journalists as the composing stick and the pen. If some editors were never called upon to use weapons to quiet complaining readers, preserved records show that a host did have to resort to arms; and doubtless many more instances could be found, were it possible to fill in or resurrect broken and destroyed newspaper files.

All editors weren't the stuff of heroes, to be sure. After leaving the *Reese River Reveille*, Fred Hart edited the *Territorial Enterprise* in Nevada's Virginia City. So situated, he undertook to style a capitalist named James G. Fair "Slippery Jim." Hart wasn't necessarily in error, but it chanced that John Mackay—later to found the Commercial Cable Company, and so forth—was at once a close friend of Fair's and part owner of the *Enterprise*. A miner in his pre-tycoon days, Mackay threatened to take the plant, as well as the thus and so of the sanctum apart.

By promising not to sin again, Fred both stayed in one piece and kept his job. There was a sequel, though, which Alf Doten ably related.

"Alas, only a month later an east wind from the brewery struck Hart again, and under the resistless impulse he steered directly into and afoul of the Alta Mining Co.—among the best patrons of the *Enterprise*. . . . There was a cloudburst, earthquake and war dance, all in one, next morning, when the Alta folks and their friends waving aloft machetes and tomahawks, came charging down upon the *Enterprise* office with blood in their eyes. Poor little Fred got wind of the coming cyclone and struck out through the sage brush." He got clear out of Nevada, too, and spent the rest of his years in California.

A frontier journalist might be objected to on other grounds than his editorial policy. Tom McNeal, once of the Medicine Lodge, Kansas *Cresset*, made this plain in one of the episodes in his volume of reminiscences titled *When Kansas Was Young*.

In 1878, according to McNeal, a man named M. C. Cochran was publishing the *Barber County Mail* in Medicine Lodge, where he was disliked for two reasons. One was the sloppy printing which made his rag hard to read, and the second was his eye for other people's women.

Wishing to tar and feather the editor on these two counts, the citizens of Medicine Lodge were hampered by (a) the absence of tar, and (b) the fact that nobody could spare the feathers of a quilt, the season being dog's-nose cold. There was, however, molasses available, while nature had been locally lavish in the matter of sandburs. With these materials Cochran's ill wishers called upon him by night and, after coating him with them, rode him about a town he was asked not to see again, on a split cedar bronco.

Some that stole upon editors after dark were even less kindly disposed than the subscribers of the *Barber County Mail.* C. L. Minor of the Yuma, Arizona *Sentinel* noted as much in 1872. "In the days of Machiavelli," he opened, "one of the distinguishing features of Italian society was the midnight assassin. That the race of murderers of this class has not died out yet, was made alarmingly evident from an experience of ours last Saturday night. At about the hour of 12 o'clock . . . while we were sitting at our desk . . . we were suddenly startled by the report of a pistol, and the hiss of flying bullets, uncomfortably close."

A similar experience was recorded by Stanley Bagg, editor of the Tombstone, Arizona *Prospector,* in 1899. "Last night, soon after eleven o'clock, some gentleman whose identity is unknown to us, fired a charge of buckshot through the side window of our editorial room directly at the spot where our cot is usually placed. Had the cot been there, we should have been inquested and buried ere this. But the cot wasn't there. We are not purty, but we are no hayseed. We haven't slept twice in the same spot for the last twelve weeks. We have learned the ways of this community at a considerable cost and trouble, and we don't propose to plant ourselves as a midnight target."

Usually such visitors as those described by the *Sentinel* and the *Prospector* were the emissaries of outlaw gangs that objected to editorial notice. A prolonged war between an editor and desperadoes was described some years after the event by the Oskaloosa, Kansas *Independent.* It had been founded in 1860 by John Roberts, and during the Civil War years that followed, jayhawking, or pilfering executed in the name of patriotism was the curse of the state.

"The *Independent* editorially denounced jayhawking," a successor of John's remembered. "During all the years of the war this newspaper continued with heavy indictments of this unlawful business, and became thereby the object of hatred and threatened revenge of the horse thief crowd, which grew to considerable numbers in these parts."

"Toward the close of the war its editor, J. W. Roberts, was repeatedly threatened and plots were made to do him bodily harm and destroy his property. Men followed him about the unlighted streets, whistled their signals in the darkness and at one time . . . plotted the burning of the printing office. Warned of this mob action, a party of 16 armed citizens of the town took positions at the windows of the office and stood guard during the night. . . .

"At another time three of the gang were appointed to go to the editor's residence in the night, call him out and beat him up." Whether they would have got to lay hands on the man who customarily slept with three guns for bed companions is questionable. But in any case the plot was discovered because, "a neighbor woman sitting up with a sick child saw the three fellows go by the house and hide in a big patch of jimson weeds in the barn lot."

But at times men of print were attacked by bands which neither took advantage of covering darkness nor the secrecy of ambush. Such a thing befell John Hanson Beadle, while he was editing the Corinne, Utah *Reporter*. In an 1869 issue the *Reporter* published the following bulletin:

"War Declared! A Horrible Outrage! J. H. Beadle was knocked down and brutally beaten in the streets of Brigham City. . . . Mr. Beadle at this writing, 10 P.M., lies in a critical condition."

"A few weeks before," to give John Hanson's own account, "I had published a severe criticism of . . . Judge Smith. His 'strikers' now had me at court as defendant, in a town of 1200 Mormons, and only half a dozen Gentiles with me. The facts brought out on trial were so clearly in my favor that I gained the suit. About sundown I started with the crowd to pass out of the Court House, and was stepping off the portico when I heard the words, 'You're the man that wrote that lie about my father,' and at the same instant received a violent blow on the back of the neck and head which sent me upon my face in the gravel walk. I remember nothing more than a succession of blows followed by the trampling of heavy boots, and next I was being raised by my friends, covered with blood and only not quite senseless. I was hauled seven miles to Corinne, where a medical examination showed that my collar bone was broken in two places, my temple badly cut, my right eye injured, a section of my scalp torn off, and a few internal injuries received."

Legh Freeman, as he recalled in an 1883 number of the Butte, Montana *Union-Freeman,* was almost rubbed out by a mob, as opposed to a small gang. Many hundreds strong, the would-be lynchers had been sicked on the editor by capitalists who were displeased with a newspaper he had earlier established. This was the here-today and gone-tomorrow *Frontier Index.* Launched in the lee of Fort Kearny, Nebraska in 1866, it had a subsequent history that Legh fitted into a nutshell. "After the Union Pacific Railroad came along, our print became the advertising medium which built up ten of the terminal towns of that national artery of commerce."

One of these was Bear River City, not since a large mark on Utah's map, but then jammed with railroad workers, caterers to these, opportunists at large, and representatives of an international banking house's American branch. Speculators in land, they wanted a monopoly which the *Index* opposed.

"When we thought we had a right to lay out towns, independent of the Credit Mobilier ring, we did so," as Freeman put it, "and for this, and for exposing the frauds of that hydra headed monster, its chief had a riot brought on us . . . composed of several thousand graders, headed by cut-throats of the most desperate type who were paid $15,000 to head the mob."

Because Mrs. Freeman managed to send a wire to the Salt Lake City *Telegraph,* details of the furor at Bear River were published in that paper's issue of November 20, 1868. "Some 200 [probably a typo; the figure should have been at least 2000, according to Legh] rioters have possession of the city; they have burnt down the office of the *Frontier Index* and fears are entertained that the whole city will be destroyed. The muss arose from the action taken by the Vigilance Committee in hanging the three men on the eleventh instant."

Whether Legh knew the names he was accused of withholding is not now plain reading, but on November 23 he was in the hot water described by the Salt Lake City *Tribune*. The paper's information source was again a telegram sent by Mrs. Freeman, who had herself been in danger because she helped her husband publish the *Frontier Index*. But she had managed to make her way to some nearby settlement and wire the *Tribune* from there.

"Mr. Freeman, the editor of the *Index,* was captured by the mob, composed entirely of Cheeseborough and McGee's men, and threatened with instant death if he did not reveal the names of the Vigilantes who hanged the friends of the rioters. Mr. Freeman at once drew his 'iron,' but found half a dozen at his head and breast in a second." There were two schools of thought as to what should be done with the editor, though. According to the *Tribune,* some yelled, "Hang him!" while, "Shoot him!" was urged by others.

Legh got out of the corner he was in partly through the intervention of Bear River Tom Smith, later marshal of Abilene, when that Kansas burg was the roaring railhead of the Chisholm Trail. Tom and a man for whose assistance he called diverted the attention of the crowd, allowing Freeman to duck into a saloon and thence out its back door to safety.

"The crowd became incensed at his escape . . . and at once began to search," the *Tribune* continued. It also told how Legh beat the Credit Mobilier's mob by ringing in the U.S. Cavalry. "Mr. Freeman struck for Ft. Bridger and at once got troops dispatched. . . ."

Once the horsemen in blue had pulled their classic run to restore order, all were peaceful at Bear River City, including the fourteen killed and thirty-five wounded in the course of the pacifying process. The over-all casualties were more numerous, however. "Counting the number killed by the citizens and those slain at the wakes," to give Freeman's cheerful tally, "thirty-nine of the mob bit the dust."

With less buoyance he reported the state of his own affairs. "Our office was burned to a grease spot, the marble imposing stones were reduced to lime and the type ran down the hillside as a molten masse."

Legh wasn't discouraged, though. "The printing office and the [Bear River] jail will be rebuilt at once," the Salt Lake City *Tribune* assured its readers. "Mr. Freeman has telegraphed to Chicago for a new press and 'out-fit' generally. The *Frontier Index* will be on wheels again in a few weeks."

If the United States Army made it possible for Legh to start over again, it was the villain of a piece involving another pioneer paper. And like the *Frontier Index*, the *Oklahoma War Chief* was given to moving about.

The *Chief's* brain, if not always its official editor, was David L. Payne. He only had one idea, but it was a pretty big one. It panned out, too, though David never got to enjoy his dream's fulfillment.

What he strove to bring about was the abolition of the Indian Territory and the substitution of a state of the union for that unreconstructed American island. Payne had no more than a lone opponent worth reckoning with, but that happened to be the United States government. Committed to the fiction that captive Indian tribes were autonomous nations, Washington preferred to maintain the iron curtain it had hung around a hapless, multitribal hodgepodge.

With the federal administration on one side and a single newspaperman on the other, it didn't look like an even contest. But both Uncle Sam and Payne understood that a shift in public opinion could change the odds. With that in mind, David published the *Oklahoma War Chief* in several Kansas towns in the early 1880s. Also thinking of it, Washington looked for ways to suppress the sheet.

Its chance came when the *War Chief* stole into Oklahoma for the first time and began publishing at a scratch settlement called

Rock Falls in 1884. As the Boomer Run that signified Payne's ulti-mate success was five years in the offing, Rock Falls was in Indian Territory and off limits for paleface editors with opinions of their own. So Army troops swooped and destroyed the plant of a paper without finances enough to recover from that blow.

Officers of the law also joined the game of giving pioneer journalists a bad time. The first sheet to break the monopoly which had been enjoyed in Salt Lake City by the *Deseret News* was Kirk Anderson's *Valley Tan*. Originally applied to leather which had been locally processed, rather than imported from the States, "valley tan" had come to mean anything homemade; and the Boise *Statesman's* Thomas Donaldson remembered in *Idaho's Yesterdays* that Mormons of that territory so styled the moonshine they lapped at frolics.

Anderson, then, had picked out a name designed to give the idea that he and his sheet were indigenous; but that wasn't the case. Kirk was a Gentile in a land where a man didn't have to be a Christian to qualify. John Beadle noted that Utah was the only spot on earth where a Jew could bump into the novel ex-perience of being spoken of as a Gentile, undifferentiated from all others in that category. If Anderson wasn't a Jew, neither was he a Mormon, and that brand of chosen people resented the en-trance of dissenting religionists into what they looked on as their private preserve.

Kirk's publishing venture wouldn't have been possible before his starting year of 1858, as a matter of fact. Earlier in it Albert Sidney Johnston had led into Salt Lake City the military expedi-tion which had established there the hitherto defied authority of the United States. It then became possible for Gentiles to compete commercially with Latter-Day Saints, though a toler-ance forced at gun point couldn't have been expected to produce any "welcome to our city" spirit.

While Johnston's troops were in the Mormon capital, the *Deseret News* was published at various outlying points. By the time it was again being issued in Salt Lake, it was confronted by the *Valley Tan's* competition.

Or opposition would be a better word. If the *News* was the

printed voice of the angered Saints, Anderson's paper was the equally militant organ of the Gentile invaders.

"We had scarcely commenced our publication before the Utah Legislature declared the *Valley Tan* 'a libelous and scurrilous sheet,'" Kirk stated. Then he threw the gage back at his enemies. "The judgment . . . pronounced upon us by a Mormon Senate we most gratuitously accept. . . . We have warred against the corruption and crimes that have existed here and against the Church which has protected them."

As that church had never been backward about intimidating rebellious members of its own flock, it is more deplorable than astounding that Anderson suffered the official bullying of which he complained in the *Valley Tan*'s columns. He and his assistant, John Harnell, as he declared, were stopped on the street by "at least eight men . . . armed with guns, and who as we approached within a few feet of them, cocked their guns and placed themselves in front of us in a hostile manner. . . . One of the number fired a pistol," though apparently with a view to frightening rather than hitting the newspapermen.

Kirk then pointed out that the armed jostlers were all members of Salt Lake City's constabulary. "We desire to enter complaint against certain policemen (the above-mentioned eight) for acting contrary to law."

The enemies-in-chief of William Cowper Brann were supposedly men dedicated to the service of higher education. The *Iconoclast* was published in Waco, Texas, which was also the seat of Baylor University. Brann was a skeptic in religious matters and a practicer of self-expression. The Baptist sponsors of the university were fundamentalists who believed in imposing limits on the freedom of the press, especially where Baylor was concerned.

What got sparks and tinder together was Brann's belief that a coed at the U. had been made way with before she could become an unwedded mother. When he made a noise about it, Baylor's backers accused him of trying to destroy the university, because it was on God's side and the editor wasn't.

The outcry excited the students. Shouting such slogans as

"Lynch the atheist," they once seemed about to dangle William Cowper from a campus tree. Possibly seeing that this wouldn't have formed the best public relations for the old school, they let themselves be talked out of it by a Baylor official, however.

But Brann stayed on in a town where he was roughed up more than once, and as the 1890s waned, the *Iconoclast* was still publishing whatever its editor thought his subscribers would be interested in reading. As Baylor continued to be a subject, the blood pressure of the school's trainers and handlers kept on mounting.

In 1898 the thought of the university's critic was more than the boiler of a Baptist elder named Thomas E. Davis could hold. Whether he planned to bushwhack Brann, or couldn't pass up the chance when it was unexpectedly offered, Thomas stepped from a real estate office that the editor had just passed and shot him in the back.

Of course heeled himself, Brann whirled and scored four hits on Davis, while stopping two more slugs himself. Then both folded, William Cowper later that day and Thomas on the morrow.

In two other celebrated encounters the victims were San Francisco editors. In the first of these, the exchange of shots was sanctioned by the code duello.

In 1852 Edward Gilbert, of the *Alta California,* published statements about James Denver—for whom Colorado's capital city was named—which James thought he ought to do something about. He therefore sent a challenge which resulted in a meeting at which rifles were the weapons agreed upon.

An expert shot, Denver had no intention of taking advantage of a man who was not; his purpose was merely to press home the need for better editorial manners in the future. So, according to Ned McGowan, who was there, James said he was satisfied when the first exchange drew no claret from either. But when Gilbert insisted they should try again, Denver reasoned that it was time to look after himself. Bearing down, he drilled Edward; but the man of print got posthumously even. Many years later, when James seemed due to win the Democratic presidential nomination, an opposer killed his bid by bringing the death of Gilbert to the notice of the convention.

The other mentioned fatality was a more involved matter. Embroiled at the outset were Charles de Young, editor of the San Francisco *Chronicle*, and a fellow who was at times a journalist, too.

The Reverend Isaac S. Kalloch could have had quite a scrapbook, if he had collected his Western press notices. In 1859, for instance, the Sioux Falls *Dakota Democrat* cited him as a divine who was given to ginning and seduction. In 1871 a brochure published at Lawrence announced him as editor of the *Kansas Spirit,* "a Journal of Home and Husbandry." By 1880 he was making headlines in San Francisco as mayor of that city.

The campaign preceding his election had been a bitter one, marked by charges flung by and at de Young. After Kalloch was in office, Charles found himself so aggravated that he tried to assassinate the mayor and did badly wound him.

For the *Chronicle*'s editor such a method of showing his disapproval was nothing new. He was always shooting at somebody, though he usually gave opponents a fairer break. Yet his trigger happiness had brought him no serious consequences, and even his attempt to slay an unprepared man in the presence of a horde of witnesses for a while did not. Disappointed at his faulty aim but not one to brood, Charles returned to the business of putting out the *Chronicle* in partnership with his brother, Michel.

But where his luck let him down was the existence of a Reverend Isaac Kalloch in addition to the one he'd put out of action for a while. His middle initial M. and not S., the mayor's son eventually decided to make his way to the *Chronicle*'s sanctum. With no more warning than had been given his father, the minister put bullets in de Young that kept him down for keeps.

The unexpected enemy was an occupational hazard which was peculiarly hard to guard against by men who spent much of their time gazing at what they were writing. At times, however, an enraged visitor would unintentionally give an editor an even chance because of an urge to bleat of his wrongs before meting punishment.

An early experience of Wells Drury should suffice as illustration. On the day in the 1870s which first saw him at work on the Gold Hill, Nevada *News,* Wells was left in charge of the editorial department while the old hands went out for lunch. The only companion he had was the office pistol, dubbed "the family Bible" by Alf Doten, who pointed out that it had an uncommonly quick trigger. Alf and the rest hadn't long gone, when in stormed an outraged politico, horsewhip in hand. Had he chosen to wield it right away, Drury would have been in a sorry fix, but instead the fellow wanted to make an oration first. While he was shouting, Wells remembered the family Bible and picked it up. He had thought to do no more than discourage the owner of the whip, but the pistol lived up to advance billing. Hardly had the reporter leveled it than it belched a shot which nearly hit the politico. With a squeal of alarm, he fled premises to which he never afterward returned.

Women could not be counted out as dangerous callers either. When the famous Matilda Heron performed a tragedy or so in Virginia City in 1863, Joe Goodman undertook to put her on the pan in the *Territorial Enterprise.* Thereupon La Heron brought a furled umbrella into a sanctum of which Joe wasn't long an occupant.

The girls could make night visits, too. Once in the winter of 1857–58 Ned McGowan awoke in his hotel room to find a gun not far from his head. Holding it was one Helene Wingate, who fancied that Ned had attacked her deceased husband in the Sacramento *Phoenix.* Ned hadn't come of a long line of Blarney Stone kissers for nothing, however. The episode's finale was mutual admiration voiced over a champagne breakfast.

By no means isolated incidents, these two give poignance to a complaint published by Jim Chatham in the Short Creek, Kansas *Daily Republican* in 1880. "What this community needs just now is a society for the prevention of cruelty to writing men, otherwise editors. There is entirely too much blood on the moon and the air is getting too fragrant of the smoke of battle. There are too many bloodthirsty women on the warpath and unless some steps are taken pretty soon to secure a cessation of hostilities, there is liable to be a number of vacant chairs.

"For three days a woman in a violent rage has been promenading the streets of this town, looking for the man who writes up articles for the Republican. . . . She doesn't know him when she sees him, and thanks to a generous public, no one will point him out. She boils over at every street corner, and the object of her search hasn't eaten a hearty meal for three days, and besides his hair is rapidly turning gray.

"One woman has brought suit against the paper for libel and wants three thousand dollars to patch up her wounded reputation. We don't care for that, however. She has only to call and the money will be paid in without a grumble, but the cowhide and that pistol or perhaps loaded cane is what is causing a great deal of uneasiness. We want to resign in favor of a solid, cast-iron man with a Bogardus kicker [an invention of the then celebrated James Bogardus] attached to each heel.

"We no longer have a free press. We have been muzzled, and that, too, by women who seem determined not only to rule but to ruin also."

10

INTRA-MURAL SPORTS

IF WABUSKA, NEVADA, was an actual town, its *Mangler* was a figment, created by Sam Davis as a butt for the Carson City *Appeal*. When short of other matter, that is, Davis would "reprint" items from the *Mangler*, then castigate his gingerbread man as a disgrace to journalism.

The best part of Sam's joke was that the existence of the voice of Wabuska was not for some while doubted by Carson's other newspapermen. Neither were they surprised at the *Appeal's* savagery, nor at the amount of space it devoted to the business of running another sheet into the ground.

Sam's conduct seemed perfectly normal to his colleagues, because they were in general a contentious lot. Not satisfied with battles involving the rest of society, many of them turned their guns as well as their pens against fellows of their fraternity.

To take up the inked lead first, those who slung it had a choice of techniques. They could name rival editors outright or they could join Sam Davis and hammer at an institutional target. Usually that target was of the same town, and everybody in it would know who was being indirectly insulted; but at least there was a pretense of avoiding personalities.

Los Angeles was, in particular, the home of this limited form of verbal warfare. There was a difference of opinion among its editors, however, as to just how far from professional courtesy the printed word should stray. Relatively mild, for example, was the Los Angeles *News* when considering the L.A. *Irresistable* in 1865.

"This five column page of trash is called a newspaper. What's in a name? It favors the election [for U.S. Senator] of Phineas Banning. Considering that the *Irresistable* belongs body and breeches, to Mr. Banning, it would be natural to suppose that pa-

per would support its owner. The columns of balderdash which
have already appeared in Mr. Banning's 'paper' have disgusted
even the bolters . . . let the 'paper' keep on in its present style,
and it will make votes for its owner 'in a horn.'"

In 1873 the Los Angeles *Star* took off one glove when dealing
with the neighboring *Express*. "HOODLUM ORGAN. The vile
handbill across the way in its issue of last evening offends the sen-
sibilities of its readers by a lot of rubbish intended to be abusive
of the *Star*. How long a sensible community will tolerate the ut-
terances of that windy intestine . . . remains to be seen."

The Los Angeles *Broad-Axe* exposed both sets of bare knuckles
when swinging at the L.A. *Independent* in 1873. "The hired tool
of Black Republicanism . . . is still pegging away at the *Broad-
Axe*. . . . You cannot raise to the dignity of a sycophant, or a
yellow bobtailed, mangy dog . . . and your efforts have sunk low
down into the cesspool of corruption from which you emigrated."

Sometimes the warfare went beyond common newspaper feud-
ing and stemmed from the rivalry between neighboring queen
cities. That was the case when the White Cloud, *Kansas Chief*
jumped on the *Democratic Platform* in 1860 and fulminated a
play upon words.

"We call the attention of the wholesale news dealers to the
sheet published in this territory called the Democratic Platform—
Office, Number 123 Broadway, Marysville. . . . Marysville is a
city of a dozen or twenty log huts, principally used as whiskey
shops, scattered about with as much regularity as buffalo chips on
the plains. Dealers cannot fail to make a speculation by the sale
of this paper, as it overflows with wit, sarcasm and originality of
the most 'sockmatical' kind. Somehow its excruciatingly *ass toot*
editors have taken a fancy to us, and the excruciatingly cute, cut-
ting and penetrating witticisms that they get off at our expense
are indescribably funny. . . . The following is all original with the
editors of the Platform. It required the united intellect of both
to get it off."

The *Kansas Chief's* Sol Miller then proceeded to show why he
was wrathful. The issuers of the other rag hadn't insulted him,

but they had done far worse by printing a quip which questioned the metropolitan grandeur of White Cloud:

"Our city is fast filling up."—Chief.
"Especially in the vicinity of the grave yard."—Platform.

Miller came nearer to the insult direct in 1859, when the *Kansas Chief* was at odds with the voice of *Iowa Point*. But although he seemed beside himself, he didn't quite reach the point of identifying the qualities he ascribed with a named man.

"We have heard of hybrids of various descriptions, but only once of a cross between a quadruped and an insect. That isolated case is the editor of the Iowa Point Dispatch—he is half fyste and half tumble bug. His quadruped nature is indicated by his bark, and his insect nature by the substance he delights to revel in!"

Neither did Thomas J. Dryer, of the Portland *Oregonian,* name the city of roses rival to whom he tossed this bouquet in 1853: "Strayed, stolen, lost, absquatulated, mimeloosed [Chinook for dead or slain] or run away . . . formerly editor, proprietor, compositor, pressman, roller boy, extra seller, libeler, item gatherer, affidavit maker, slanderer general and pimp generalissimo of a small, cheap paper."

The line dividing the institutional insult from the personal one had, however, been crossed some years earlier by San Francisco's *California Star.* Later a Golden Gate paper itself, the *Californian* was still being published in Monterey when the *Star* was started in 1847 by Sam Brannan. Because of his sponsorship, the Monterey sheet had joshed the San Francisco one on the score of being a Mormon rag. This so annoyed the *Star's* non-Mormon editor, a Dr. Elbert Jones, that he sent this shot south:

"We have received two late numbers of the Californian, a dim, dirty little paper printed at Monterey, on the worn out material of one of the old California war presses. It is published and edited by Walter Colton and Robert Semple, the one a lying sycophant and the other an overgrown lickspittle."

Certain editors developed what modern poets would call private symbols for colleagues they singled out. For instance, William L. Adams of the Portland *Argus* referred to Asahel Bush of the Salem, Oregon *Statesman* as "Ass of Hell," while John Marion of the Prescott, Arizona *Miner* coined "the Black Cricket" for the Tucson *Citizen's* John Wasson.

One passage in which he did so shows that it was not meant as a pet name. Prescott's voice began by quoting a *Citizen* statement which averred that "Marion of the Miner has been more filthy than usual in his present campaign."

"So," Marion's rebuttal commenced, "says the Black Cricket, recently imported from Nevada by [Richard] McCormick & Co., to act as a liar, affidavit man, scavenger, scullion and valet de chambre for the outfit. We dare this abominable beggar, who has just been placed on horseback for his dirty services . . . to show where we have been filthy. But this is a way thieves and blackguards have for drawing attention from their own foul deeds and expressions. . . . Back, dog, to your foul kennel."

There were editors at odds who addressed each other in their columns, as though they were carrying on a telephone conversation. In 1868 John P. Cone, of the Seneca, Kansas *Nemeha Courier*, received this person-to-person call from the editor of the Marysville *Enterprise:*

"Cone, for the three hundred and fifty seventh time, refers to our being in the guard house on one occasion. We have acknowledged that fact so often that it is useless to do any more. Cone—you idiot—you jackass—red headed, frizzle-headed, mush-headed, slab sided, brainless deformity and counterfeit imitation of a diseased polecat—we inform you again, once more and emphatically—we *were* there. But it wasn't for stealing type."

Then there was M. Schiffgen, of the Cimarron, Kansas *Jacksonian*, who didn't boggle at inviting a brother of the craft to give him the salute intimate in 1889. "We are 'onto' the lop-eared, lantern-jawed, half-bred and half-born, whiskey soaked, pox eaten pup who pretends to edit that worthless wad of subdued outhouse bung fodder, known as the *Ingalls Messenger.* He is just starting out to climb the journalistic bannister and wants us to knock the hayseed out of his hair, pull the splinters out of his stern and push him up. We'll fool him. No free advertising from us. Murphy, k.m.a."

None of the above passages seem to have been written by men who had physical battle in mind. Extant, however, are two broadsides issued by men of print, furious because disappointed in their hopes of drawing blood from colleagues. Both bulletins involve, although in different capacities, authors of some note. Pilloried in one was Jesse Quinn Thornton, now remembered as the author of a piece of Americana titled *Oregon and California in 1848*. The writer of the other blast was Richard Realf, a poet whose work still occasionally turns up in anthologies.

An adherent of John Brown, Realf was a red-hot member of the free labor side when "Bleeding Kansas" was an apt term for that territory. Yet it wasn't because of a pro-slavery partisan that Realf raised his ruff in 1857. The fellow whose blood he yearned to add to the general flow was technically a brother in arms. Cheated of the duel he'd hoped for, the bard got the job shop of whatever Lawrence paper he was scribbling for to dish this up for distribution:

NOTICE!!
To the Public!

"I, the undersigned, on my personal honor and responsibility, do hereby publicly declare G. [eorge] W. Brown, Editor of the Herald of Freedom, to be a wilful LIAR, a malicious SLANDERER, and a most contemptible COWARD: all of which charges I hold myself in readiness to prove."

Richard Realf
Lawrence, July 14, 1857

On the receiving end, ten years earlier, was historian Thornton. Hurling was James N. Nesmith, of the Oregon City *Spectator*. To put his offer in perspective, Oregon was then a year short of being organized as a United States territory, and its metropolis wasn't elsewhere regarded as the globe's hub. Living in a queen city, however, the man of print aimed this item at his fourth-estate fellow:

TO THE WORLD

"J. Quinn Thornton, having resorted to low, cowardly and dishonorable means, for the purpose of injuring my character and my standing, and having refused honorable satisfaction which I demanded, I avail myself of the opportunity of publishing him to the world as a reclaimless liar, an infamous scoundrel, a black hearted villain, an arrant coward, a worthless vagabond and an imported miscreant, a disgrace to the profession and a dishonor to his country."

James W. Nesmith
Oregon City, June 7, 1847

But there were challenges, from and to frontier newspapermen, which were accepted. Tom Fitch sent the invitation heeded to Joe Goodman—likewise of Nevada's Virginia City—twice in fact. The second effort was necessary, because the first was a failure due to circumstances over which the duelists had no mastery.

Why they reached for pistols, and what occurred to balk them, was narrated by Mark Twain in the August 2, 1863 issue of the *Territorial Enterprise.* "Whereas Thomas Fitch, editor of the Union, having taken umbrage at an article headed 'The Virginia Union, not the Federal,' written by Joseph T. Goodman, our chief editor, and published in these columns; and whereas said Fitch having challenged said Goodman to mortal combat, naming John Church as his 'friend'; and whereas the said Goodman having accepted said challenge, and chosen Thomas Peasley to appoint the means of death——

"Therefore, on Friday afternoon it was agreed between the two seconds that the battle should transpire at nine o'clock yesterday morning (which would have been late in the day for most duelists, but it was fearfully early for newspapermen to get up)— place, the foot of the canyon below the Gould and Curry Mill; weapons navy six shooters; distance, fifteen paces, conditions, the first fire to be delivered at the word, the others to follow at the pleasure of the targets, as long as a chamber in their pistols remained loaded. To say that we felt a little proud to think that in our official capacity we were about to rise above the recording of ordinary street brawls and the monotonous transactions of the Police Court to delineate the ghastly transaction of a real duel would be to use the mildest language. Much as we deplored the state of things which was about to invest us with a new dignity, we could not help taking much comfort in the reflection that it was out of our power and also antagonistic to the principles of our class to prevent the state of things above mentioned. All conscientious scruples—all generous feelings must give way to our inexorable duty—which is to keep the public mind in a healthy state of excitement, and experience has taught us that blood alone can do this. . . .

"But we lost our bloody item . . . for Marshal Perry arrived early with a detachment of constables, and also Deputy Sheriff Blodgett with a lot of blasted Sheriffs, and the battle ground lying and being in Storey county, these miserable, meddling whelps arrested the whole party and marched them back to town."

Bound to keep the peace, Tom and Joe did for a month but in September they crossed over into California's Stampede Valley, duello bent; and this time they did swap bullets. Joe fired one more than Tom wanted, indeed. It lodged in one knee, giving him a gimpy leg for the rest of his life.

Yet not all editors were marksmen enough to be able to make a good showing on the field of honor. A case in point was the meeting which took place between Edward Ephraim Cross and Sylvester Mowry—author of a descriptive work titled *Arizona and Sonora*—in 1859. Both men were at one time or another connected with the Tubac *Arizonian;* but Cross was then its editor, and he had published affronts which led to a confrontation with Burnside rifles.

Billed as deadly weapons, these didn't prove so. After whanging away at each other, and drawing Maggie's drawers with each of several shots apiece, the foemen forgot they had ever been peeved. In mutual relief at having come through the ordeal unscathed, they rushed into each other's arms and were friends from then on.

In addition to meetings arranged and supervised by seconds, the Western code duello countenanced semi-formal exchanges of shots, referred to as affrays. The procedure in such cases was for the aggrieved party to warn the man who had offended him that he had better be armed when next they met. At that time the aggressor had another obligation. While still out of range of his enemy, he was supposed to call attention to his approach and the gun he hadn't yet drawn with a cry of, "Defend yourself."

Pioneer editors were given to affrays when at outs with each other, and it was one such encounter that led to the seizure of San Francisco by opportunists styling themselves the S. F. Committee of Vigilance of 1856. That wildest of all Western stories bristles with so many newspaper angles, in fact, that some special attention is due it here.

It began as a bicker between Tom King—later editor of the San Francisco *Evening Bulletin,* but then assisting his older brother, James King, of William—and James P. Casey, publisher of a Sunday number called the *Times.* Tom boiled over at something Casey had printed about him and threatened gunplay, if James P. didn't tell who had written the offending item by the time he next asked.

Faced with an affray and not a gun toter, Casey sought the cooperation of somebody he knew to be well supplied with weapons. This was Ned McGowan, who didn't feel well dressed without a revolver and two derringers, and was, besides, something of a collector of guns. Ned gave James P. a pistola and a bit of coaching, but placed a bet that Tom King would wilt in a showdown. Interested to see whether he was right, he next undertook to tail Tom.

"I followed the Polecat at a short distance," as McGowan later reminisced. "Casey and Tom met between Moult Nickerson's and the segar store near the Bulletin office. I stepped into the segar store to see the fun and watch the movements of the Slippery individual. The moment he saw Casey he approached and demanded the name of the writer of the article in question. Casey all the while looking him in the eye, both parties having their hands on their pistols. King again spoke and told him he would give him till a stated hour, which he named, to produce the author. Casey stepped back and replied in a firm tone, he did not wish for a moment longer, that he alone was responsible. Tom quailed

under the eye of Casey and could scarcely articulate that he
thought a gentleman had written it; and turned to go away."

That appeared to have chopped the episode short. But Ned
thought the story worth telling, and when James King of William
heard of the barroom joy at Tom's expense, the *Bulletin's* head
man revived the feud. His method was to publish the libel that,
before leaving New York, Casey had whiled away some of his
time in Sing Sing Penitentiary. When the welterweight editor of
the *Times* got only threats of violence, upon protesting to the
heavyweight director of the *Bulletin*, he followed the rule book
for affrays by telling King to be on his guard in the future.

As Casey meant nothing but business, the gun borrowed from
McGowan for use against Tom King was in practice aimed at
James. That editor, as he was fond of declaring in print, always
went armed himself. Nor did he depart from custom on 1856's
May 14, for a multi-barreled variant of the standard revolver was
found upon him, pursuant to an encounter witnessed by James
Madison Estell, of such Sacramento papers as the *Tribune* and the
California American.

Although San Francisco's vigilantes raised the hue that Casey
had shot an unprepared and unarmed man, Estell subsequently
published his own account of what had taken place. "Not with-
standing all the testimony got up under the fire of the Vigilance
Committee, I now state that Mr. King was shot by Casey when
they were forty-five feet apart, and after he had given him ample
warning; indeed warning sufficient for him to have discharged
every barrel of his revolver before Casey fired. I do not deny but
that Casey would have commenced firing as soon as Mr. King, but
I mean to say that Mr. King appeared to be attempting to in-
dignantly look him down when he should have been preparing to
defend himself. As soon as Mr. King was struck, instead of making fight as he had advertised, he cried aloud and retreated into
the [Pacific] express office, without making a single demonstration toward defense."

Probably the best explanation as to why King didn't draw was
offered by Casey, as quoted in a San Francisco sheet known as

Varieties: "Seeing he did not fire, and believing him a dung hill, I did not shoot again."

However that might be, the shooting of King—who was not hit in a vital spot—was town-cried as an assassination and used as the excuse for the usurpation of power by the San Francisco Committee of Vigilance of 1856. This body began trying the editor of the *Times* for murder before he of the *Bulletin* died of poor medical treatment some days later.

When James King finally did go under, the *Times* folded because Casey was lynched. Another development was that Tom King became the *Bulletin's* director. Aside from remembering Ned McGowan's mirth, re the street meeting near the "segar store," Tom had been picked up for theft in Philadelphia, and in a district of Pennsylvania's metropolis of which Ned had been police superintendent prior to becoming a forty-niner. In the *Bulletin's* saddle the younger King accused McGowan of having sicked Casey on dead James.

There were two sets of teeth in the trap that then yawned for Ned, for the vigilantes not only charged him with murder themselves but squeezed an indictment out of a convening grand jury. McGowan was then in the impossible position of being hunted by outlaws and posted by peace officers. Nor did he dare stand trial in San Francisco County, for Casey had been in custody, awaiting court action, when the vigilantes rolled a cannon up to the jail door and got possession of the editor by that writ of authority.

How Ned got out of his jam is one of the world's great true adventure stories, of which some notice will be taken in another chapter. Suffice it at this point to say that a change of venue to Napa was at length arranged for McGowan's case; and that was when Augustus Heslep—a lawyer as well as editor of the San Francisco *Plain Dealer*—rang himself in as one of the prosecutors.

As the evidence against Ned turned out to be nothing worth weighing, the jury only took ten minutes to agree to set him free, among other things, to start the Sacramento *Phoenix*. The purpose of that paper was to probe for flaws in the characters of Ned's vigilante enemies, and in due course it told of a moth hole in the moral armor of the *Plain Dealer's* director. Heslep, according to the *Phoenix*, had seduced his own daughter.

Claiming that he had been libeled, Augustus boated to Sacramento to file a suit which drew him nothing but a thwacking. A charmed observer, Mortimer J. Smith, published an account of this 1858 event in his Sacramento *Watch-Dog*.

"He [Heslep] came up from the Bay on Wednesday night to prosecute his case of libel against Judge McGowan, and on the opening of the Recorder's court yesterday morning, the case was called, but the old rat not being present to prosecute, though the defendant was on hand and ready for examination, the Recorder very properly dismissed the charge. . . . After the adjournment Heslep made his appearance, but was met by McGowan . . . who proceeded to castigate the Vigilante cur in a manner richly merited. After spitting in his face, and giving him a 'right hand' or two, McGowan wrenched a cane out of the hand of Heslep and applied it smartly to his back. Heslep, like all the cowardly Vigilantes received the castigation without daring to defend himself, although he was armed and was called upon by McGowan to draw."

Another wielder of a walking stick was Sam Post of the Carson City *Appeal*. While footing it along one of the corridors of Nevada's capitol in 1883, Sam was said by Wells Drury to have become brave-bull furious because of seeing C. N. Harris of the Carson *Index*. Although Drury didn't say what the vendetta was about, he did make it clear that when Sam Davis had an impulse, he didn't risk giving himself a complex by fighting it. At sight of the approaching Harris, he leapt forward with a howl and laid his enemy out cold with an adroit swipe of his cane.

On occasion weapons were dispensed with; witness an 1876 report of the Cheyenne, Wyoming *Sun* bearing on the career of Legh Freeman. No longer with the flitabout *Frontier Index*, Legh had temporarily cast anchor at Ogden, Utah.

"The editor of the Ogden Freeman recently whipped Joseph Blyman, a newspaperman, formerly of Denver, within an inch of his life," the *Sun* affirmed of a man whose sheet now had the same name as himself. "The Mormon authorities chucked Freeman in jail, and now the editor doesn't know whether he is a 'freeman' or not."

Still, guns were the most popular means of dealing with a colleague, and many editors were in such haste to shoot that they couldn't be bothered with the advanced warnings called for by affrays. They just saw to it that their shooting irons were ready for use and made for the offices of the colleagues they meant to use them on.

In one famous case a man of print didn't even have to leave the plant where he scribbled in order to bag the game he wanted. Earlier of the Panamint *News*, the Darwin *Coso Mining News*, and the Bodie *Standard*, Thomas S. Harris was reporting for the Los Angeles *Republican* in 1884. The *Republican*'s editor for part of that year was Charles Whitehead. Perhaps if he'd thought more about Tom's background he would have handled a man who was used to being his own boss more diplomatically. But, as it was, supervision so chafed a man who'd been schooled in Panamint and Bodie that he reached for his cannon and finished Whitehead with one pull of the trigger.

But wars between the editors of separate papers were the norm, and a common procedure was for one sanctum occupant to barge into the lair of another with a view to making sure that he could not again print offensive statements. That was what Sam H. Wall of the Tacoma, Washington *Evening Telegraph* did, when annoyed by remarks about him that had been published by Herbert S. Harcourt of the Tacoma *News* in 1886. Sam would have achieved his purpose, too, if Herb hadn't been such a dude. But, as it was, the shot with which Wall let daylight through Harcourt failed of being lethal because it was deflected by a tie clip.

In some instances rival staffs, and not merely single parties, were mortally embroiled. When Dan Anthony of the Leavenworth, Kansas *Conservative* felt himself insulted by J. C. Satterlee, of the same town's *Herald* in 1861, he went looking for his enemy with a man to back him. As the *Herald*'s editor, when found, had a partisan also, there were casualties on both sides. The *Conservative* won the engagement, though, for while somebody in the other camp scored a hit on Anthony's assistant, Dan himself put Satterlee where he wouldn't wound anybody's feelings again.

Another battle involving team play pitted William Thompson and a fellow writer for the Roseburg, Oregon *Plaindealer* against Henry and Thomas Hale of the Roseburg *Guard*. This ended in a draw, with Thompson hit several times and Henry Hale badly wounded.

To return from doubles play to singles, J. K. Mercer of the Portland *Bee* slew A. C. McDonald of the rival *Telegram* as the climax of a street engagement, in which eight shots were exchanged. The list could be strung into a long one, but it will be cut short here to make way for the story of gunfire whose purpose was to admonish rather than to wound or kill.

As of 1882, John Wasson—disliked by John Marion of the Prescott *Miner*—no longer ruled the Tucson, Arizona *Citizen*. In his place was J. A. Whitmore, whose claim to immortality is vested in the shot taken at him by Charles D. Poston.

As early as 1859, Poston had begun his long career as an Arizona journalist by contributing to the previously mentioned Tubac *Arizonian*. Just how he was engaged, when Whitmore undertook to give him adverse notice in the *Citizen*, was neither stated nor of importance to the anecdote. But the next 1882 day he took the remedial action reported by an eyewitness and published in the Tucson *Star*.

"Colonel Poston appeared upon the plaza of Porter's Hotel some minutes after nine o'clock. He was soon joined by Judge Porter and the two stepped to the bar and took drinks. They then walked out of the saloon door and were engaged in general conversation for a few minutes. Colonel Poston then walked with the Judge to the southeast corner of the hotel . . . and paced back, passing the saloon door and proceeding several feet beyond. . . . During these few minutes he showed no symptoms of excitement or anxiety.

"In the meantime Mr. Whitmore had left the dining-room, where he had breakfasted, and proceeding across the bar-room, intended passing through the outer door of that apartment. At this place he was brought face to face with Colonel Poston who upon seeing him . . . with some deliberation, drew from the right pocket of his pantaloons a six shooter and fired at his enemy. The ball, however, missed its mark, passing through the woodwork to the right of Whitmore and across the bar-room. . . . Its course was within six inches of the editor's right arm and on a level with his chest. He abruptly turned and ran across the bar-room into the wash-room, while the Colonel stepped into the doorway, watching the retreat of his intended victim. He then passed back to the plaza, after pocketing his revolver, and calmly conversed with some friends for a few minutes before starting down town."

Whitmore didn't return from the gents' room, as he skinned out its window and fled via the alley into which it admitted him. It is not on record that he was again critical of Poston in print.

Having acted on behalf of good editorial manners, the Colonel was meanwhile satisfied that he had obtained his end. His placid attitude is well preserved by the reporter for the *Star* who interviewed him concerning the episode.

"An editorial in the Citizen impugned my political, moral and social character in a manner not to be overlooked. . . . Later I was passing the Citizen's office, when Whitmore was sitting in an armchair in front, but observing our approach [although he began with the first person singular, the veteran journalist shifted naturally into the editorial plural] he rapidly retired to the sanctum and when we arrived he was not there."

As Whitmore had dodged confrontation, Poston decided to lay for him, as for an elk at a water hole. "This morning, having been informed that the editor had gone to breakfast at Porter's Hotel, I thitherward went, and having imbibed a delicate brandy cocktail with Judge Porter at the bar, was fuming a Havana upon the porch when Whitmore appeared at the door, and I therefore leveled a shot, with a very wild range."

Part II

SIDELIGHTS AND SPECIALTIES

11

THE PRESS AND THE SWORD

THE PURPOSE OF this work's first section was to sketch the internal workings of journalism as practiced on the frontier. The aim of the second will be to show the relations of the profession to sundry institutions and assorted lines of endeavor.

The one with which men of print were involved from the outset of their adventure in the West was war; specifically, war in Texas. In a previous chapter, that province's break with Mexico was no more than touched upon. It thus remains unfinished business which will now be taken up.

Following a series of armed uprisings, the Texas Revolution—at first but a movement for forcing better treatment for American colonists—jelled with a formal declaration of purpose on October 5, 1836. Five days later Gail Borden, his brother, Thomas, and one Joseph Baker commenced publication of the *Telegraph and Texas Register* at San Felipe de Austin.

The thinker at the helm, Gail was later more renowned as a purveyor of canned milk than as a journalist. But he saw that a newspaper was an indispensable tool for a pickup team of warriors, who were at times more of a peril to one another than to the Mexicans. As earlier periodicals had by then lapsed, the residents of scattered settlements looked to the *Telegraph and Texas Register* for word of what was going on. Because the editors were plugging a cause and not seeking to advance their own political interests, the paper was a unifying force. It might almost be said to have been the only one in a movement which came near failing, because of factions operating in defiance of President Henry Smith and General in Chief Sam Houston.

The turning point came when the *Telegraph*'s job shop published a broadside dated March 16, 1836. It was signed by Thomas

Gay, writing for the colonists' Standing Committee of Safety. Gay wasn't long on orthography, but he had an important message. "Felow Citizens, I have just received information by Col. William T. Austin of the fall of the Alimo and masacre of our countrymen in that garrison."

The hastily assembled army which Houston was then able to command wasn't strong enough to confront the Mexican punitive expedition which soon began marching east from San Antonio. Washington, the revolutionary capital, had to be abandoned, and when San Felipe, too, had to be left in enemy hands, the staff and equipment of the *Telegraph* swelled the numbers and baggage of the retreating governmental party.

Thomas Borden and Baker quit the paper to join the army, but Gail grasped that a news organ was as crucial to the Texan cause as it had ever been. Nor was he less in danger than the soldiery. When he took his stand in Harrisburg to issue the April 14 number of his sheet, the Mexicans seized the town before he could have his gear packed and rolled away. If Gail escaped scathe, his press did not. It and the *Telegraph*'s type were dumped into Buffalo Bayou.

But at least one of the copies of the April 14 issue—only a few had been printed before the Mexicans arrived and destroyed all they could find—was saved by Borden when he fled. As critical papers of the provisional government of Texas had not survived the scramble of retreat, the lone number of the *Telegraph* published at Harrisburg turned out to be the sole documentary proof that such a body had been legally in operation.

Evidence was important, because after Houston had made the revolution a success at the Battle of San Jacinto, the Texans began wrangling as to how it should be capitalized on, and who should be the chief capitalizers. Organization would have broken down entirely but for a circumstance noted with satisfaction by Gail on January 18, 1837. By then in Columbia as editor of the resurrected *Telegraph and Texas Register,* he told how print had saved the game.

After observing that other proofs had been flight casualties in April of 1836, Borden cited the *Telegraph*'s brief stay on the

THE PRESS AND THE SWORD

marge of Buffalo Bayou. There, as he said, "a paper was issued on the executive ordinance, the only link unbroken which in the chain of government could hold Texas as a nation." The original had turned up missing at a bad time, for Gail went to point out, with reference to said ordinance, "the importance of which was remembered by many, when last fall the powers of the government *ad interim* were doubted—the archives ransacked to find the authority, when lo! it was found in the only number of the *Telegraph* printed at Harrisburg, which we preserved from the general destruction of that place."

When the republic formed with the *Telegraph's* aid had become one of the United States, the first of America's two wars with Mexico resulted. The declaration of hostilities in the spring of 1846 gave Sam Bangs a new idea. After launching the West's first daily at Galveston in 1839, Sam had published the *Musquito* at Houston for a couple of years, but then had returned to the island where he had worked a press for filibuster Francisco Mina in 1817. Moving out of Galveston again twenty-nine years later, Bangs set up his press by the headquarters of General Zachary Taylor. While Old Rough and Ready was preparing for the invasion of Mexico, which he soon headed, Sam began issuing the Corpus Christi *Gazette*.

After battles had cleared the way and American troops were south of the Rio Grande, Bangs was there, too, as publisher of the Matamoros *Reveille*. But not all generals are close friends with publicity, as exercised by practicers of the free press theory, and this one seemed to have had reservations about it. On grounds not now plain, Taylor sounded Taps for the *Reveille;* but Bangs had already made his mark on military history. He was the first publisher of papers designed to serve United States troops in the field.

Westward and much farther up the Rio Grande, General Stephen Watts Kearny made his shotless conquest of New Mexico not much later. Hearing of the press which had once printed the earlier mentioned *El Crepúsculo de la Libertad,* Kearny decided to use it as a bridge to span the gap between American authority and Mexican understanding of the new rules in force in the province of which Santa Fe was the capital.

Among the volunteers who had hiked down the Santa Fe Trail as a member of Alexander Doniphan's famous regiment was the keeper of a subsequently published journal named George R. Gibson. Having looked the confiscated outfit over with a professional's eye, he thus wrote of it:

"A small printing press was brought from Taos, the type badly pied and but little [of it]. Workmen are sorting and distributing it and trying to put the office in a condition to print the public documents, proclamations, orders by the governor, etc. Being a Spanish concern, there are no 'Ws,' but they probably can use the capital 'M'."

General Kearny had been authorized to set up a civil government in New Mexico, prior to pushing on to California. Prerequisite was imparting to a people of Spanish speech and traditions some comprehension of what their rights and obligations as American citizens would be. A lawyer as well as a military officer, Colonel Doniphan drew up a legal code, and after it had been translated, the little Ramage made it available to such among a largely illiterate populace as could read it.

Then, in an order datelined Santa Fe, September 22, 1846, the press quoted Kearny as follows. "Notice being duly authorized by the President of the United States of America, I hereby make the following appointments for the Government of New Mexico, a territory of the United States. . . ." Heading the slate as governor was Charles Bent, founder of a fur-trading empire and the celebrated post known as Bent's Fort.

Thereafter the printing equipment, brought to New Mexico at the behest of one Antonio Barreiro twelve years earlier, made no noticed history until it scored a dramatic finish in 1877. In that year it was being used to publish the Cimarron *News*, or it was up to the time that its editor complained in print that the cowboys who used the town as a filling station were boorish in their cups. He wasn't soon able to reprint the charge, because the waddies roped the Ramage and dragged it into the Cimarron River.

But to return to its period of Army service in 1846: In coastal California, meanwhile, American invaders had found and used the press which Don Augustin V. Zamorano had imported in 1834.

When the United States man-of-war *Savannah* sailed into the harbor of Monterey in the summer of 1846, the Reverend Walter Colton—already the author of *Ship and Shore* and later to father a couple of other books—was serving as chaplain. Subsequently relieved of his divine deck duties, he was made Monterey's *alcalde*, or combination of mayor and magistrate.

In the course of casing the town he was ruling by right of conquest, Colton learned that the long departed Zamorano had left his press behind; and being a man of letters, he took it over. The parson wasn't a printer, but one was on hand. A veteran of Fremont's recent Bear Flag revolution, Robert Semple had earlier been a Kentucky hunter, a dentist somewhere, and editor of the Philadelphia *North American*.

A brother was supposed to have said of Robert that if he could have been kept locked up, so he couldn't botch the wonderful ideas which emerged from his genius, that he would have prospered boundlessly. Colton incorporated nothing but praise of Semple in a one-sentence sketch. "He is in buckskin dress and fox skin cap; he is true with his rifle, ready with his pen and quick at the type case."

Associated as partners, Walter and Robert were to draw the previously described fire of San Francisco's *California Star*. Not yet so stigmatized in the summer of 1846, they launched the Monterey *Californian*, a bilingual paper designed both to serve American settlers and to make reconstructed Mexicans acquainted with their new lot.

There were some preliminaries for Dr. Semple, though. Gone Zamorano's type hadn't been used for so long that it was as rusty as only metal exposed to salt air can get. If there had ever been any rules, or leads for spacing, they were lost and had to be improvised. There was no newsprint, so a deal was made with a tobacconist for sheets which had been imported for the purpose of wrapping cigars. There was one lack the man of print couldn't make up for, though. The Spanish alphabet didn't have any 'Ws', so pairs of 'Vs' were yoked, in place of the inverted 'Ms' suggested in the journal of George R. Gibson.

On August 15, 1846, California's first newspaper—for, unlike New Mexico, there had been no Hispanic forerunner—hit the street. *The Californian* had news for the largely Spanish speaking populace of Monterey, too. It told a people who had changed nationalities at gunpoint that war between the United States and Mexico had been declared.

Subsequently *The Californian* made the mentioned hegira to San Francisco. As for Zamorano's press, it met with as violent an end as the one which military authorities had confiscated in New Mexico. For in 1853 it was burned in Columbia, California, by a man who'd lost possession through failure to pay all that had been agreed.

To go again, however, with the Mexican War of 1846–48: After it was over, print and the armed services continued to flourish together on the frontier. At times they were officially linked, while at others editors set up their presses close to army posts, because settlers had clustered where they could thus be reasonably safe from Indian attacks. Such, as has been mentioned, was the beginning of Legh Freeman's *Frontier Index*, which was at Fort Kearny, Nebraska, before the Union Pacific put it on wheels.

The Prescott *Arizona Miner* went through what might be called a military larval stage before it was able to operate independently. When Arizona was organized as a territory separate from New Mexico in 1863, Richard C. McCormick was appointed Secretary of State by Lincoln's administration. Because he was a man of print, he took a press with him, upon starting westward with other members of the governmental party.

Traveling across the plains, Arizona's civil officers had to have a military escort, and after they reached the new territory they still needed armed protection. Most governments have a capital to hole up in, but this one didn't. There was a town available, to be sure, but 1863 was a Civil War year, and Tucson was Confederate as to sympathy. On that account Arizona's rulers had been ordered to set up shop far away from the only considerable gathering of those under their jurisdiction.

The government without a citizenry crossed the territorial boundary just above parallel thirty-five, whereas Tucson lay well below thirty-three. Safely out of contact with any constituents, the administrators functioned—after the turn of 1864—at two military compounds, both known as Fort Whipple. At the second one McCormick unpacked his press, which began printing a sheet called the *Arizona Miner* in March.

By that time a gold rush to central Arizona had brought settlers to the *Miner's* vicinity, so the government could rub shoulders with some people, if it was willing to compromise a little. Deciding that was in order, Governor John Goodwin asked the commandant of Fort Whipple to move once again. So the post was shifted south, into the heart of the gold-seeking excitement, and the *Arizona Miner* came with it.

Christened by Richard McCormick, who named it for his favorite historian, the town of Prescott emerged as a capital in which the fugitive government was at last able to operate on a respectable political basis. Emancipated from Fort Whipple, too, the Prescott *Miner* commenced its civil career.

Published as morale boosters for men stationed at lonely posts, other papers were military productions from start to finish. One such was the Fort Rice, Dakota Territory *Frontier Scout.* In 1864 a paper of the same name had been issued at Fort Union— the old headquarters of the American Fur Company's Western Division—which the army had taken over. Also in what is now North Dakota, it was on the north bank of the Missouri, a few miles above its confluence with the Yellowstone.

Toward the end of 1864, a part of the garrison of Fort Union was detailed to build Fort Rice. Located on the Missouri, just north of the Cannonball's mouth, the site was already fixed in Western lore, because it was there that the Arikara massacred the Langevin fur-trading expedition in 1823. The founding units of the Thirtieth Wisconsin took the *Frontier Scout's* press down stream with them, but, before it could be put to work, the First United States Volunteer Infantry arrived as a replacement outfit.

One of its officers was Captain Enoch George Adams, later editor of the St. Helena, Oregon *Columbian* and the Vancouver, Washington *Register*. In June of 1865 he brought the *Frontier Scout* to life again. At Fort Union it had not been a noteworthy newspaper. At Fort Rice—alike on account of what Adams was and what he was not—it became both interesting and exasperating.

The captain was a literary cove, who might have become a writer of some importance, had he either learned more about verse or cared less for it and framed his ideas in prose, where he was more at home. Yet he had a perceptive mind, and because of one of its bents, Adams can't be denied a place in the history of American poetry.

Previously the nation's versifiers had dealt with Indians in a variety of ways, but even when most sympathetic, the poets had measured redskins with a white man's yardstick. Most of them, to be sure, had never seen a savage warrior outside of pipe dreams or the pages of a book. But Enoch George had fought against them, and known them, too, as allies, in the form of the post's Indian scouts. So he racked up a first by writing convincingly of a renegade—or white-aiding Indian—as seen through the eyes of a Sioux patriot.

The parties involved in his poem were a celebrated chief, called Santee, and an Indian scout for General Alfred Sully, who was in charge of operations against the Sioux as of that period. Fool-Dog was not an epithet; it was a name earned by the scout's general elusiveness and specific ability to spy on an Indian encampment without drawing even canine notice. So much for the background of the piece which Adams titled *Santee Vs. Fool-Dog*.

> My anger it burns with a heat that is white
> Whenever the Fool-Dog appears in my sight.
> His heart rings true to the white man's touch
> As the white iron rings in the trader's clutch;
> He forgetteth his people, his kith and his kin,
> And letteth our foe to his wigwam in;
> He hath led in safety o'er every trail
> That accursed race with their faces pale. . . .

There's an arrow I long have hid in my quiver
To plant in that traitor Fool-Dog's liver.
He may fool the dogs so they cannot scent
What was the way that his foot steps went,
But he cannot elude with his cunning the hater
That will have his revenge, be it sooner or later.
If he goes till his sight is weakened and dim
In the shadow of age I will punish him. . . .

After a passage which portrays the pioneer era from the Indian
viewpoint, Santee tells just what he means to do to the renegade
who has helped defeat the Dakotas. And here Enoch George suc-
ceeds in imparting, in some measure, the true ring of implacabil-
ity waiting its moment.

No wonder for Fool-Dog my heart is too narrow,
That I make for his bosom a death-dealing arrow,
For the day when the moons of his life are all reckoned
I will tear off his scalp in the lapse of a second
And hang on my belt when my people assemble
For traitors like him to, beholding it, tremble.
He led the Chief Sully with his band of marauders
To the heart of our kingdom away from its borders,
Who purpled the Black Hills with a sunset of slaughter
While our veins emptied blood as the clouds empty water. . . .
And vengeance alone is my wish and my care;
Like his shadow I'll follow him everywhere.
In a moment unguarded, not thinking of danger,
I will tear out the heart that is warm for the stranger
I will squeeze the blood from it and paint my cheeks gory
And never will wash off that trophy of glory.

Years before the dying cowboy of a well-known ballad voiced
the petition, "Bury me not on the lone prairie," Adams put an
almost identical plea in the mouth of a Sioux. Again looking
through Indian eyes, the captain pictured, in *The Dying Indian's
Request*, the advantages of being lofted on a platform—Dakota
fashion—as compared with the white man's practice of interment.

O bury me not in the midst of the earth
In a cavern of dreamless night
Where comes not the voice of living mirth
Or the gash of living light.

But build me a stage of the greenwood tree,
And arrayed in my warlike gear,
Unbandaged, unswathed, uncoffined and free,
Let me lie, as I'm lying here. . . .

To Adams' credit, too, must be placed a vivid verse sketch of what life at a completely isolated post was like. A prominent feature of it seems to have been the amateur theatricals—*Uncle Tom's Cabin* was apparently one play that was staged—with which the soldiers solaced themselves during off-duty hours that would else be barren. As for the rest of it, anybody who's been in military service will find his fiddle strings twanged by the tribute paid "detail" in *Life at Fort Rice.*

Everything by detail goes,
Even blowing of the nose.
By that holy oath St. Patrick,
We are on detail theatric,
And tomorrow, so the chance is,
It depends on circumstances,
We'll be detailed for court martial.
Meting justice out impartial,
So we go from gay to solemn
As we change from flank to column.
Like manoeuvres military,
So our occupations vary.
Now as officer we figure,
Next we personate a "nigger."
Nothing meddles, naught infringes,
Round we move like well oiled hinges. . . .
If we're living or we're dying,
We're detailed, there's no denying.
Just so many must be sick;
One that's over totes a stick.
Every day is made a coffin
Detailed man to carry off in,
And the rations he would eat
Is deducted from our meat.
This is done by strong potations
Of the Army regulations.
This is not untrue or libel;
'Tis the soldier's chart and Bible.

Just how many presses were in operation at frontier military posts cannot now be told. Application to the archival division of the Defense Department has revealed the fact that it was an army activity of which no record was kept. But at least one commissioned man of print had a private press, which he operated when not fighting Apaches. In 1877 an issue of the Prescott *Miner* carried the following item. "Captain Corliss at Camp McDowell has a miniature press on which he has printed several opuscula and is now engaged in publication of a monthly magazine which he is distributing among friends in the East."

Perhaps a descendant of one of the captain's Eastern fans will some day dredge from an attic samples of said little works and copies of the periodical. Unless that happens, the notation in the *Miner* will remain the sole monument to the determination of a lonely printer-journalist to work a press and find an audience for what it issued.

There is another military solitaire who must be dealt with in this chapter. On duty in San Diego, as of the summer of 1853, was Lieutenant George Horatio Derby, of the United States Army's Corps of Topographical Engineers. That was but one of the lives he led, though. When not on duty, he was a then much admired humorist who signed his squibs and jingles John Phoenix or Squibob.

Everything happened to Judson Ames of the San Diego *Herald*. During the winter of 1852–53, as has been related, Jud's office, together with much of his income, was commandeered by William Walton. The following fall he mistakenly put his paper in the hands of the merry Lieutenant Derby.

Not content with backing California's Democratic ticket with the *Herald*, Ames decided to go to San Francisco and there throw his personal support behind John Bigler, then running for governor a second time. Going north to do so in September of 1853, he made his friend Squibob, or perhaps it was John Phoenix, the *Herald's* policy director.

Overnight the voice of San Diego deserted the Democrats and began cheering for the ticket headed by William Waldo, the Whig gubernatorial candidate. There were other changes in the paper's tone and temper, too; for Derby thought he was a very comical man, and he was out to have as much fun as he could during the six weeks that Ames was gone.

The lieutenant's wit was of his period only. But if it withered when his coevals did, it convulsed them. All California was over-joyed by the Derby-edited numbers of the *Herald,* and even Jud was amused enough to overlook the dirty political trick which had been played upon him.

"Here we are again!" Ames wrote, upon his return. "Phoenix has played the 'devil' during our absence, but he has done it in such a good humored manner that we have nothing to say. He has done things which he ought not to have done . . . but as the evil he has done cannot be undone, we may as well 'dry up' and let it slide."

As a capper for this chapter, another look will be taken at the *Frontier Scout,* though as published at Fort Union in 1864 and not at Fort Rice the following year. If the Fort Union *Scout* was in general undistinguished, it published one paragraph which tells of a frontier newspaperman's hazard not elsewhere chroni-cled.

The editor's subject was the post's "BBs. We have seen them in battalions, in division, in army corps, all sizes, regularly organized, thoroughly drilled. Not content with disturbing our sleep, they are on the paper when we sit down to write. If we have a game of cards, bed bugs form the hearts, spades, diamonds and clubs."

12

IMPOLITIC POLITICIANS

IN THE WEST, as elsewhere, the field of politics was a more usual battleground for editors than the Campus Martius. One cause of wrangling was the location of the state or territorial capital.

When Helena, for example, became the capital of Montana Territory in 1874, it took the prize away from Virginia City the younger. There were preliminary electoral fights, however, in which the original seat of government won out. Nor was this fact overlooked by Virginia City's *Weekly Republican*.

In thumbing its nose at the beaten aspirant, the *Republican* invoked a now neglected musical instrument called the hew-gag. This was both an actuality and a Pacific Coast myth. In the former capacity it was a wind instrument, not unlike the kazoo, though fashioned of wood instead of tin. As a gong to be whammed, it was a figment of the brain that begot E. Clampus Vitus, a society formed by California gold-rush old timers for the purpose of shaking greenhorns down for drinks.

No doubt once a member of this single-minded fraternal order, the *Republican's* editor featured the gong in the headlines he wrote for the story of a capital temporarily saved.

Beat the Hew-Gag

Virginia Keeps the Capital

301 Majority

Helena Must Wait

Old Madison [County] Roars—Deer Lodge Thunders

How are You, Capital?

We will Remember Our Friends

Western fourth estaters seldom forgot enemies either. But more prevalent than their occupation of bickering about the sites of capitals was rowing over the location of county seats.

The newspaper publisher who operated where a county's government did could count on some or all of the public printing gravy, depending on whether or not he had local competition. Then, in addition to patronage, there were such perquisites as legal ads and the publishing of briefs. These were large stakes for shoestringers, and they were battled for accordingly.

There were three campaign possibilities, of which the least common was a setup in which no county seat had as yet been designated. The other two situations emerged when a territorial government, or some other federal agency, picked a site which might or might not be the one which drew a decisive number of settlers. If it attracted no more than its nearest county rival, there was bound to be a contest, of which either might be the winner. But should it be plainly overmatched, population-wise, the original seat was apt to be stripped of its honors, to the tune of jeers and hoots from the editor who had engineered the pilfering.

The men of print were not nice to each other at any stage of such a tournament. Typical was the 1887 struggle for the seat of Garfield County, Kansas. Hoping to keep the advantage for Ravanna, the *Chieftain* took a severe look at not only Eminence but also at the editor of that town's *Call*.

"Although we desire that this enterprising, God-fearing and progressive city of Ravanna shall be and remain the permanent county seat" rather than "that nondescript collection of bug infested huts which its few and scabby inhabitants have the supreme gall to call a town . . . we refuse to descend to the depths of filth and indecency indulged in by that loathsome creature who sets type for an alleged newspaper in that God-forsaken collection of places unworthy to be called human habitations."

Just how the *Call*'s editor had shocked the *Chieftain*'s wasn't recorded, but the man of Ravanna had more to say about his rival. After remarking that the voice of Eminence caused "staid farm horses to break their halters and run away when they see him coming down the road," the *Chieftain* further opined that "he is the kind of a man who sleeps on a manure pile from choice and whose breath has been known to turn the stomach of a veteran skunk."

But, alas for Garfield County's center of culture, the barbarians proved too tricky for its upright denizens. A review of the census shows that neither town had more than 400 voters, when the issue of the shire's capital was settled at the polls. Yet the count of the returns revealed that Eminence—with 18,000 backers to Ravanna's 17,000—won the capital on the strength of more imagination.

How crucial a newspaper was in settling such matters was demonstrated in the reminiscences of one E. C. Cole. A resident of Crawford County, Kansas, he took the lead in beating off the challenge of Crawfordsville in the 1860s.

"I saw there was one thing lacking, and very much needed for our success, and that deficiency was a newspaper," he affirmed. "Our rival had such a small sheet called the Crawfordsville Times. . . . I had learned there was a second-hand Washington hand-press and a few fonts of type for sale or trade at the town of Osage Mission. . . . I borrowed a horse and struck out for the coveted prize. . . . In due course I arrived, and soon made a bargain with Mr. Oliver, the owner, for a half interest.

"Two days later found us unloading and setting up our printing office in a modest board house, 12 × 16. . . . My partner, Mr. Oliver, took charge of the labor and the mechanical end of the business, and your humble servant assumed the role of editor and manager. Everything being in readiness, on the 10th day of April, 1869, the Girard News . . . went forth dressed in its spring garb of mechanical and editorial beauty to the waiting throng on the outside, and was considered by all a masterpiece . . . this five column 12 × 16 sheet.

It was masterpiece enough to blow Crawfordsville off the map, which is more than Detroit's *Western News* could do when battling Abilene for the seat of Dickenson County, Kansas, in 1870. "ABILENE IS DEAD and will be BURIED next TUESDAY," the voice of Detroit declared when the election was imminent.

But after the polls closed, it was learned that the rumor of the famous cow town's demise was not well founded.

Yet even when not fighting to promote their towns, and consequently their own fortunes, the pioneer men of print were furious politicians. They snarled over party principles in verse as well as prose, and in at least two instances attacks took the form of poetic drama.

In 1852 the Whigs, as represented by the Portland *Oregonian,* were sounding off against the Democrats, in particular Asahel Bush, of the Salem, Oregon *Statesman.* In the course of this ideological war the *Oregonian* published *A Melodrama Entitled 'Treason, Stratagems and Spoils' by Breakspear.*

Written by William L. Adams, it was also published in pamphlet form the same year. In each case it began with the warning: "Prepare for rhymes—I'll publish right or wrong. Fools are my theme—let satire be my song."

Twelve years later there was an intra-Republican fight in Kansas. The chief spokesmen for the two factions were the *Times* and *Conservative* of Leavenworth, which was then the state's metropolis. The biggest gun fired in this war was another five-act play, a parody of *Macbeth,* though written in rhyme rather than blank verse.

The author was the *Conservative's* H. Clay Wright. He called his 1864 offering *Burlesque Statesmanship or the Gubernatorial —Senatorial—Editorial—Conclavical, Fizzletorial Coup d'Etat.*

Of the school of Thomas Middleton's famous but little read *A Game at Chesse,* these clever efforts share with their Elizabethan forebear the drawback of demanding acquaintance with the political infighting of the day in order to be comprehensible. As there is no room in this narrative for accounts of the causes and personalities which were exciting Oregon and Kansas in the middle of the nineteenth century, both plays will be merely pointed to as examples of the virtuosity often displayed by frontier journalists.

There is one feature of *Burlesque Statesmanship* which makes it briefly a matter of general interest, however. Toward the end of his play, Wright brought Abraham Lincoln on stage as a speaking character. This may well have been Abe's first appearance behind footlights.

Both works stood in subtle contrast to the unvarnished abuse which was a usual feature of Western political attacks. At that type of composition, Sol Miller of the White Cloud *Chief* was as forthright a hand as any.

A Democrat in the frenzied Kansas of 1860, Sol had no use for the surging sons of the Elephant and did all in his editorial power to keep them in check. "Muzzle the Hound!" the *Chief* roared on one occasion. "Jim Lane, the whore monger and murderer, is peregrinating the Territory, for the ostensible purpose of denouncing the Territorial Claim Bonds, authorized by the Legislature, but in reality to gratify a personal spite and abuse Governor Robinson. In this despicable business he is encouraged by Republicans and generally makes it convenient to ease himself of his overflowing bile at Republican County Conventions. . . ."

Feeling as strongly as they did about things political, the men of print usually worked only for papers which spoke their minds. An exception, though, was recorded by Tom Donaldson of the Boise, Idaho *Statesman*.

In his memoirs he recalled that although the *Statesman's* editor, James S. Reynolds, was a fervid Republican, printer Judson A. Boyakin—earlier noticed as advertising for the return of a stolen gun—was an equally warm Democrat. They remained friends, nevertheless, in spite of conversations such as one that Donaldson reported as typical.

"Boyakin set up the editorials and often when he read a line which hurled invective against the Democratic Party, he would say to Reynolds, 'Does this thing go in?'

"'Yep,' Reynolds would retort.

"'Well, it's a damned lie.'

"'Indeed?' Jim would remark. 'Well, she goes in all the same.'

"'All right, Jim, you're the boss,' Jud would say. 'Only you know it's a damned lie. Democrats ain't built that way.'"

Occasionally pioneer editors took the "a curse on both your houses" stand. In such instances, though, they were not forswearing allegiance to the national parties to which they belonged, but were pointing fingers at state or territorial officeholders of poor mark.

In his recollections Moses K. Armstrong of the Yankton *Union and Dakotaian* found it hard to distinguish between the politicos of Dakota Territory and the Indians who also at times pillaged it. Musing on the similarity, he summed it up in a Rubaiyat-type quatrain in which assonance was substituted for rhyme.

> Dakota's Politicians and Indians:
> The first are tricky; the second are evil;
> Neither one has a trail you can travel
> And to follow them both, I'm sure it would trouble
> The wit of the gods or the scent of the devil.

Dave Day was no better moved to admiration by Colorado's public figures. A feature of the Ouray *Solid Muldoon* for a while was a column called "Muldoon's Primer." In this the Solid Zulu for virgin would reply to a youngster whose curiosity had been stirred by official antics. One such dialogue could just as easily have applied to the burying of evidence in the U.S. Senate's modern Baker case.

"Is that a Salvation Army?" the *Muldoon* was asked.

"No, my child, that is a Band of Horse Thieves."

"What are they Doing that they Look so excited?"

"They are suspicioned by the People, and are Debating a motion to investigate the Charges."

"What is an Investigation?"

"Investigation, my Child, is a preparation of Self-amalgamated Whitewash introduced by the Colorado legislature in the Latter part of the 19th Century."

Yet it would be wrong to think of Western journalists as functioning only as partisan spokesmen, or critics at large of local political activities. Many of them were themselves officeholders and more were willing to be.

Issuing a newspaper was in fact a recognized political gambit, and Will Porter's Austin, Texas *Rolling Stone* was being no more than realistic when it described the dual activities of the man at the helm of the fictive *Plunkville Patriot*. Colonel Aristotle

Jordan was, its masthead assured readers, not only "Editor" but "Candidate for County Judge."

At times frontier journalists set their sights notches higher than Colonel Jordan did. Richard McCormick used the Prescott *Arizona Miner* as a lever to pry Charles Poston out of his berth as Territorial Delegate to Congress and as a springboard to boost himself in. With his Tucson *Star* to point up his usefulness to the Democratic Party, Louis C. Hughes won the appointment as Arizona's first non-carpetbagging governor.

Many times multiplied, those two cases from one territory give an idea of the link between journalism and political aspirations throughout the West. A true-to-life picture, though, would reveal that scores could have followed the lead of Aristotle Jordan, had they possessed his frankness. After a ferocious but futile campaign, conducted via the columns of the *Plunkville Patriot*, the colonel resigned himself to carrying on as "Editor and Ex-candidate for County Judge."

The men of print grabbed for patronage, too. The commonest prize—but available only to a man who belonged to the party nationally in power—was the town postmastership. Thus Cad Davis of the *Chronicle* won that plum in Leadville, Colorado; John Clum of the *Epitaph* did so in Tombstone, Arizona; and Bill Nye of the *Boomerang* got the P. O. gravy in Laramie, Wyoming.

Political organizing was another endeavor of pioneer editors. Robert Semple, of the Monterey and San Francisco *Californian*, presided over the convention at which a constitution was illegally but successfully drawn up for a state which had not yet been recognized as such by Congress. On the other hand, a bold bid that didn't work out was promulgated by a newspaper fronting for "Cimarron Territory."

This Western version of Ruritania was appropriately set up in "No Man's Land." Oklahoma's Panhandle was so known for many years, as it was neither included in the Indian Territory nor attached to any of the reservations for palefaces surrounding its other three sides.

But Beaver City was located there, its organ was the *Terri-*

torial Advocate, and the editor of that paper meant to see to it that Congress did the right thing by a region that never made the map under the name used in his paper's dateline. Because of the *Advocate,* besides, a non-existent province was able to father an imprint. An undated broadside, issued in "Cimarron Territory," reads in part as follows: "Repudiating all other platforms, we ask for territorial government, a U. S. District Court and U. S. Land Office in the borders of the Public Land Strip, as other territories have."

If the *Advocate's* editor was trying to add an entity to the United States, this was not a universal concern of frontier men of print. That is as much as to say that their part in trying to keep Mormon Deseret separate from America should not be overlooked.

Utah was only one room of the mansion they had in mind. All or parts of Arizona, Idaho, Nevada, Southern California, and Western Wyoming were also in the realm hoped for by Latter-Day Saints planners. It was an empire worth striving for, and the strivers saw that the only chance of gaining it was to inculcate a feeling of racial separateness in the people of Deseret, as marked as their religious one. A great deal of ingenuity, therefore, was lavished on ways to develop national passions, on the one hand, and hostility to everything American on the other.

From the point of view of this narrative the most interesting device was a special Mormon alphabet, or quasi-alphabet. An extant card, undoubtedly printed in Salt Lake City, though not stating where and when it was issued, shows that there were thirty-seven letters or characters representative of letter combinations.

For many years after the Utah Expedition supposedly did away with Deseret in 1858, this cultural war of separation was still being waged. Published at Salt Lake City in 1872, for instance, was a work printed in the Mormon alphabet but prefaced by a hoot in the standard one, so that non-Saints could grasp the insult.

This item was titled *A New Nursery Ballad, Embellished With Finely Engraved Portraits of some of the Most Emmanent Men of the Day.* Opposite the title page were three sets of playing-card jacks—or knaves, as the designers wished them to be considered. Interlarded were two pairs of donkeys. The caption below this array of villains and asses assured the examiner that they were "Portraits of some EMMANENT AMERICAN and ENGLISH CITIZENS. Below this again, fine print stated that the price "to English subscribers" would be one million pounds.

The English were obviously rung in because of forming America's basic racial stock and because of being identified with the language spoken in the United States. The hope of the publisher of *A New Nursery Ballad* then was to snap both the strong ties binding Deseret to the country from which Mormon die-hards were still trying to secede.

Outside of the alphabet which Sequoyah developed for the Cherokees, the Mormon one seems to have been the only set of letters devised in America whose purpose was to serve a separate nationality. Its weakness as a cultural fence-raiser, however, was that, unlike that of the Cherokees, it did not enshrine a separate language. It was merely another, and more difficult, way of writing the one shared with Americans and English, whether EMMANENT or not. But if a political failure, it was a brave try and not least of the interesting odds and ends which Western presses added to the national printing budget.

Yet sometimes, as has been pointed out, pioneer editors functioned politically while away from the sanctum or the composing room. Other ways in which they did so have been mentioned, but as yet no notice has been taken of their activity as party officers.

For this the reminiscences of Ned McGowan form incomparably the best source of information. Aside from the fact that a passion for politics was his ruling one, Ned was a party leader during a particularly tumultuous period in the political history of California.

For a number of years McGowan was one of the aides of state Democratic chieftain David Broderick, and in 1853 he was San Francisco County Chairman of the Democratic Party. As the Republicans had yet to emerge, the opposition consisted of first the Whigs and then the American Party, as the "Know-Nothings" were officially styled.

A vivid picture of that curious political phenomenon is presented in the following McGowan paragraph: "In 1854 the Know-nothing party carried the city of San Francisco. A paid organizer for this secret order was sent to California from the East who inaugurated 'wigwams' in every county in the state. The 'dark lantern' party merged in it all of the Whig party and many Southern democrats and a few from non-slave holding states. They held their meetings in secret, and to be admitted to their lodges you had to be initiated and put in possession of their grips, signs and passwords. It was a kind of Freemasonry; they could distinguish each other by their signs; and when any brother was in distress or wanted help politically, he could bring members within call by bellowing at the top of his voice, "ki-eye, ki-eye!" . . . I remember the first time I heard this ki-eyeing call was in the Fourth Ward on the day of the election, and they came running to the scene faster and more numerous than rats from a burning slaughter house."

In California at large, however, the Democrats found it harder to get along with each other than with their political foes. The cause of the split was the rivalry between Broderick, who wished to be in the U.S. Senate, and William Gwin, who was already there and wanted to stay. Respectively they headed a wing of the party dominantly recruited from former Easterners and one made up principally of immigrants from the South. On account of the different hair-dos affected by members of these factions, they were known as Short Hairs and Long Hairs.

The high moment of their vendetta was the assembly of party delegates held at Sacramento in 1854, which came to be known as the Short and Long Hair Convention. As both factions had slates of candidates they were determined to have nominated, both were alike eager to install the convention chairman. The trouble was, though, that the post was considered so dangerous that nobody wanted the honor.

"Each section met without fraternizing or consulting what the plan of proceedings would be on the morrow," as Ned wrote;

"and every member and their friends were armed to the teeth, anticipating bloody work when they assembled to organize the convention. The presidency of our wing of the party went a-begging. . . . Judge Wells and Ben Lippincott both declined. Mr. Broderick, in his dilemma, fell back as usual on me. I informed him I would accept but the chances were I would be killed, and in that event I wanted them to look after my family."

Things were at that pass when a delegate's gun went off by accident, "shooting into the floor and wounding him in a tender place." It panicked the convention, which was held in a church, through whose stained-glass windows Short Hairs and Long now crashed in their eagerness to cut stick.

Soon after things quieted, the uproar was renewed, because neither faction would accept a representative of the other as a replacement for Broderick, temporarily presiding in his capacity of California State Chairman of the Democratic Party. It thus came about that Ned and a Long Hair named John McDougall advanced to the rostrum simultaneously.

On the spot himself, McGowan later learned that the man he was fronting for was on even more shaky ground. "My chances for life, if the 'ball did open,' were ten to one better than his," McGowan affirmed, "for General Estell [of the Sacramento *Tribune*, etc.] and several others told me afterwards that Broderick was surrounded by a score of pistols, all ready, and that he [Estell] had one inside his coat, cocked and with his hand on it, pointing at Mr. Broderick's stomach."

Although the ball didn't open, Ned found himself faced with another hazard. When cocktails were brought to the pair on the rostrum, both chairmen "looked wistfully at the drinks but neither dared to touch them, for fear of being dosed." At length, though, McGowan was inspired to pour part of each cocktail into the other. "It's a long time between drinks," he said, while offering a glass to McDougall, "and if there has been any dosing of the liquor, we are both in for it."

13

BOUTS WITH BACCHUS

BEING IN THE Siamese class of inseparability, printer's ink and hearty drink went West together. They stayed East together also, to be sure, but by no means so pervasively. In much of the West, drinking was every other man's way of life until the nineteenth century began to sag, so the atmosphere encouraged the practice of liberating spirits by pulling corks. With all that competition it wasn't easy to shine as tosspots; but because of original ways of thinking, certain journalists made the grade.

One was John A. Joyce, of the Leadville, Colorado *Chronicle;* or for a while he was. Cad Davis finally had to can him, because when John got tight, he refused to have any truck with anything as pedestrian as prose.

Joyce's preferred medium of expression was verse, in a word, and his doggedness in this direction earned him one claim to eminence. Probably he is the only American poet whose work was ever processed by a probate court. But John's official last will and testament was written in a form which at least has the virtue of conciseness:

> To my daughters, Libbie and Florence
>   In equal proportions to share,
> I give all my cash and property
>   When my spirit is soaring in air,
>
> And appoint Mrs. James J. Lampton
>   To execute this, my last will,
> When I rest 'neath the bloomy flowers
>   In lot 444 on Oak Hill.

Another of his footholds on literature stems from lines, usually ascribed to Ella Wheeler Wilcox, reading

> Laugh and the world laughs with you
> Weep and you weep alone, etc.

As noted in *Hoyt's New Cyclopaedia of Practical Quotations,* Joyce always claimed that he was the real author of the piece, and that Ella had purloined it from him. And Cad Davis in his *Olden Times in Colorado* backed up his former employee. Cad said he knew the barrel house where John had dashed off the poem.

In Davis' opinion, though, Joyce was a better hand at prose, and it was to write articles in this medium that he hired a man who had the history of a periodic. For months he'd stay away from the bars and never touch an iamb or a trochee. Then, wham! he'd fall off the wagon and be his lyric self again.

For months John supplied the *Chronicle* with just the stuff its editor wanted. Then one day he hung on the hook a batch of copy that was different. Looking it over, Cad decided not to publish any of it, though he was interested enough to make a note of the titles. Included were *An Apostrophe to the Moon, A Tribute to My Landlady,* a sonnet addressed to *The Sylph of My Neighbor's Kitchen, Lines on a Stage Horse,* and verses celebrating *The Red-eyed Blue Haired Biscuit Shover of the Vendome.*

Sam Simpson, of various Oregon sheets, was as different from John Joyce as north from south. He only wanted to write verse when he was sober, and, as that seldom happened, he was chary of using a genuine talent. Some fellow of the press described him as "the most drunken poet, and the most poetical drunkard that ever made the Muses smile or weep." He wasn't in Oregon's literary doghouse, though, for he was commonly referred to as the state's laureate.

But riding Pegasus or staggering arm and arm with John Barleycorn, Sam was a newspaperman. Beginning with the Corvallis *Gazette,* he had played the wandering editor's circuit for a couple of dozen years by 1893. As of then he was working for the Astoria *Budget.*

The year is important, because it marked the launching of the battleship *Oregon.* This was to become one of the most famous men-of-war in America's naval history. In 1898 she surged from Puget Sound around Cape Horn to the West Indies, arriving just in time to play a key role in the sea fight off Santiago, Cuba. She was later in the Philippines, too, and around the world with the famous squadron dispatched by Theodore Roosevelt to impress other nations with this country's maritime might.

The ship was built at San Francisco, and because of the relative nearness, quite a delegation of Oregonians fared to see a vessel, named in honor of their state, take its first dip in the sea. A scheduled highlight of the attendant ceremonies was the reading of a poem just before a swung champagne bottle started the battlewagon on its way. Nor was there any doubt in the minds of those drawing up the program as to who would compose this bardic send-off. The piece would inevitably be by Oregon's laureate.

Sam, this while, was in his usual state of being solidly canned. In that condition he could handle his newspaper work with aplomb; but the word that he would be called on to give a warship a literary blessing shook him. Worse yet, he was conscious of fans waiting for him to go into his poetical act, and getting more tense about it with every day shed from the calendar. To steady his nerves, he got four sheets to the wind instead of his normal three.

Fuddled herself by this time, Simpson's Muse didn't deliver. Down in San Francisco, meanwhile, workmen kept inexorably hammering on the *Oregon;* and up in Astoria Mrs. Narcissa White Kinney wanted to practice spouting the verses she was due to recite in California.

Narcissa eventually went south with no manuscript in her purse, but she was not without hopes of being able to perform as slated. Tired of asking Sam how he was coming along with the poem, Astorians kidnaped him and dried him out at the home of Oscar Dunbar, the *Budget's* publisher. A kitty had, in the meantime, been fed by him and other businessmen of the town, so that the verses could be wired to San Francisco, assuming they could be bullied out of Sam in time.

While all Oregonians held their breath in dread of poetic de-

falcation, the laureate sobered enough to realize he wasn't going
to be allowed back in the pickle jar until he saved the team by
kicking a Parnassian goal. Taking pen in hand as well as a man
with the shakes can, he turned out *The Launching of the Oregon.*

> Oh, ship, like crested Pallas armed,
> Oh bride, the hoary god hath charmed,
> Leap to his strong and proud embrace——
> In Freedom's squadron take thy place!
>
> Northward in sheen of crystal mail,
> A scarf of cloud upon his breast,
> Our mighty monarch, Hood, will hail
> The mighty daughter of the West. . . .
>
> Launched on the golden gated bay,
> Be thine a royal bridal day,
> And with the wave's exultant kiss
> Come dreams of olden Salamis,
> When Greece was life's white morning star;
> Come, welcome to a scene like this
> The memories of Trafalgar,
> And Erie's crash of thunder telling
> How Perry's warrior heart was swelling——
>
> Come throbbing through the dusk of years
> Decatur's drum beat in Algiers,
> And from a hero's frosting lip
> The whisper, "Don't give up the ship!" . . .

Running to seventy-eight lines, *The Launching of the Oregon*
is perhaps the longest metrical message ever sent over telegraphic
wires. The men who paid for it got their money's worth, too.
While no study of this sub-department of literature has as yet
been made, the *Oregon* probably took to the waves with as good
a blessing as any battlewagon in the fleet could boast.

Sleeping cars got mixed up with Western ink and hard liquor,
as well as a warship. That happened in Colorado while Eugene
Field was there. If now he is thought of as the author of sentimental nursery rhymes—which he cheerfully referred to as
"mother rot," according to Cad Davis—he had other propensities.

Field was as demonic a japester as the frontier ever rejoiced
in. He was furthermore a grand hand with hooch; and in these

twin capacities he was the hero of a revel whose *mise en scène* was Denver.

The editor of that city's *Tribune,* he was favored by a public relations operative for the Pullman Company, on its way up and fighting the battle of railroad rates with all Western legislatures. As this chap had become an industrialist of stature by the time biographers began working over Gene's career, his right name was prudently withheld. Specific about that, Slason Thompson —a former writer for the San Francisco *Golden Era* and *Call*— substituted "Wickersham" in his life of Field; and Thompson's cue will be taken here.

Whatever he was like by the time he got in the blue chips, Wickersham was a lively boy when young. Fronting for Pullman's sleeping cars, he commanded the purse of a company which needed the good will of a capital's newspapermen. So he was authorized to be lavish in entertaining them. That's as much as to say that he could buy booze in unlimited amounts; and whenever he bought for others, he drank, too.

Along with his other talents, Gene was an able managing editor. Because he made the *Tribune* Denver's most influential journal, as of 1881–83, Wickersham favored its staff members above all others. When he met any of them, it was never too early for snifters, while it was always, too, the shank of the evening for him, no matter how late the hour.

Field liked Wickersham fine, but being a pal of Gene's didn't make it safer for anyone, when a joke occurred to the author of *Little Boy Blue* and kindred tear jerkers. In this case, Field decided to see how a glad hander would react if he suddenly found himself in the midst of cronies too busy to notice him.

So when Pullman's public relations hand next sent word that he would be in Denver, Gene persuaded his crew to aid him in his psychological experiment. When the jolly boy breezed into the *Tribune*'s city room, nobody more than threw him a greeting before bearing down on work again. When he suggested drinks, heads were impatiently shaken by men who had no time for such frivolities.

Bewildered by the freeze-out, Wickersham at length left to

brood upon it in saloon solitude. After just so many drinks he decided to strike back at men who had misused him. Waiting until the staff of a morning paper had gone out for supper, he tore up all the copy he could find in the city room, broke pens, spilled ink, smeared paste, and otherwise told of his displeasure.

If the returning newspapermen were ever in doubt as to who had fouled their nest, they were soon convinced of the truth by the Vandal himself. Having laughed about his vengeance in company with a few more drinks, Wickersham renewed hostilities. One of his weapons was a barrage of catcalls designed to interfere with editorial concentration. His heavier artillery took the form of a dismantled ash barrel, whose staves he hurled through windows—open then, if they had not been before.

They of the *Tribune* bore with this out of their faith in Gene. He promised them that if they would get the paper out, he would see to it that their wrongs would not go unavenged.

The editor's first move was to comb saloons known to him for dependable assistants. Or, as Slason Thompson said, Gene "gathered to his aid as fine a collection of Bohemian 'thoroughbreds' as ever made the revels of Mardi Gras look like a Sunday-school picnic."

One of these was a Kentuckian named Jones. Because he had an apartment which was always blessed with a heavy fall of blue-grass dew, it was the agreed headquarters for that night's campaign. Another pal undertook to ferret out a police sergeant upon whom Field knew he could rely. A third looked up "Possum Jim," the colored owner of a rickety express wagon and horse to match, and got him to report to the generalissimo.

When all in the drama to come had been assigned their parts, Gene armed himself with a bottle and sauntered to the hotel, whither Wickersham had been tailed by a fourth ally. The public relations man was by then abed; but he was glad to see a man who was sportsman enough to return the good of bourbon for the evil of the practical joke that had been wreaked on the *Tribune's* staff. Pelion piled on Ossa, the drinks made him ready for anything Gene suggested. So they set forth with gaiety in one heart and guile in the other.

They hadn't left the hotel far behind when who should come jogging along but "Possum Jim." Flagging the makeshift express wagon down, Field haggled with the owner for its hire, while Wickersham chortled at the thought of the splash they'd make, touring downtown Denver in such a chariot.

Gene, however, had an even shinier idea for amusing the city's night crawlers; and he dazzled Pullman's glad hander with a vision of how he'd be laughed with, should he get in harness and pull the cart past some of the city's brightest lights.

The future capitalist had no sooner been hitched between the shafts than the rehearsed police sergeant and several of his men appeared. As the editor of the *Tribune* had ceased to be present, references to him only made Wickersham's drunk and disorderly condition more apparent.

Waving the treasury of the Pullman Company, its operative offered handsome bribes, only to find that Denver's constables were above corruption. A ruined career was all that Wickersham could see before him then. Sagging, and with all the hooch turned to whey in his veins, he was carried off—but not to police headquarters. His destination was the apartment of Kentuckian Jones, where Gene and the other Bohemian thoroughbreds were waiting amid soldiers, dead and yet to fall.

Along with *Dutch Lullaby*—the Wynken, Blynken, and Nod thing—Field wrote *The Clink of the Ice*. Written by a connoisseur, it is a matchless tribute to that descent from the stratosphere known as a hangover.

Gene, in a word, showed his devotion to liquor with his pen as well as his readiness to imbibe. He was not alone in this among Western men of print. Charles Poston, for example, even went so far as to compose his autobiography in terms of where and with whom he had given bottles the sunwise turn, especially at the Christmas season. Although never published separately, it was read at a festivity covered by a December 1895 issue of the Phoenix, *Arizona Republican*.

One of the most diversely acquainted men in American annals, Poston had sopped it up with everybody from Garibaldi to Li Hung Chang, and he had braced himself with Christmas snorts in places as separate as Fort Yuma, California, and the desert about Egypt's pyramids. All in all, though, his most improbable choice as a spot for Yuletide tippling was the Great Wall of China.

This was done in the company of John Ross Browne, an extremely able pioneer man of print, not earlier noticed because of professional habits which excluded him from discussion in previous chapters. Partly because he was as skilled at illustrating as at writing, Browne had established himself as a contributor to national magazines before he went West. Being able to crack these, he wasn't engaged in frontier journalism in the same sense that the others were. If he perhaps now and again wrote for California sheets, all the items on which his reputation rests were printed on the Atlantic seaboard. This was true, to cite instances, of *A Peep at Washoe* and *Adventures in the Apache Country.*

That last work celebrated a trip Browne had taken at the invitation of Poston, when he was Arizona's Indian agent in 1864. Several years later they were both off for the Orient under circumstances noted by Charles in his bibulous autobiography.

"The Christmas [season] of 1868 found me in Peking, where I had been sent by the State Department to deliver the Burlingame Treaty to the Emperor of China.

"My compagnon du voyage was my old friend of California and travelling companion of Arizona, J. Ross Browne, who had been appointed Ambassador [actually Minister] from the United States to the Celestial Empire. . . .

"After we had exhausted the festivities incidental to our arrival in Peking, which is called in the slang of diplomacy, eating and drinking them in, the Ambassador and myself concluded to make a journey to the Great Wall of China, to spend the Christmas; as the holy day is unknown to the 'heathen Chinee.' We accordingly accomplished this journey in a couple of carts without springs as they do not know of that luxury in China.

"We had scarcely got established in the Caravanserai at the Nankou Gate when a nondescript relic of humanity presented himself and offered his services as a guide; presenting some letters of recommendation, one of which I will endeavor to repeat.

> This filthy cuss, whose name is Chang
> Solicits of this Christian gang
> A letter to commend him;
> He'll show you China's greatest wall,
> Her mountains, streams, Ming tombs and all
> And may the devil mend him.

"Chang had a suit of clothes which Noah must have worn in the Ark . . . but he was a good guide, and knew every hole and corner in the great Wall. . . .

"The next day was Christmas, and as the Ambassador woke, the Asiatic sun was illuminating the great wall in its sinuous course over mountain and stream. Mr. Browne, according to custom, enquired if I had anything to drink.

"I replied, according to custom—'Yes!, there was whiskey, sugar, bitters, and nutmeg, and I could make a cocktail fit for the emperor'; but being a Kentuckian said, 'My God, Mr. Browne, are we going to spend this Christmas in this heathen country without egg-nog?'

"He said, 'I don't know, Poston; we have had them together in Louisville, Washington, New York, San Francisco and Arizona, but where is the milk? Call up Chang and see what he can do.' I called the handy Chang and made known our wants. He replied, 'Oh yes, my wife had a child last week, and I can get you milk for half a dollar.'

"We took our egg-nog *straight* under the shadow of the Great Wall of China and bade farewell to Chang and his milky wife."

Eight years after that 1868 development, journalistic and Bacchic history were alike made in the city room of the San Francisco *Daily Mail*. When started by Davison Dalziel, its offices had been set up in an abandoned bordello with an expensive décor. Desks for reporters and cases for compositors stood in rooms which featured erotic pictures and statuary, with a background of passionate wallpaper.

As elsewhere noted, the *Mail* had been started to promote the senatorial candidacy of a moneybags named Mark McDonald. It missed its goal, but Mark hadn't yet found that out, and consequently withdrawn the paper's supporting funds, in the summer of 1876. Usually San Francisco keeps its summer months under control, but that year an August day—not now precisely identifiable, because the *Mail's* files are deficient—got out of hand. The situation didn't, however. As the paper had always been operated on an informal basis, refreshment was not wanting.

Not yet an editor, the celebrated muckraker Fremont Older was foreman of the *Mail's* composing room. Because of his position, Older was the link between the paper's printers and its writers. He was therefore able to know what was going on in the editorial department, though as an outsider he got only an occasional drink. On that account he stayed sober enough to become the narrator of a hero lay of which the previously noticed Arthur McEwen was the protagonist. In his published reminiscences, it is true, Fremont singled out no one. But orally he named Arthur to Ernest J. Hopkins, an authority on such nineteenth-century newspapermen of mark as Ambrose Bierce and Older himself. When asked about the frontier journalists he had known, Fremont would unhesitatingly style Arthur McEwen the greatest in his experience; and he had this tale to tell in support of his opinion:

As the *Daily Mail* was a morning paper, its reporters began assembling early in the afternoon. On the aforementioned torrid day one of them showed up with equipment designed to alleviate painful working conditions. His burdens were (a) three quarts of claret (b) a package of lemons (c) a pound or so of sugar (d) a tin dipper (e) a tin pail with a capacity of several gallons and (f) the big chunk of ice the bucket already held.

A careful man, the unidentified journalist poured "a" over "f" into "e" and used "d" to stir in just the right amounts of "c" and the juice of "b." When sure that he had wrought well, he swigged from the dipper and announced, "This is the stuff for a hot day."

While not quarreling with his major premise, certain of his colleagues inserted amendments. Via flasks drawn from desks, some whiskey and rum were added. But the chief increment of hard liquor was supplied by a reporter who undertook to procure three bottles of Martell brandy.

Everybody was satisfied with the beverage then until publisher

Davison Dalziel showed up. After he had lifted the dipper, he proved a constructive critic.

"Boys," he said, "I think a little champagne would improve that."

Davison's notion of a little champagne turned out to be three liters. With that leaven, what had started out as a modest claret punch became a brew of more character than conscience.

Undaunted, and likewise unmindful of time, the San Francisco men of print kept passing the dipper to the tune of much chat and no work. Yet, as the afternoon wore on, the long-handled flagon was raised by ever fewer hands. A law of nature brought this about, for the combination of tanglefoot and unseasonable heat induced what old Samuel Daniel called "Care-charmer Sleep."

By six o'clock the only man in the editorial department who hadn't been charmed out of care was Arthur McEwen. The hour was significant because of the *Daily Mail's* operation schedule. During the afternoon only Fremont Older and a few needed to set up ads had been on deck in the composing room, but at six the whole staff of printers stood by to receive the day's output of editorial matter.

Entering the city room to see if anything could be done about securing copy, Older found that McEwen was himself aware of the crisis. He didn't rise to meet the situation, as that was beyond his means. But he had wriggled on his belly to the desk which held the office shears; and, as Fremont watched, Arthur got hold of them by tugging a newspaper which dangled low enough to be within reach.

Possessed of this method of filling news columns, McEwen went to work. If the *Mail* was unlike other journals in some respects, it was like them in having a city room carpeted with out-of-town sheets—examined and tossed aside during the days preceding the weekly Saturday cleanup. Coursing here and there on his navel, Arthur began clipping out stories for copy boys to rush to the composing room.

The paper which Older remembered as contributing most was one of the latest issues of the Philadelphia *Public Ledger* to reach the West Coast. Other drawn-upon journals represented Chicago, New York, and London.

Subscribers to the *Mail*, the next morning, were puzzled to find detailed coverage of matters bearing on the above-named cities, and not a line about San Francisco. But Fremont Older was right about the stature of Arthur McEwen. Where thousands would have failed, he had soared above self and seen to it that his paper didn't suffer the disgrace of missing an edition.

14

VIRGINIA WAS A CITY

WHILE THE EMPHASIS here has so far been on shoestring operation, references have been made to more complex and solidly financed enterprises. As this report would be incomplete without an examination of what one of these was like, that will now fall due.

Although the treasures dug out of many parts of the West seldom rubbed off on pioneer journalists, there was one place where solid wealth was the prime conditioner of their activities. This was the Nevada vicinity known as the Comstock.

The designation stemmed from the name of the greatest silver bonanza of the fabulous Washoe mining district. But the Comstock was more complex than that suggests. An ample supply of gold was also for a while on hand, and the community consisted of not one boom camp but two.

Primary was Virginia City. Yet nearby Gold Hill was large enough to have ranked as a metropolis in almost any other section of the West. Only a mile separated the centers of the towns, which came to merge as indistinguishably as modern Oakland and Berkeley, California.

Between 1860 and 1880 the Comstock was second only to San Francisco both as to population and financial importance. Unlike the usual hectic boom communities, it held out solid promises of opportunity, which spoke to men of ability in a wide range of fields. It was thus not by accident that a feature of the Comstock was an array of journalists whose match was not to be found outside of the nation's largest cities.

Not so known upon his arrival, Mark Twain was one. Others, whose work appeared between book covers during their lifetimes, were Dan De Quille, Samuel Davis, Artemus Ward, Fred Hart, Charles C. Goodwin, Rollin M. Daggett, and Joseph T. Goodman. Brilliant, if never seeking book publication, were Arthur McEwen, Semblens Forbes, Tom Fitch, and Denis McCarthy. Then there were Alf Doten and Wells Drury, the first the keeper of an inimitable journal and the second the bequeather of fascinating reminiscences.

Yet before there can be newspapermen, there must be sheets for them to write for. Many were published at the Comstock: at Gold Hill in a few cases but mostly in Virginia City. Of these the nonpareil—unchallenged for primacy by even the papers of San Francisco—was the *Territorial Enterprise*.

The beginning of this institution has already been glanced at. For during the discussion of the legal difficulties which beset pioneer publishers, it was remarked that William Jernegan jerked his press east of the Sierra Nevadas to keep it from being impounded by a sheriff stationed on the western slope of that range.

Jernegan holed up in Genoa. Previously the best that the settlement had been able to boast in the way of a news organ was a manuscript journal called the *Scorpion*. But when William and a partner named Alfred James set up the saved press, they began printing the *Territorial Enterprise*. It was as good a handle as any, for nobody was quite sure in whose territory Genoa was. Utah, as well as California, claimed a place that had at first been known as Mormon Station. Nevada didn't put in a bid, as in 1858 it didn't exist.

The conditions under which the *Enterprise* was first published are known because of an editorial printed after the paper had fled to Carson City in December of 1859. Jernegan was so bucked up by the better hole found at the Carson stand that he told what the old one had been like, in order to explain his pleasure to his new set of subscribers.

"One year ago today the first number of the *Territorial Enterprise* was issued at Genoa. Our publishing room was in Singleton's Hall, Nevada Hotel, a room indiscriminately used by preachers, debating clubs, secret societies and once, at least, for a prison. Upon the latter occasion we had a man accused of a crime chained to our printing press for two days and a half. . . . Many a time in the past year we have suffered for lack of fuel and been pinched for the actual necessities of life. But so far we have struggled on successfully, and today we find ourselves in more comfortable circumstances in many respects. To be sure, we still have to descend from the editorial tripod to supervise the cooking of breakfast, and seasoning of bean soup or the concoction of a pot of coffee. . . . But as we have said, we feel that we have made a step in advance."

Yet as business in Carson City was poky, Jernegan and James sold their paper to Jonathan Williams and I. B. Wollard within a few months. Not much later the Virginia City boom moved these two to take the *Territorial Enterprise* to the Comstock in November of 1860. For several months thereafter it remained a weekly, but in March of 1861 Joseph Goodman hit town.

A veteran of the San Francisco *Golden Era's* composing room, Joe teamed with fellow printer Denis McCarthy to put the *Enterprise* out six days a week. Williams was originally with them, but complained that the pace of a daily was too fast for him and bowed out.

The hectic beginning of this profitable phase of the paper's existence was described by Dan De Quille in *The Big Bonanza*. "The office in which the *Enterprise* was first published in Virginia City was a small, one-story frame building with a shed or lean-to on one side, and was a queerly arranged establishment. The proprietors had the shed part fitted up as a kitchen-and-dining and lodging place. Bunks were arranged along the sides of the room, one above another, as on ship-board, and here editors, printers, proprietors, and all hands 'bunked' after the style of the miners in their cabins. A Chinaman, 'Old Joe,' did the cooking, and three times each day the whole crowd of 'newspaper men' were called out to the long table in the shed to get their 'square meal.' The 'devil' went for numerous lunches between meals and often came flying into the composition room with a large piece of pie in his mouth, and the old Chinaman at his heels."

It need hardly be added that the two young partners, who put their sheet out each day under these circumstances, were without capital worth mentioning. But because they were first in the field, where men in other lines were piling up profits for a good few years, they made modest fortunes themselves.

Still they wouldn't have been able to do that, and to keep the inside track in spite of numerous challenges, had they not offered a first-class product. For Comstockers could afford to pay for quality, and the sharp men on the make who flavored the community wanted their money's worth or else.

Through being top hands themselves and hiring others, Goodman and McCarthy built up a paper which they were soon able to move into comfortable quarters, and outfit with the best equipment on the market. That meant, among other things, the installation of main and job presses powered by steam.

As for the staff, it was a relatively diversified one. Joe and Denis wrote editorials, as well as attending to business management. Assistants sifted the newspapers with which the *Enterprise* exchanged and drew on reports supplied by telegraphic service. Then in addition to cubs who handled routine matters, there were a couple of "locals" or city room stars. Other dailies had such operatives, too, but on the *Territorial Enterprise* they were charged with making news of the vicinity entertaining.

There were no copy readers. "Blue penciling was seldom known," as Wells Drury declared, when looking back at his own Comstock days. "Every reporter wrote what he pleased and . . . the printer set it as written."

So young men of talent were able to try out their paces, and expand as they never could have, if forced to conform to somebody else's ideas. Yet that but half accounts for the fine work done at the Comstock. The named newspapermen couldn't have performed as brilliantly as they did there, if the atmosphere of the town as a whole hadn't been peculiarly stimulating.

The nature of that incentive was finely summed by Arthur McEwen, who was with the Gold Hill *News* before operating for the San Francisco *Mail*. Of the Comstock, he declared that "it was a republic in which the ablest were first."

But after stressing that the community was a competitive field where nobody had an advantage he didn't owe to ability and effort, Arthur took up the nature of its society.

"There was a deal of drinking in Virginia when the *Enterprise* and the town were new, but it wasn't all drinking. Some of the brightest men of the country were working as well as having fun there. Lawyers, I understand, admit that the bar was about the brainiest ever gathered together in one town of the size, or ten times the size. Adventurers with keen wits and empty pockets were drawn there as naturally as gamblers seek a faro game. Rolling stones of every kind obeyed the moral law of gravitation by rolling up Mount Davidson.

"It was a city of men. If any of them were poor, that troubled them not at all, for they expected to be rich next week, and had good reason for the expectation. Those who were rich had so recently been poor that they had not forgotten it, and the circumstance was not so unusual as to be deemed a title to others' deference. Everybody was rated for what he was, not what he had. There were no classes, only individuals. Pretentiousness was out of order. Not to be a man of sense, frank, free handed and without prejudice, was to find oneself a second or third grader. The men most distinguished for ability were the best fellows, the heartiest roisterers, the most democratic."

Into this best of crucibles was tossed the still untested ore of the man who was to enrich American literature with the largest body of first-rate reading matter ever contributed to it by one hand. He was so unformed that he didn't even know he was Mark Twain until months after he'd joined the staff of the *Territorial Enterprise* in 1862.

His first connection with the paper was not that intimate. A printer and pilot in his pre-Western days, Sam Clemens had turned prospector after reaching Nevada Territory. Finding nothing but experience in Aurora, he braced his spirits by writing up such comic matters as met his eye and mailing his efforts to the paper he thought most likely to use them. As it was an era when pseudonyms were the rage, he used one, too. His choice was Josh.

Doubtless one thing which encouraged him to apply to the *Territorial Enterprise* was that it regularly published the work of a writer belonging to the literary school which Josh aspired to join. This was William Wright, who had become so identified

with his pen name of Dan De Quille that nobody thought of
calling him anything else.

Six years older than Josh, Dan hadn't applied for a job on the
Enterprise. Joe Goodman had "brought him out of the brush,"
as he put it, after De Quille had scored a big regional hit by
contributing to San Francisco's *Golden Era* installments of a narrative dealing with a prospecting trip, since published in book
form under the title of *Washoe Rambles.*

That was a solid journalistic accomplishment. But amusing aspects of it were what prompted Goodman to reach for a drifting
free lance. Installed on the *Enterprise* as a "local," De Quille
had the job of brightening up the paper in any way that occurred
to him.

The important role of the hoax in frontier journalism has previously received treatment here. One of the genre's eminent practitioners, Dan specialized in the scientific hoax. To his credit were
several served up with such cunning that they bamboozled the
technically trained. His story of a windmill designed to move
loads of sand and gravel had, for example, drawn interested queries from engineers. And once De Quille was rewarded by having
one of his spoofs turn up in a London professional journal.

Now the funny thing about a man who can be successful in
this field is that he must himself be endowed with a genuine, if
undeveloped, bent for invention. In one of Dan's items, which
will be the one used for illustration of his talents here, he came
within an ace of creating the air-cooling device for making the
desert livable that eventually materialized in the 1930s.

"SAD FATE OF AN INVENTOR. A gentleman who had just
arrived from the borax fields of the desert regions surrounding
the town of Columbus in the eastern part of this State, gave us
the following account of the sad fate of Mr. Jonathan Newhouse,
a man of considerable inventive genius. Mr. Newhouse had constructed what he called "solar armor," an apparatus intended to
protect the wearer from the fierce heat of the sun in crossing
deserts. . . . The armor consisted of a long, close-fitting jacket
made of common sponge and a cap or hood of the same material,
both jacket and hood being about an inch in thickness. Before

starting across the desert this armor was to be saturated with water. Under the right arm was suspended an India-rubber sack filled with water and having a small gutta percha tube leading to the top of the hood. In order to keep the armor moist, all that was necessary to be done by the traveler as he progressed over the burning sands, was to press the sack occasionally, when a small quantity of water would be forced up and thoroughly saturate the hood and jacket below it. Thus by evaporation of the moisture in the armor, it was calculated, might be produced any degree of cold. Mr. Newhouse went down to Death Valley, determined to try the experiment of crossing that terrible place in his armor. He started out into the valley one morning from the camp nearest its borders, telling the men at the camp that he would return in two days. The next day an Indian who could speak but a few words of English came to the camp in a great state of excitement. He made the men understand that he wanted them to follow him. At the distance of about twenty miles out into the desert the Indian pointed to a human figure seated against a rock. Approaching, they found it to be Newhouse still in his armor. He was dead and frozen stiff."

This that stole so near to possibility was not offered as a hoax; it was for laughs only. That was the third string of an *Enterprise* local's fiddle. In addition to coming up with fictions which wouldn't be recognized as such, he could treat the factual comically and the comic soberly. Good at all three, Dan was the dean of Virginia City's fourth estate and admired throughout the Comstock.

But in the summer of 1862 De Quille wanted to visit kinsmen beyond the Mississippi. Having meanwhile been favorably impressed by contributions sent in from Aurora, Joe Goodman brought Josh out of the brush as a replacement.

Going on twenty-seven, a man who'd received no previous recognition arrived to make his way in what Arthur McEwen called "a republic in which the ablest were first." The *Territorial Enterprise* proffered special perquisites besides. A prestigious sheet, it exchanged with the best journals in the nation, and by-

line writers for it got a chance to be favorably known—as De
Quille already was—to editors elsewhere.

Although making good, Josh was not thought of as living up
to Dan's marks. He never was so recognized throughout his stay
in Virginia City in fact.

"Isn't it so singular that Mark Twain should live and Dan De
Quille fade out?" as Goodman was to write, after the two in
question had found their respective literary niches. "If anyone
had asked me in 1863 which was to be an immortal name, I
should have unhesitatingly said Dan De Quille."

Joe specified 1863, because it was in February of that year that
Sam Clemens turned his back on Josh for keeps, becoming Mark
Twain from there on out. If he had been found competent enough
to have been kept on, after Dan's return, he had caused no stir
in Virginia City. Yet he was profiting from his association with a
crack set of colleagues, and De Quille in particular. The two became warm friends and they shared one professional peculiarity.
Both trained as printers, they preferred to do their writing
amidst the bustle of setting type, and otherwise readying the
paper for the press, rather than to use their city-room desks.

After Mark Twain had been that for some while, he finally
drew Comstock notice—but not of the kind he had counted on
exciting. For what was dubbed a hoax—and which operated as
one in as much as it was nonsense which readers took seriously—
was intended by him as no such thing.

Before letting him tell what he did have in mind, it should be
pointed out that the hero or villain of his otherwise complete
fiction was an actual person. He was, in fact, that same Pete
Hopkins, master of the Magnolia Saloon in Carson City, to whom
Semblens Forbes addressed the quoted warm tribute in the *Humboldt Register*.

The piece which made Twain's first real mark was headed,
*Massacre in the Giant Forest Surrounding Dutch Nick's, on the
Carson River*. The reaction was so astonishing to the author that
he devoted an article about it in a collection of sketches subsequently published in book form.

"I stole upon the public unawares with my scathing satire on the dividend-cooking system. In about half a column of imaginary human carnage I told how a citizen had murdered his wife and nine children and then committed suicide. And I said slyly at the bottom, that the sudden madness of which this melancholy massacre was the result, had been brought about by his having allowed himself to be persuaded by the California papers to sell his sound and lucrative Nevada silver stocks, and buy into Spring Valley, just in time to get cooked along with the company's fancy dividend, and sink every cent he had in the world. . . . But I made the horrible details so carefully and conscientiously interesting that the public devoured *them* greedily, and wholly overlooked the following distinctly stated facts, to wit:——

"The murderer was perfectly well known to every creature in the land as a bachelor and consequently could not murder his wife and nine children; he murdered them 'in his splendid dressed-stone mansion just in the edge of the great pine forest between Empire City and Dutch Nick's' when even the very pickled oysters that came on our tables knew that there was not a dressed-stone mansion in all Nevada Territory; also that so far from there being a great pine forest between Empire City and Dutch Nick's, there wasn't a solitary tree within fifteen miles of either place; and finally it was patent and notorious that Empire City and Dutch Nick's were one and the same place . . . and consequently there could be no forest between them; and on top of all those absurdities I stated that this diabolic murderer, after inflicting a wound upon himself that the reader ought to have seen would kill an elephant in the twinkling of an eye, jumped on his horse and rode *four miles,* waving his wife's reeking scalp in the air, and thus performing entered Carson City with tremendous éclat, and dropped dead in front of the chief saloon, the envy and admiration of all beholders."

In company with De Quille, Mark was able to observe one reader in the process of reacting to his burlesque of a horror story. "Dan and I (Dan was my reportorial associate) took our seats on either side of our customary table in the Eagle Restaurant, and as I unfolded the shred they used to call a napkin in that establishment, I saw at the next table two stalwart innocents with that sort of dandruff sprinkled about their clothing which was the sign and evidence that they were in from the Truckee with a load of hay. The one facing me had the morning paper folded to a narrow strip, and I knew, without any telling, that the strip represented the column that contained my pleasant financial satire. From the way he was mumbling, I saw that the heedless son of a hay mow was skipping . . . in order to get to the bloody details as soon as possible; and so he was missing the guide boards I had set up to warn him that the whole thing was a fraud.

"Presently . . . just as his jaws swung asunder to take in a potato approaching it on a fork . . . the face lit up, and the whole man was on fire with excitement. Then he broke into a disjointed checking off of the particulars—his potato cooling in mid-air meantime. . . . At last he looked his . . . comrade . . . in the face, and said with an expression of concentrated awe——

"'Jim he b'iled his baby, and he took the old 'oman's skelp. Cuss'd if I want any breakfast. . . .'

"He *never got down*," Mark continued, "to where the satire part of it began. Nobody ever did. They found the thrilling particulars sufficient. . . . The idea that anybody could ever take my massacre for a genuine occurrence never once suggested itself to me. But I found out then, and never have forgotten since, that we never *read* the dull explanatory surroundings of marvelously exciting things. . . . We skip all that, and hasten to revel in the blood-curdling particulars and be happy."

Another thing that Mark learned was that people who had fooled themselves wouldn't admit that they had taken palpable nonsense seriously. They therefore insisted that Twain had perpetrated a singularly convincing hoax, and his name first began to be one to conjure with on that account.

That was true not only in the Comstock but elsewhere. Through the exchange system the atrocities committed by Pete Hopkins had been picked out for reprinting by editors far and near. After the blood bath at Dutch Nick's was revealed as fake news, a hoax that was none came to be recognized as one of the most famous in the annals of the newspaper profession.

Admitted to renown by that back door, America's greatest

writer began to reach for the mantle he was to wear. It was while with the *Territorial Enterprise* that Mark renewed long abandoned efforts to get a foothold in Eastern journalism.

He did it in such a desultory manner, though, that he could not be said to be making any serious effort to set himself up as a free-lance writer. Nor did he attempt anything as ambitious as had Dan De Quille, in the instance of *Washoe Rambles.*

In assessing the reputation ultimately attained by the two, Joe Goodman wrote that "they had about equal talent and sense of humor, but the difference was the way in which they used their gifts. One shrank from the world; the other braved it, and it recognized his audacity."

That suggests that Mark had charged forth from Virginia City, determined to gain the recognition he knew to be his due. Yet strutting boldly forth from a place and leaving it because it isn't safe to stay are not the same thing. It was this last that Twain did; and if he later mumbled he was tired of the Comstock anyhow, why that might or might not have been a move to blur the fact that his 1864 exit was a furtive one.

What made it necessary was a duel he contracted for, the other party being a writer for the Virginia City *Daily Union* named James Laird. Steve Gillis, of the *Enterprise's* composing room, and Rollin Daggett, of the paper's editorial staff, were Twain's seconds, after an acid editorial exchange had brought on an accepted challenge.

Not pistoleers, neither of the combatants was happy about the situation into which they had worked themselves; but Laird was nervous to the point of being jittery. Sensing as much, Gillis decided to see if the *Union's* man could be stampeded.

The sharpshooter that Mark was not, Steve got his chance, when a sage hen was flushed as the duelists approached their chosen battle ground. Seeing that nobody was watching him, Gillis snatched his principal's revolver, shot the bird's head off, slipped the smoking gun back to Twain, and complimented him for showing such a keen eye when testing his weapon.

As that eye was scheduled to be lethally turned his way, Laird wished no part of it. He left the field and the Comstock.

But—and probably because Twain and his friends couldn't keep the joke to themselves—word that a duel had been planned reached the ears of a Nevada official whom Mark had put on the printed pan. On the strength of a law which voided the code duello, the politico swore out a warrant for the arrest of his newspaper critic.

As only a bird's blood had been shed, the chances are that a Western jury would have laughed the case out of court; but Mark didn't want to take a chance. He was able to go on the lam without the onus of being officially a fugitive from justice, because of the friendship of Governor James W. Nye. Pleased with the way that Twain had covered Carson City while Nevada's legislature was in session, the governor sent word that a warrant had been sworn out, but that he could delay service for twenty-four hours.

Before that period had lapsed, Mark was over the border and on the way to San Francisco. As of May 1864 he was also on his way to begin the career as a free lance that he might not have had were it not for his fizzled duel with a fellow man of print.

Having many friends and owning a good job on what was recognized as the finest paper in the West, he might well have stayed in Virginia City and played out his string as the local man of letters that Dan De Quille settled for remaining. Perhaps destiny would have pried Twain loose from the joys of the Comstock in some other fashion, but the record's the record. As things stand, American literature owes a debt of incalculable magnitude to James Laird, Steve Gillis, and the sage hen slain on the field of honor.

Yet if Twain left Virginia City physically, he never ceased to be a citizen of it, or a writer for its leading paper, in the opinion of Arthur McEwen. After citing the Comstock, Arthur declared, "It was there that Mark got his point of view—that shrewd, graceless, good humored, cynical way of looking at things as they in fact are—unbullied by authority and indifferent to traditions—which has made the world laugh."

15

A MESS OF MISCELLANIES

THE DISTINCTION BETWEEN newspaper and magazine journalism—now so clearly drawn—was not honored by a host of pioneer men of print. As they wrote in any way that happened to occur to them at any given moment, and scrambled their papers together with the aid of anything that was within reach, their sheets were often closer in tone to periodicals belonging to the entertainment or hobby fields than to those in the strictly reportorial one. Then, through the exchange system or piracy, some rags were regularly multiple as to authorship, tone, and subject matter.

With such a little way to go, in order to leave the newspaper field and become avowedly something different, it is not surprising that the shift was often undertaken. That does not necessarily imply the production of items that would now be recognized as magazines. The difference was apt to lie in the purpose rather than the format. It has been pointed out that the Greenwater, California *Chuck-Walla* looked like a magazine but by nature was a community's news organ. Contrastively there were journals which were magazines in point of aspiration but which had the outward seeming of newspapers.

As early as its days as a republic, Texas was occasionally offered publications which assured subscribers, if any, that they were "literary" journals. And throughout the nineteenth century things that purported to be "literary" miscellanies kept popping up and collapsing all over the West.

There were genuine magazines, too. In communities so small that issuing a weekly newspaper in them would have strained most men's optimism, pioneer editors launched multi-paged cultural ventures which they didn't know how to continue, even if they could have found some means of supporting them. All that was needed to trigger a salute to enlightenment was the conviction that any given empty plot of Western space should have such a thing in order to realize its possibilities. The magazine, in other words, was visualized as a tap which would release a flow of informed immigrants—some of them eager contributors.

A variant of this Quixotism was to joust for the Muses in hardboiled commercial burgs where something of a more practical nature might possibly have found subscribers. Such knights of the pen were Elias T. L. Harrison and Edward Wheelock Tullidge. Of the many lances they broke for culture in Salt Lake City, the earliest was a weekly called *The Peep o'Day*, an 1864 number billed as a "magazine of science, literature and art."

At times cultural groups rather than yearning men of print fostered literary miscellanies in the midst of a frontier market town's hurly-burly. In the 1880s, to cite but one, certain eager spirits brought the Latin Quarter of Paris, France, close to the cattle pens of Fort Worth, Texas, by publishing *Our Bohemia* there.

Such a package was undoubtedly floated by angels. But those issued by such men of print as Harrison and Tullidge were meant as commercial undertakings. Prerequisite for any hopes of success, meanwhile, were qualities owned by but one Western city. As only a minor percentage of residents in any town are culturally inclined, a burg has to be really sizable in order to hold enough of them to support a literary miscellany. Far rarer than the needed sort of subscriber, besides, is the resident of a provincial city who is capable of regularly contributing readable matter to a literary periodical.

The only town in the West large enough to contain both these indispensable factors in even marginal quantities was San Francisco. The history of Western cultural miscellanies—whether resembling newspapers as to format or cast in the forms of magazines—is therefore almost wholly a matter of the periodicals issued in California's nineteenth-century metropolis.

Its earliest genuine magazine was called the *Pioneer*. Begun in 1854 and edited by Ferdinand Ewer, it chiefly served to support the above offered arguments that such a journal can't flourish away from population in depth. As Ewer's standards were too high and San Francisco's ability to meet them were too low, the result was satisfactory to neither. After two years, during which it was chiefly notable for publishing some good pieces by "Old Block" Delano, it died and had few mourners.

Yet a literary miscellany with a significant history had beat the *Pioneer* into print. San Francisco had only about 35,000 residents when the *Golden Era* was launched in 1852, nor were its literati more numerous than when Ewer's magazine was started. But when J. Macdonough Foard and Rollin M. Daggett commenced issuing a periodical which had the form of a newspaper, they had their feet planted in realism.

The old man of the firm, Foard was twenty-two. In terms of literary experience, he and Daggett were of the age of the editors of today's college journals. Their notions of what was practical, however, had been shaped by living in Eldorado's mining camps as well as its capital city.

What they grasped was the fact that they could neither find enough subscribers for, or contributions to, a publication aimed at the mature professional men who formed San Francisco's cultural elite. So they scrapped the concept of sophistication in favor of seeking a broad, non-metropolitan audience.

Their plan also called for saving the money they couldn't afford to invest in writing talent, had much been available. What they saw as feasible, in sum, was a literary organ aimed at, and soliciting manuscripts from, the residents of mining camps. As the rush of forty-nine had been primarily a dash of youngsters seeking a short-cut to prosperity, the prospectors of the gold towns were coevals of Daggett and Foard. Having been Argonauts themselves, the editors knew what stuff would go down; and they also knew that among the toilers in the mines were amateur scribblers, for whom seeing their work in print would be all the pay required.

To foster this scheme, Daggett left Foard to hold down the office. Donning the red shirt which he had once worn when swinging a pick or sluicing a cradle himself, Rollin traipsed all over the Mother Lode region, picking up subscribers and contributors as he went.

The triumph of the *Golden Era* wasn't immediate, of course. Foard's report of the struggle to keep the journal from being killed by the sheriff has been quoted in an earlier chapter. But within two or three years, the *Era* was solidly established, and could begin paying favored contributors.

Thus tinged with professionalism, it was on the way to becoming the different publication that ultimately developed. But before it began appealing to another order of readers, The *Golden Era* was an eye looking into the collective mind of the young, bachelor fortune seekers who read and wrote for it. Written by amateurs, the serious items are too painful for repetition. Some of the humor was palatable when taken in small quantities, though. In 1855, for a sample, the *Era* ran stanzas celebrating the tragedy of a couple named Reuben and Phoebe. In view of its subject and tone, the piece might just as well have appeared in a twentieth-century college humor magazine. The form is interesting, though, as it showed familiarity with Albert Pike's great ballad—published in 1853—about "A fine Arkansas gentleman, close to the Choctaw line!" Pike seems to have been the first to use the strung out last line, which long withholds the shoe of rhyme before dropping it.

But to get back to Reuben and the former Phoebe Brown, they had eloped, when her parents had refused to countenance the wedding. In an effort to gain a post-marital blessing, they had repaired to the home of the bride, only to find adamant in her father's heart. So much for the body of the tragedy; now for the catastrophe.

> Old Brown then took a deadly aim
>   Toward young Reuben's head,
> But oh, it was a bleeding shame,
> He made a mistake and shot his only daughter and
>   had the unspeakable anguish of seeing
> her drop down dead.

The *Golden Era* didn't stay of this juvenile spirit, for the prospectors who had come to California as teenagers or not much more than that didn't hold on to those ages any longer than the gold camps remained the swagger towns they had been. These either folded up or settled down as communities where such gold as was mined was in the hands of the corporations which alone could afford to exploit it. And the men who remained to flourish in such towns were gaited for a different type of reading matter than they had once enjoyed.

So the *Golden Era* had the choice of changing its policy or going out of business. Yet it was toward the end of its first phase that it offered its best piece written strictly in the spirit of footloose bachelor prospectors. Published serially, the work was the afore-mentioned *Washoe Rambles* of Dan De Quille.

In 1861 Dan and a pair of partners had made a tour of a mineral region which had not yet settled on Virginia City as its capital. The account of it is not such a report as would have been written for another audience. Thinking of his readers in terms of fellow prospectors, De Quille gave them back their own style of living complete with boozing, practical jokes, rough trail experiences, and campfire yarns without a moral.

Back in their starting point of Silver City, Nevada, Dan and one of his partners are pleased to find that their return and the Fourth of July are both being celebrated there. The climax of the narrative, it will do as well as any to give its flavor.

"At night, Jones and I go up town to hear the 'Kannins Rore,' and see the fire works let off. We stood for a long time in silence watching divers and sundry splendid rockets dart up in fiery haste toward the blue dome, etc., when Jones broke the silence.

" 'I wish,' he said, 'I were a rocket.'

" 'Good Heavens! Jones, what on earth should cause you to make such a wish? You're excited, Jones. Jones, I beg of you, be calm, be cool, be as you see me! I fear your excitable temper will yet ruin your brain; "the day we celebrate" has been too much for you. But why do you wish yourself a rocket?'

" 'Because,' said Jones, 'I could then make a raise.'

" 'Oh, Jones,' I cried. . . . 'Jones, you have killed me! I shall never smile again.'

"Jones took the hint, and hastening to the nearest saloon, we both smiled—several times.

"I don't know but what we—that is, I mean Jones—became too good natured.

"Said Jones—in answer to some very cogent reason I was giving why the comet, then flaming in the northwestern sky, had a tail growing out of its head and no tail to its tail—'Bald'n keeps a bes' branny of any fel-elyer in town, I believe—enhow's er bigges'. . . .'

" 'No, taint,' said I. 'I know ware'd Dush feller got sum—sum's heap bigger! . . . I see er big strong man t'orrer day strrrugle worse way to take down two bi's worf and wen er got 't down, save is soul he *couldn't keep it down.*' "

That clincher was the last paragraph of *Washoe Rambles* except one of farewell addressed to the paper's following. "Now as I am safely housed in my casa, and for fear of making bad worse, I will close these long, rambling, zigzag sketches, with my best wishes to my brethren and sisters of the Era—that is if they will acknowledge me as being one of the Eraites. . . ."

In that signing-off passage, Dan took note of a constituency not counted on by Foard and Daggett when founding the *Era*. For he referred to female readers.

The miscellany had feminine writers as well as ditto subscribers, moreover. This was a change which Foard went on record as bemoaning.

"Oh, yes!" he said, when interviewed after the journal had finally been deadlettered in 1893. "The *Golden Era* was a great paper, and if the same policy had been continued, it would be a great paper today. But I will tell you where we made the mistake, and that was when we let the women write for it. Yes, they killed it—they literally killed it, with their namby-pamby school girl trash."

That was an old man looking back at the golden era of Argonaut striving as well as the periodical named for it. Actually the miscellany's important phase came later, and after its original editors had dropped it. This they did because it no longer reflected only the spirit of shaggy but hopeful young bachelorhood that it had spoken for when founded.

Disgusted at not being able to keep time from marching on, its owners sold the *Golden Era* in 1860. The future career of Foard is not pertinent to this chapter; but Rollin Daggett left California, to relive the excitement of the gold rush in the silver-happy Comstock region. In the upshot he became Joe Goodman's chief editorial assistant on the *Territorial Enterprise,* and was one of Mark's seconds in the abortive duel which caused Twain to take it on the lam for San Francisco in 1864.

Before that happened, an event took place in Virginia City which Mark remembered when writing *Roughing It* some years later. "A crowded police court docket is the surest of all signs that trade is brisk and money plenty. Still there is one other sign; it comes last, but when it does come it establishes beyond cavil that the 'flush times' are at the flood. This is the birth of a literary paper. The Weekly Occidental, 'devoted to literature,' made its appearance in Virginia. All the literary people were to write for it. Mr. F. [Tom Fitch, into whose knee Joe Goodman slung the mentioned code duello bullet] was to edit it."

The most ambitious feature of the *Occidental* was a novel of composite authorship. Started by Tom, it was continued by at least two other hands. Mark was supposed to make his debut as a novelist by contributing a chapter, but before his turn came due the miscellany had run its brief course.

Robbed of this opportunity, Twain had never published anything but newspaper copy and a few sketches contributed to Eastern journals when he reached San Francisco two months after the *Occidental* bloomed and withered in March of 1864. That he might live by free-lancing could not have occurred to him, for the institution had never existed in the West. Finding there was an opening on the San Francisco *Call,* he caught on as an employee of that paper.

Had his work been more pleasant, he might have continued to play it safe. The stimulating professional associations he had found on the *Territorial Enterprise* were missing from the *Call,* though; and he was denied there the freedom to write as he wished that he'd enjoyed in Virginia City. Bored and fed up with taking guff from incompetents, he walked out after two months.

A year earlier Mark would have had to run for cover to some other newspaper job, whether in San Francisco or out. But in the year 1864 there were developments which for the first time made free-lancing by the Golden Gate a possibility. Preparatory was the new role of the *Golden Era* under the guidance of Joseph Lawrence. A city of over 100,000, San Francisco towered as never before over the towns of a mining region which had lost all expectations of grandeur themselves, and Lawrence had determined to capitalize on that situation in two ways.

In the first place, he reasoned that San Francisco was now large enough to furnish an adequate quota of subscribers to a literary miscellany—if it was aimed at metropolitan readers and not provincials. As for residents in the quieted mining towns, Lawrence understood that a fair percentage of possible subscribers would be willing to align themselves culturally with the big city by accepting its viewpoints in preference to local ones. So whereas the *Golden Era* had begun as something made in the metropolis especially for the provinces, it wound up as a metropolitan journal.

With the paper's center of gravity shifted, most of the copy for it was written in San Francisco, in place of being supplied from without. By catering to city residents, besides, the *Era* upped its circulation and supplied itself with a firmer advertising base. As it could afford to pay reasonably well for contributions, that was one market which Twain found waiting for him when he left the *Call*. By signing up for a regular number of sketches a month, he precariously became an independent writer.

The problem of office space was solved when Charles and Michel de Young commenced a stage-door-johnnie publication called the *Dramatic Chronicle*. To develop into the yet flourishing San Francisco *Chronicle*, it was a shoestring outfit in 1864. So the de Young brothers gave notice that they would offer desk space and a professional address in return for copy.

Mark was but one of several writers, later all nationally known, who made book with the *Chronicle's* owners. Bret Harte, Prentice Mulford, and Charles Warren Stoddard were three other contributors to the *Golden Era* who were willing to trade play reviews and squibs for a place to work and pick up their mail.

On the staff of the *Era* at this time was Charles Henry Webb, a journalist later to become briefly famous in the East as the author of a humorous item called *John Paul's Book*. The success of Lawrence's miscellany, together with the presence of qualified contributors in some abundance, made him decide to launch the *Californian.* So before 1864 closed, Twain had two major outlets. As he could sell occasional pieces to the *Territorial Enterprise* and the also highly regarded Sacramento *Union,* moreover, he was making a fairly good living.

Additionally he sent a few pieces to Eastern miscellanies, and as one of these was *The Celebrated Jumping Frog of Calaveras County,* he suddenly found himself as famed nationally as the athletic frog was in Angel's Camp. He was therefore able to talk the *Union* into sending him to the Sandwich Islands in 1866; and the letters he wrote back were so well received that in December of that year San Francisco's *Alta California* commissioned him to make a tour of the globe. But though he returned to the Golden Gate's city in completion of that assignment, he had become too big for its literary market, and in 1867 the West saw the last of him.

As a sphere for writers in general, San Francisco had depreciated by then. For in 1866 Webb had gone East, leaving the *Californian* to flounder and founder. Eclipsed for a while by its rival, the *Golden Era* was once again the city's chief cultural organ.

At times that miscellany had hidden more writing talent in its composing room than it exhibited in its columns. Joe Goodman, Bret Harte, and Henry George had been among its typesetters; and if Joe had left, the other two were still in town. Then in addition to Mulford and Stoddard, there was Ambrose Bierce. Having arrived in 1866, he had contributed a piece or so to the *Era,* though he was chiefly known as the writer of "The Town Crier" column for a sheet called *News-Letter.*

Looking the field over in 1868, Bret Harte wasn't convinced that it was a strong enough one with which to undertake to publish a full-fledged cultural magazine. He therefore at first objected to a proposition made him by the head of a prosperous printing establishment named Anton Roman. Yet as Anton was able to supply the inducement of a good salary and sound general financing for the publication, Bret quit arguing and commenced editing the *Overland Monthly.*

Now though Bierce and George were to achieve greatness, and

Mulford the reputation of being a sort of seagoing Thoreau, Harte was right in judging that they and the rest of San Francisco's literati weren't then up to filling a magazine of respectable quality month in and month out. But the periodical's editor had one hole card that he had entirely overlooked; and that was his own not yet exploited talent for masquerading sentimentality as rugged realism.

He had to fight stockholders in order to get the first of these accepted by the *Overland*. What shook them with fear that they'd lose subscribers and their investment was an item that Bret wrote for the second number called *The Luck of Roaring Camp*. Central to the story was an infant born out of wedlock; and the directors figured that, after reading it, Queen Victoria would reach clean over to San Francisco and cut the *Overland Monthly's* water off.

Not knowing he'd struck oil, but feeling he'd turned out a publishable piece of work, Harte refused to reject the story which wound up by making him and his magazine famous in England as well as America's East. For it developed that people elsewhere were charmed by a combination of toughness and tenderness that they wouldn't have credited, had it been found in their respective regions. But they were willing to believe it intrinsic to the West, especially when published in a magazine printed in that faraway land.

On the strength of *The Luck of Roaring Camp* and followers in the same appreciated vein, the *Overland Monthly* was successful for two years. Then Harte fired a shot which he didn't know would be startling a second time. In 1870 he wrote his ballad about two American gamblers who get taken by a Chinaman they'd tried to fleece at poker, its title being *Plain Language from Truthful James*.

Tossed off at a time when there was much excitement about immigration from the Celestial Empire, its punch line was the cry of one of the disillusioned gamblers, "We are ruined by Chinese cheap labor!" Considered as a topical piece, it was only so-so, and Bret didn't think too much of it himself. He kept it in his desk for a couple of months until, as a deadline neared, there was a hole in the make-up which the ballad exactly fitted.

It made no impression on other Californians, who were like the author in seeing only its topical bearing. But as in the East there was no concern about the competition offered by thronging Orientals, all that was apparent was a narrative of two big, tough wiseacres outsmarted by their seemingly helpless little victim. The mirth was so ecstatic that Boston's *Atlantic Monthly* decided to buy the services of the man who could both inspire it and write convincingly of golden-hearted tarts and blacklegs.

The *Atlantic* got stung, as Harte had already spent his cleverness on the magazine of his own editing. But that was finished, too, though it limped along, on the strength of the prestige with which Bret had supplied it, for another five years.

The *Golden Era* was still alive, meanwhile, but it was never again as lustrous as it had seemed before a handsomely designed magazine had absorbed the best efforts of its chief contributors. Then in 1877, or two years after the *Overland Monthly* quit publication, it was outshone again.

The founder of the *Argonaut* is now remembered because of Ambrose Bierce's epitaph: "Here lies Frank Pixley, as usual." The magazine itself had more claims to fame. Aside from running Bierce's own inimitable "Prattle" column, it published some fine sketches and short stories by Sam Davis, the Nevada newspaperman, and a lawyer—once of the fourth estate—named James Gally.

Both Davis and Gally had other jobs, in a word, and wrote for the *Argonaut* as well as the *Overland* (when it was revived in 1883), as a never regularly pursued sideline. Formerly of the *News Letter* and later of the *Wasp* as well as the *Examiner*, Bierce turned out his columns as a staff member. The great cham of Western letters for much of his long career, Ambrose was only able to operate independently for a few years—and they were spent in London. By the time he returned to California in 1875, the brief period when it was possible to free-lance in the West's metropolis was a long-gone thing.

In the absence of professional free-lances, the story of the *Argonaut*, the *Overland*, and numerous lesser San Francisco miscellanies was one tale. The occasional good things they published were needles in haystacks piled up by the dilettantes and yearners on whom they alone could depend for a sufficient flow of contributions.

What was true of the West's capital city was trebly true elsewhere. Usually short of any talent but that of the editor, the literary sheets and magazines published in the lesser towns were hopeless projects with short histories.

There was one such journal, however, which was so much of a hit that it outgrew its frontier breeches and wound up with offices on both shores of the Atlantic. This was *Texas Siftings*, which began in 1869 as "San Antonio Siftings," a humorous column contributed to the *Express* by Alexander E. Sweet. Moving to what had once been Sam Bangs' Galveston *News* in 1878, Alex there won such applause that he decided to sift on a larger and more profitable scale.

In 1881, accordingly, he and another sharp journalist named John Armoy Knox started a paper called *Texas Siftings* in Austin. One of their jointly written features was *Through Texas on a Mexican Mustang*, serialized in their sheet before being issued in book form. Yet Alex and John didn't long have to provide all the copy for their rag. Via the exchange system, it got to be known all over the country; and Eugene Field and Bill Nye were among the authors who began adding the siftings of other sections of the United States to those gleaned in Texas.

Solidly established as a national institution in 1884, *Texas Siftings* shifted its office to New York. Although it moved out of range of this chronicle in so doing, it will be added that three years later it began putting out a London edition.

Back on the frontier, meanwhile, Edward and Harvey Mickle were showing that they knew a thing or two. Not content with being publishers of the Brownwood, Texas *Banner*, this pair issued from their isolated small town a fiction and feature magazine which was a popular hit for a few of the 1880s. At its peak the *Sunny South* had a circulation of 150,000, and ads were pouring in from all over the country. As for contributors, the editors could afford to pay for them, so professionals kicked in by mail.

What did the Mickle brethren understand that other men of print did not? Why, that people would buy even reading matter, if they had a chance to cop a prize. Wherefore the subscription department of the *Sunny South* conducted a lottery with premiums ranging from cheap watches to 160 acres of land.

Pleased with their profits, the editors moved their base of operations from Brownwood to comparatively metropolitan Waco. But in common with Icarus, they weren't helped by getting nearer the sun. Soreheads who'd drawn fifty-cent timepieces instead of quarter sections began beefing to federal authorities, who took their good thing away from the Mickles on the ground that they had used the mails to defraud.

Two more miscellanies—both also Texas ones—cannot be ignored because of the fame of their respective editors. Having interlocking histories, these were Will Porter's *Rolling Stone* and William Cowper Brann's *Iconoclast*.

How the first got started was remembered by a partner of Will's, a man of print who had somehow come to be called Doc Daniels. "It was in the spring of 1894 that I floated into Austin, and I got a place in the State printing office. I had been working there for a short time when I heard that a man named Porter had bought out the old Iconoclast plant—known everywhere as Brann's Iconoclast—and was looking for a printer to go in the game with him. I went around to see him, and that was the first time I met O. Henry. . . . I talked things over with him, the proposition looked good, and we formed a partnership then and there. We christened the paper the *Rolling Stone* after a few discussions, and in smaller type across the full page head we printed 'Out for the Moss.' Which is exactly what we were out for. Our idea was to run this weekly with a lot of current events treated in humorous fashion, and also to run short sketches, drawings and verse. I had been doing a lot of chalk plate work . . . and Porter was the most versatile man I had ever met. He was a fine singer, could write remarkably clever stuff under all circumstances, and was a good hand at sketching. . . ."

With a staff thus equipped, the paper got off the blocks well, and even glistened politically for a while. "The Populist party was coming in for all sorts of publicity at this time," Doc Daniels went on, "and the famous 'Sockless Simpson,' of Kansas, was running for Congress. Porter worked out a series of 'Tictocq, the Great French Detective,' in burlesque of Lecocq; and in one story, I remember, had a deep-laid conspiracy to locate a pair of socks in Simpson's luggage, thus discrediting him with his political followers."

This scoop notwithstanding, the *Rolling Stone* stopped, after making a year of progress. Among other causes was the fact that its sponsors failed to save the moss collected en route. To go with Daniels again, "The Rolling Stone met with unusual success at the start, and we had in our files letters from men like Bill Nye and John Kendrick Bangs praising us for the quality of the sheet. We were doing nicely, getting the paper out every Saturday—approximately—and blowing the receipts every night. Then we began to strike snags."

Unable to beat past these with squandered sinews of war, the partners had to let their paper die in 1895. Brann revived the *Iconoclast* that same year, as it happened, though at Waco rather than Austin.

The sheet's purpose was implicit in its name. William Cowper was a dedicated smasher of popular fetishes; and a bold one, too, as he stayed in business until one of the numerous threats to extinguish him was carried out, as earlier related. The *Iconoclast* was nevertheless as "out for the moss" as the *Rolling Stone*, and one of Brann's ways of gathering same ill accorded with the dignity of a professional sage. For William Cowper seems to have been the first American journalist to have used an international beauty contest as a circulation builder.

Dropping the editorial "we," Brann voiced personal yearning when commencing this dodge. "I will pay $500," he announced in 1896, "for the blessed privilege of looking for five minutes at the most beautiful woman in the world."

In another take he had a fit of prose poetry. "I have heard her [the global beauty champ's] voice in the low sweet anthem of the summer sea at Night's high noon; I have caught fitful glimpses of the dark eyes' splendor in waking dreams, and when demons rose upon the storm of passion and murder shrieked within my soul, I have felt her dewy breath upon my fevered cheek, her cool tresses floating like leaves of the lotus flower across my face. . . ."

It developed that a lot of widely situated owners of cool tresses aspired to be the editor's realized dream. "Up to the present writing," as the *Iconoclast* eventually analyzed the returns, "the countries represented in the contest are as follows: the United States, Canada, Mexico, Cuba, Peru, Brazil, Scotland, Ireland, Wales, France, Italy and Denmark."

Presumably the entries submitted portraits, though fair features were not all that was demanded in Waco then, any more than in Atlantic City at a later period. "Bust and waist measurements would materially assist the judges in determining the contest," the *Iconoclast* underscored the need for well-stemmed lotus flowers.

Unfortunately there's no record of who walked off with Brann's golden apple, or rather who racked up $100 for each of five minutes by letting the man of print give her a connoisseur's appraisal. But the contest was obviously not in disfavor with the serious [male] thinkers from all over the country who largely made up William Cowper's following. Amazingly well supported for a paper aimed at such a clientele, the *Iconoclast* had over 100,000 subscribers by the time bullets put it out of business in 1898.

16

CRITICISM UNLIMITED

WHETHER WRITING FOR miscellanies or newspapers, the field of aesthetics was one that the Western men of print by no means left unexplored. Individually editors were apt to serve as the literary, dramatic, music, and art critics of their respective sheets. Collectively they spoke for the cultural outlook of a region which had broken with tradition where most things were concerned.

So they could be interested in the arts without being awed by them. And whether or not approving of any given work or performance, they could be counted on to look at it with their own eyes. As they belonged to no schools of criticism and catered to no intellectual claques, nothing but personal taste moved them.

Neither did they feel compelled to parade the pose of omniscience affected by so many culture vultures [good old Henry Clewes] of the twentieth century. They could be educated without itching on that account.

This relaxed attitude was illustrated by Tom Donaldson, of the Boise *Statesman,* when recalling an Idaho colleague named Thomas Butler. "Long Tom," as Butler was known because of his stringiness, had formerly belonged to California's fourth estate and was later to join that of Arizona.

"He gave me one of the best pointers of my youthful days," Donaldson declared. "I was perplexed, on one occasion, to find the name of the author of a poetical quotation which I placed at the head of an editorial. Butler looked over my shoulder, rubbed his hand slowly across his chin and drawled, 'Sonny, don't let things like that bother you in life. Do as I do when I'm in your fix. Simply write down, "Old Poet."'"

Whether or not he remembered the name of the dead-and-gone bard he borrowed from, the *Solid Muldoon*'s Dave Day didn't boggle at adding lines of his own to a pair by Goldsmith. Nor did he feel compelled to take Oliver's laissez-faire attitude toward fallen femininity.

"A shootin' affray occurred at Lake City," the *Muldoon* reported, when both leaning on Goldsmith and taking issue with him. "We are reliably informed that there was a woman at the bottom:

> When lovely woman stoops to folly
> And finds too late that men betray,
> Pater familias is eminently justified
> In loadin' his cannon and bangin' away."

Proofs of familiarity with poets might not be as direct as was the offering of Dave Day. One of the editors of the Greenwater, California *Chuck-Walla* had read Keats without feeling compelled to quote him. This he showed by paying John the compliment of writing a lyric titled *Owed to the Nightengale.*

> Here the bird is a burro, benighted,
>   With two fuzzy ears and a tail,
> And its home is a desolate desert
>   And its song less a tune than a wail.
> But the life that it leads forms a story
>   Of more interest than any bard's tale
> And far out in the wild western desert
>   Much is owed to the nightengale.

When it came to evaluation, the pioneer editor could be as little moved by chauvinism as by opinions expressed on the Atlantic seaboard or Europe. The Albany, Oregon *Democrat* made this plain, when discussing a Western bard who had become celebrated in England, pursuant to the 1871 publication there of *Songs of the Sierras.*

"C. H. [Joaquin] Miller, ex-editor of the Eugene Register, and ex-County Judge of Grant County, has published a book of poems and become a man of fame in London. The fact makes us think no more of Miller but a lot less of the Londoners."

More genial about it, Mark Twain entered the field of poetic criticism when he began contributing to San Francisco's *Californian.* In 1865 one of Mark's games was to answer the queries of fictive writers from afield. Of these one was a yearner named Melton Mowbray, with whom Twain felt called upon to be quite severe.

"This correspondent sends a lot of doggerel, and says it has been regarded as very good in Dutch Flat. I give a specimen verse:—

> The Assyrian came down like a wolf on the fold,
> And his cohorts were gleaming with purple and gold;
> And the sheen of his spears was like stars on the sea,
> When the blue waves roll nightly on deep Galilee.

"There, that will do. That may be very good Dutch Flat poetry, but it won't do in the metropolis. It is too smooth and blubbery; it reads like buttermilk gurgling through a jug. What the people ought to have is something spirited—something like 'Johnny Comes Marching Home.' However, keep on practicing, and you may succeed yet. There is genius in you but too much blubber."

To Mark's delight, Californians proved both indignant of the Dutch Flat poet's plagiarism and scornful of the columnist who hadn't recognized it. From all over the state, as he reminisced, there swooped "denunciations of the . . . author and editor, in not knowing that the lines in question were 'written by Byron.'"

A second case where Mark called a poet to account is noteworthy because of the criticized bard's name. Later in 1865 Simon Wheeler became an American immortal as the narrator of the fortunes of Jim Smiley of Calaveras County and his broad jumping frog. In his column written for the *Californian*, Twain hadn't yet settled Simon in Angel's Camp; he represented Mr. Wheeler as dwelling in a Tuolumne rather than a Calaveras gold-rush camp.

Simon Wheeler. . . . The following simple and touching remarks and accompanying poem have just come in from the gold mining region of Sonora:

To Mr. Mark Twain: The within parson, which I have set to poetry under the name and style of 'He done His Level Best' was one among the whitest men I ever see, and it ain't every man that knowed him can find it in his heart to say he's glad the poor cuss is busted and gone home to the States. He was here in an early day, and he was the handiest man about takin' hold of anythin' that come along you most ever see, I judge. He was a cheerful, stirrin' cretur, always doin' somethin', and no man can say he ever seen him do anythin' by halvers. Preachin' was his natural gait, but he warn't a man to lay back and twiddle his thumbs, because there didn't happen to be nothin' doin' in his own especial line— no, sir, he was a man who would meander forth and stir up some-thin' for hisself. His last act was to go his pile on 'kings-and' (calkalatin' to fill, which he didn't fill), when there was a flush out agin him and naterally, you see, he went under. And so he was cleaned out as you may say, and he struck the home-trail, cheerful but flat broke. I knowed this talonted man in Arkansaw, and if you would print this humbly tribute to his gorgis abilities, you would greatly obleege his onhappy friend.

HE DONE HIS LEVEL BEST

Was he a mining on the flat——
　　He done it with a zest;
Was he a leading of the choir——
　　He done his level best.

If he'd a reg'lar task to do,
　　He never took no rest;
Or if 'twas off-and-on—the same——
　　He done his level best.

If he was preachin' on his beat,
　　He'd tramp from east to west
And north to south—in cold and heat
　　He done his level best.

He'd yank a sinner outen Hell
　　And land him with the blest;
Then snatch a prayer'n waltz in again,
　　And do his level best.

He'd cuss and sing and howl and pray
　　And dance and drink and jest
And lie and steal—all one to him——
　　He done his level best.

Whate'er this man was sot to do,
　　He done it with a zest;
No matter *what* his contract was,
　　He'd do his level best.

Having created, in Simon Wheeler, a character he wasn't to forget, Mark proceeded to dust him off. "Verily, this man *was* gifted with 'gorgis abilities,' and it is a happiness to me to embalm the memory of their lustre in these columns. If it were not that the poet crop is unusually large and rank in California this year, I would encourage you to continue writing, Simon Wheeler; but as it is, perhaps it might be too risky in you to enter against so much opposition."

To turn from the spoofing of yearners to serious interpretative writing, what is undoubtedly one of the best critiques in the history of American literature appeared in the Gold Hill *News* in 1864. Its subject was not poetry, however, but a stage production.

In an earlier chapter it was related that when Matilda Heron brought her troupe to Virginia City, she was provoked into swinging an umbrella at Joe Goodman, because of adverse judgments published in the *Territorial Enterprise*. But the Comstock was a divided camp as to Matilda, for the *News* was on her side.

The play that La Heron had roused controversy with was Corneille's *Medea*. The *Enterprise* had jeered at Matilda for not portraying the glamorous sorceress whom Jason had collected at Colchis as bonus for the Golden Fleece. Philip Lynch, of the *News*, thought the actress was right in giving more attention to realism than charm. As the play was to be repeated, besides, he had the task of making understandable a stage story which had baffled many Comstock first nighters.

Wishing to encourage these to try again, as well as interest those who hadn't seen the original performance, Philip undertook to bring the tale of the ancient enchantress up to date, via a parody of Longfellow's then enormously popular *The Song of Hiawatha*. After praising Matilda's acting, Hawkins faced his readers squarely with their problem of comprehending something which many were ill equipped by education to appreciate:

> . . . . 'Tis a sad and mournful story
> Is the story of Medea.
> The scene is laid in ancient Corinth,
> In the dark and misty ages
> Of the ancient Grecian poems;

In the days of gods and heroes——
Days of goddesses and women——
Days when deities and mortals
Mixed in such conglomeration
That you can't tell which from 'tother.
Of those days and of such people
Is the story of Medea.
Consequently if the audience
Ain't well posted in their classics
They fail in due appreciation.
In short to use a coarse expression,
Medea is a huckleberry
Above the popular persimmon.

Yet, having allowed that the superficial aspects of the tragedy
were foreign to Nevada, Lynch got down to the business of showing that the reverse was true of the drama's basic elements.

But the story of Medea
Is a tale of human passions;
And the hearts of men and women
Are made of much the same material
Now as in the misty ages——
Here in Washoe as in Corinth——
And the woes of wronged Medea
Are a story *too* familiar
On the shores of the Pacific
If we lay the scene in Washoe,
We can tell Medea's story
To the better comprehension
Of the masses of the people.

In sketching the career of Jason, Philip grinned at unheroic
phases of the Piute War, a conflict in which the whites had been
outgeneraled by Chief Winnemucca, until veteran Indian fighter
Jack Coffee Hays hove in from California and got the situation in
hand. Lynch also dragged in the stone skeleton of a mammoth,
which was one of the by-products of a fad for finding such things
which Twain mocked in one of his articles for the *Territorial
Enterprise* called *The Petrified Man.* As for Truckee, it was the
chief stream of the Washoe mining district, while "hunky" did not
mean Hungarian but "in solid."

In the silver-land of Washoe
Lived a hunky boy, named Jason!
A mighty hero was this Jason
And his doughty deeds of valor
Rang from Tahoe to Reese River——
From Oregon to Arizona.
He had been with Captain Wallace
On the Walker expedition;
He it was who planned the movement
Which surrounded the "campoody". . . .
He was with the Nine-and-Twenty
Under Wells out on the Truckee;
They who slew the veteran legions——
Slew the nine-and-twenty Piutes,
Slew the squaws of Winnemucca,
Waded to the very arm pits
Through seas of guts and gore and garbage.
All alone had mighty Jason
Slain with single-barreled shotgun
The Fossil-Elephant of Truckee;
First he slew him, then he ate him,
Stripped his bones and left him lying,
A skeleton all bare and ghastly. . . .
Such a mighty man was Jason!

Lynch next considered the success Nevada's hero was bound
to have, when he coveted Virginia City's loveliest and most
prominent debutante.

Was it strange that all the women
In the silver-land of Washoe
Cast their brightest, sweetest glances
On the doughty warrior, Jason?
Was it strange that fair Creusa,
Child of old Creon the Wealthy,
Lord of all the Ledge of Comstock
Should succumb to the advances
Of the mighty warrior, Jason?

But while Jason is preparing to cinch a beautiful young bride
and the money she'll inherit, he gets word that his past on the
Atlantic-side is about to catch up with him.

> Jason proudly stalked through C Street
> To buy a ring and hire a preacher;
> Met in front of Doyle and Goodman's
> Orpheus his friend and pitcher,
> And the tale that Orpheus told him
> Made bold Jason rather weaken;
> Orpheus told him that Medea
> (His other wife from Philadelphia)
> Had come out across the Isthmus
> On the Nicaragua steamer!
> Had come out and brought the children
> For to see their daddy, Jason,
> Hero of the land of Washoe.

Not minded to give up tootsie Creusa and settle down with middle-aged Medea, Jason got a lawyer and sued for divorce in a town where his prestige was enormous, while his newly arrived wife was without influence. Retaining a fondness for his children, moreover, the big shot obtained custody of them, when he won his case.

Just as in Corneille's play, his discarded mate at first emoted but then decided upon action. Lynch didn't analyze the properties of "screw-ten-oo-ten," but it appears to have been a potion designed to go strych-nine one better.

> Medea then took the hysterics,
> Shrieked and yelled and kicked and shouted;
> Sat down in the empty court room
> Got her wind and planned her vengeance.
> Then she took a half a dollar. . . .
> Bought a half an ounce of essence
> Of the deadly Screw-ten-oo-ten
> Went then straightway to the chamber
> Of the lovely bride Creusa,
> On the bridal veil she poured it,
> Poured the deadly Screw-ten-oo-ten;
> Went then to the house of Jason
> Went and asked to see the children
> Just to see them and to kiss them.
> Jason and the fair Creusa
> Scarce were bound in holy wedlock
> By the Reverend Mr. Rising,

> When a piercing shriek resounded
> Through the Church and fair Creusa
> Succumbed to the Screw-ten-oo-ten.
> Horror-struck the wretched Jason
> Homeward rushed and found his children
> Stretched upon the parlor-carpet
> Dead from ghastly wounds inflicted
> By the dagger of Medea. . . .
> Then she raised the bloody dagger;
> In her broken heart she thrust it
> And fell down upon the bloody
> Bodies of her slaughtered children.
> That's the story of Medea.

In his windup Philip wondered why Corneille bothered to riffle through Greek lore for the makings of a tragedy, when he could easily have got what he needed by thumbing through Pacific Coast annals.

> If you'll go and search the records
> Of the Courts of California;
> If you'll overhaul the papers
> Of the First Judicial District
> Of the new state of Nevada,
> You will find the same old story,
> The wretched story of Medea,
> Told so often that you'll wonder
> That the man who wrote that drama
> Had to overhaul his classics
> And grope amid the misty ages
> To find his Jason and Medea.

Operatic troupes occasionally toured the West, too, and one of them made a stand in Laramie, Wyoming, while Bill Nye was publishing the *Boomerang* there in the 1880s. Liking some phases of the offering but not others, Bill meted praise and blame with an impartial hand.

"A few evenings ago I had the pleasure of listening to the rendition of the Bohemian Girl by Emma Abbot and her troupe at the Grand Opera House. . . . The plot of the play seems to be that Arline, a nice little chunk of a girl, is stolen by a band of gypsies owned and operated by Devilshoof, who looks some like Othello and some like Sitting Bull. Arline grows up among the gypsies and falls in love with Thaddeus. Thaddeus was played by [Pasquale] Brignoli. Brignoli was named after a thoroughbred horse.

"Arline falls asleep in the gypsy camp and dreams a large, majolica dream . . . which she tells to Thaddeus. She says that she dreamed that she dwelt in marble halls and kept a girl [a lady's maid, that is] and had a pretty fly time generally, but after all she said it tickled her more to know that Thaddeus loved her still the same, and she kept saying this to him in G and up on the upper register and down on the second added line below, and crescendo and diminuendo and duodessimo . . . till I would have given 1,000 shares of paid up, non-assessable stock in the Boomerang if I could have been Thaddeus.

"After a while the Gypsy Queen, who is jealous of Arline, puts up a job on her to get her arrested, and she was brought up before her father, who is the Justice of the Peace for that precinct and he gives her $25 and trimmings, or 30 days in the Bastille. By and by, however, he catches sight of her arm and recognizes her by a large red Goddess of Liberty tattooed on it, and he remits the fine and charges the costs up to the county. . . .

"There is a good deal of singing in this opera. . . . Emma Abbot certainly warbles first rate. . . . But Brignoli is no singer according to my aesthetic tastes. He sings like a man who hasn't taken out his second papers yet and his stomach is too large. It gets in the way and Arline has to go around it and lean up on his flank when she wants to put her head on his breast."

Semblens Forbes wasn't at all favorably impressed with a musical program which he had come to Virginia City to audit, so that he could make a report to the subscribers of his Unionville *Humboldt Register* in 1864. Although the featured performer was a celebrated French fiddler, his efforts were prefaced by those of a pianist and some singers, all of whom Semblens dealt with in an article headed A VIOLIN CONCERT.

"Stadfeldt came forward and bowed backward and seated himself within arms length of the piano. He hammered, showed a partiality for the small end of the board, and played fast and stopped quickly—a great deal of feeling but very little music in his performance."

In his critique Forbes did not overlook the professional music lovers he found in attendance. "He [Stadfeldt] was applauded. It seemed there were men there determined to applaud whenever anybody else was occupying the attention of the audience. Mrs. Wiley sang a song. It was a great effort. You could see it. Paul Julien then came down to the front. He was applauded for bowing. He had one of those steel-pen split coats onto him. Did you ever notice how the stately raven's tail dips when the raven dips up a bug? Paul's coat tail tipped up the very same way.

"He took a clean handkerchief from one side of the split and wiped his violin. He drew the hair of the horse across the bowels of a cat much to the same purpose as though the cat had been alive—a great noise followed. He could play well if custom would permit. In some portions he did descend to a tune, and the violin sounded melodiously. He is a complete master of the instrument, or he could never succeed in torturing so sweet toned a violin into the squeaks and squalls he brings from it. He stops occasionally and the claquers applaud, while he wipes the neck of the violin with that white handkerchief from the tail of his coat. Then he bows. . . ."

But like Cousin Egbert in *Ruggles of Red Gap,* Semblens could be pushed just so far before balking. "The Beermania Society sang a fine chorus," as he remarked; but that wasn't all. "Mrs. Wiley and Stadfeldt performed [again] and Julien comes back and Steudeman is dished up, and we leave long before it is out, thinking we have enough for a dollar, and that the dollar passed the wrong way."

Interested in a musician, if not necessarily admiring his performance, Will Porter told readers of the Houston *Post* just where he'd seen the artiste's like before. The *Rolling Stone* a thing of the past, Will was conducting a column called "Postscripts" in 1896. One of the ornaments of this feature followed the appearance of a noted pianist and was headed *Two Portraits.*

Wild hair flying in a matted maze,
Hand firm as iron, eyes all ablaze,
Bystanders timidly, breathlessly gaze
As o'er the keno board boldly he plays.
                    —That's Texas Bill.

Wild hair flying in a matted maze,
Hand firm as iron, eyes all ablaze,
Bystanders timidly, breathlessly gaze
As o'er the key board boldly he plays.
                    —That's Paderewski.

There was less opportunity on the frontier to appraise the visual arts than those appealing to the ear. Such a rare chance was the fortune of Legh Freeman while at the helm of the Glendale, Montana *Atlantis* in 1879. And if Freeman didn't turn the residents of a stag camp into art lovers one and all, it wasn't for the lack of trying.

"One of the prettiest pictures in town is hanging in Frank Gilg's Brewery," Legh began his critique. "It is an oil painting of a half nude maiden developed into a form voluptuous and poetical with hair falling naturally down her bosom, as she lies at full length on some mossy rocks beside a rippling stream of limpid water coursing its way through a mountain defile similar to the one in which we live. Byron's poems are spread out before her love-flashing eyes, while trout glide along the stream winking at the nymph, and the black pine squirrels and jack daws leap from bough to bough, chattering among the over hanging trees. . . . The painting is a very refined one, portraying rare and chaste beauty and virtue, and is an excellent specimen of fine art."

Yet it was Eugene Field who told how sincerely devoted to properly applied painting skill the bachelors of a frontier camp might become. In this case it was Blue Horizon, Colorado, which a brushman named Pettibone had chosen as his headquarters.

As long as he wasted canvas on Rocky Mountain superfluities, the painter drew no more admiration than did the tinker who brought Alexander the Great a metal bird which could trill like a nightingale. Alex, as he pointed out, had heard the real thing, while the prospectors of Blue Horizon had more scenic glory at hand than they knew what to do with.

Yet after he'd been in the wilds just so long, the artist himself began to think of something more fetching than snow-clad peaks with bonnets of clouds. Having developed his new idea, he brought it to the gathering of cognoscenti described by Gene.

One evenin' as we sat around the restaurant de Casey,
A singin' songs and tellin' yarns the which was sumwhat racy,

Pettibone joined a group where he'd previously been not too welcome, and flashed his portrayal of a lovely face. The silence that fell at de Casey's was broken only by the footfalls of flies tramping across the saloon's bar.

Till presently as in a dream, remarked Three-fingered Hoover;
"Onless I am mistaken, that is Pettibone's shef doover. . . ."
"Hurray!" we cried—a woman in the camp of Blue Horizon!
Step right up, Colonel Pettibone, and nominate your pizen!"

The painting promptly became the sweetheart of all in camp; and their boasts of her beauty caused miners from other settlements to make pilgrimages to Blue Horizon. Although most were satisfactorily complimentary, one visitor horrified her champions by describing the girl as the artist's "madonner."

The which we didn't take to be respectful to a lady,
So we hung him in a quiet place that was cool 'nd dry 'nd shady
Which same might not have been good law, but it *wuz* the right
    right nameuver
To give the critics due respect for Pettibone's shef doover.

17

HISTORY AND ITS COUSINS

AS THE OPERATIONS of pioneer journalists have by now been summarized, attention will be given to what was accomplished by the spending of so much energy, hardihood, and talent. For in spite of the stress that has inevitably been laid on struggles against unconquerable odds, that wasn't all the story. Of the collective men of print, it can be said on the whole that they achieved everything but success at what they set out to do.

Essentially they had one design; the founding of journals which would reflect the grandeur of the towns they fostered. Very sparingly, as has been shown, did that come to pass.

The papers they founded collapsed or achieved permanence only after control had shifted from writers and printers to businessmen skilled at neither craft. The burgs they fought and starved for vanished or settled for limited horizons. Or at best the queen cities postponed royalty until it was too late to gratify their primary admirers.

Yet between them the West's early journalists kept the record and preserved the lore of an imperial domain; and because they were themselves involved with every form of frontier life, they were able to handle the assignment with matchless thoroughness. In part they were able to do so, because issuing periodicals was but one of their professional lines. As has been mentioned, if not earlier discussed at any length, they were publishers in a comprehensive sense.

They printed state constitutions, county laws, and city charters. They issued commercial brochures, college bulletins, the programs of social groups, and the announcements of individuals. They published reports of Indian warfare, economic and scientific treatises, town and state histories, analyses of mineral and agricultural districts, travelogues, emigrant guides, political discussions, reminiscences, biographies, accounts of personal exploits, and broadsides bearing on current events. And over and above all that, they printed items belonging to all departments of creative literature. They were the writers as well as the publishers of that indigenous Western reading matter, too. But what they thus achieved will be glanced at in succeeding chapters. In this one, a look will be taken at their service as preservers of the record through other means than that of newspaper columns.

When a pioneer journal issued an "extra," to begin with, it did not follow the later practice of publishing an entire special edition of the paper. As this would have been impossible for plants of limited equipment, all that was distributed was a bulletin dealing with nothing but the scoop of the moment.

In 1876 the Yankton *Press and Dakotaian* did this, when word of the disastrous Battle of the Little Big Horn was relayed from Montana to eastern Dakota Territory in the roundabout way described in the report. Its form was a broadside in which, because of the limited information then available, almost as much space was devoted to headlines as the story.

Press and Dakotaian
EXTRA

❂ ❂ ❂

Custer Attacks the Indians

❂ ❂ ❂

His Brother, Nephew,
Brother-in-law and Himself Among
The Killed

❂ ❂ ❂

Over Three Hundred of the
Command Killed and a
Number Wounded

The Dead Were Badly Mutilated

The Seventh Cavalry Fought Like Tigers

A Son of Gen. Crittenden Among the Killed

Salt Lake, July 5—"A special correspondent of the Helena, Mt., Herald writes from Stillwater, Mt., July 2, that Muggins Taylor, a scout for Gen. Gibson, got there last night direct from the Little Horn river. Gen. Custer found an Indian camp of nearly 2000 lodges on the Little Horn and immediately attacked the camp. Nothing is known of the operations of this command only as they trace it by the dead. . . ."

Broadsides not in the class of news bulletins could be of unusual interest because of incorporating unexpected phases of Western history. One published by the job shop of the Leavenworth *Journal* tells of the effort of one Bleeding Kansas peace officer to cool a town's hotheads down by waving the threat of a Gestapo at peace breakers.

PUBLIC WARNING

"The practice of discharging fire-arms within the limits of Leavenworth, contrary to an ordinance of said city, having become so frequent as to endanger life and greatly annoy the quiet and peace of orderly citizens, I have taken this method to inform every one that I intend to enforce the Ordinance against EACH AND EVERY VIOLATOR thereof; and if found necessary, will, by the authority of the Mayor, employ a secret police for the purpose of giving information against every one thus offending.

William P. Shockley
City Marshal

July 11, 1856
Leavenworth City"

A broadside might speak the mind of a group rather than an individual. One such item told of the descent upon a pioneer community of that rarely pinned down Western figure, the professional man of guile. As this Salem, Oregon, broadside adds up to a completely told short story, it will be given in all but full.

READ AND REFLECT

"Whereas a certain C. H. De Wolfe, a professed lecturer on Phrenology, Physiology and kindred topics, has received the patronage of the intelligence and respectability in Salem and vicinity, and whereas this delectable genius, by his loud mouthed professions of virtue, gained the confidence of a large proportion of the citizens of this place, among whom were many females of the first families of Salem, and was tendered a set of complimentary resolutions by the members of the . . . Sons of Temperance of this place at a Temperance Lecture delivered by the said De Wolfe at the Methodist Church of this place not long since, and whereas his conduct has latterly completely gainsayed the high opinion many of the Salemites had formed of him; and as he was compelled to make his exit from the city in the darkened hours of the night to escape the infliction of the penalty his licentiousness had earned for him.

"In order, therefore, to counteract the influence of the aforesaid resolutions which were passed *prior* to the disgraceful exhibition of shamelessness of the rake heart of this wandering licentiate . . . and to warn the citizens of Southern Oregon, California and elsewhere to beware of the fell destroyer—this He Wolfe in sheep's clothing, whose only object is to seek out victims on whom to satiate the brutal lusts of his corrupted and extremely vitiated carcass, We, the undersigned, citizens of Salem and vicinity in Indignation Meeting assembled, this 20th day of November, 1861, unanimously resolve:

"First. That Dr. H. C. De Wolfe is an inflated mountebank, a thorough going, rotten hearted hypocrite; a miserable, low bred, self-abandoned and licentious profligate, and an itinerate libertine, unfit to run at large, and unworthy the appelation of a man.

"Second. That Dr. H. C. De Wolfe is an unscrupulous liar, an unprinciple slanderer and that we heartily despise a wretch who would wantonly insult a respectable female, and then ruthlessly assault her womanly virtue [this apparently verbally, by claiming she'd given him the come hither] to vindicate and justify such diabolic outrage.

"Third. That the monkey menial who attends this celebrated teacher of morality is only fitted to do the bidding of the master now employing him. . . .

"Fourth. That we . . . are prepared to establish that the pol-

luted and designing Doctor and his man Friday, have given sufficient cause to warrant the publication of these resolutions, and
we earnestly solicit the perambulating quack Doctor, and his
'capping' servant, to return to Salem and receive at the hands
of an outraged community the merited chastisement so well deserved."

Leaving the cits of Salem breathing tautological fire, this chapter will now turn to less passionate aspects of the record. One
sort was provided at large by Robert E. Strahorn. Leaving his
post on the Denver *Agriculturist and Stockman,* he rambled all
over the northern moiety of the West, issuing now valued
pamphlets as he went. *The Handbook to Wyoming and Guide
to the Black Hills,* Cheyenne, 1877, was one; *To the Rockies and
Beyond,* Omaha, 1878, was a second; *The Resources of Montana
Territory,* Helena, 1879, a third; *The Resources and Attractions
of Idaho Territory,* Boise City, 1881, a fourth; and *Where Rolls
the Oregon,* Denver, 1882, a fifth.

Of the same category, but more localized, was a work by Matt
Alderson, whose authorship of a carriers' petition for the Butte,
Montana *Daily Miner* has already been noticed. At one time
editor of the Bozeman *Avant Courier,* Matt put through its job
shop, in 1883, a pamphlet called *Bozeman, a guide to its places
of recreation and a synopsis of its superior natural resources.*

Then there were chronicles of communities by newspapermen
who couldn't wait for cabin and shanty burgs to flourish for a
decade before furnishing them with accounts of their ancient
beginnings and illustrious annals since. In 1859 Denver had been
so unsure of what it was to be called that William Byers had
hedged by stating only that the *Rocky Mountain News* was published on the banks of Cherry Creek. Yet seven years later *News*
editor Junius E. Wharton published *History of the City of Denver from its Earliest Settlement to the Present Time.*

A score of years after Joe Ellis Johnson had used the stump of
a tree as his sanctum at Omaha, that town was treated to glimpses
of its distant youth by Albert R. Sorenson of the Omaha *Bee.*
Published in 1876, his work was titled *Early History of Omaha, or
Walks and Talks among the Old Settlers.*

It might be thought that these were as rare and rickety as Spanish-American War veterans in the mid-twentieth century. As most of said settlers were young when they followed Joe across the wide Missouri, however, the old timers among them were mostly in their forties or even late thirties, when Sorenson interviewed them.

Yet there was one pioneer community chronicle which had better things to report of the past than the present. This was Dan De Quille's *History of the Comstock Lode and Mines,* published at Virginia City in 1889.

That was Nevada's entry, of course. Montana's Virginia City had stormy criminal annals which found their narrator in Thomas Dimsdale, editor of the *Post.* Serialized in that paper in 1865, the story of the malign Henry Plummer gang, and of how these were dealt with by the citizenry, was published in book form a year later.

The broadside with which the author promoted *The Vigilantes of Montana, or Popular Justice in the Rockies* is interesting because of showing that Dimsdale thought the local system of currency superior to that of the federal government. "Now complete and for sale. An impartial and correct history of the Vigilantes of Montana Territory. Price per copy in dust, $2.00; in green backs, $2.25."

Inevitably bracketed with this work, because it also deals with localized Western violence, was a book covering Wyoming's Johnson County War, between small- and large-scale cattle raisers. Its author was Asa Shinn Mercer, who had published sheets in Oregon and Texas before launching the *Northwest Livestock Journal* in Cheyenne. There in 1894 he published a book that has joined Dimsdale's as a classic of its kind, the title being *The Banditti of the Plains.*

Accounts of Indian wars—John Wesley Wilbarger's *Indian Depredations in Texas,* Austin, 1889, is but the most generally familiar title—crop up among the imprints of all the Western states. As for the many tales of enslavement by Indians, the one which has drawn most notice is *The Captivity of the Oatman Girls,* published in San Francisco, as of 1857, by Royal Stratton.

Formidable as to bulk, this body of first-line historical source material makes for the most part grim reading. More cheerful looks at the redskins were occasionally taken, however. In the course of a series of articles contributed to *Overland Monthly* in 1894—later issued in book form under the title *Building a State in Apache Land*—the several times noticed Charles Poston did this.

Charles knew a lot about the aborigines, too, having had particular occasion for studying them while he was serving as Arizona's first Indian agent in 1864. That mostly meant association with the friendly Pimas, of whose methods of reasoning he was pleased to report a couple.

"In my intercourse with these Indians for many years they frequently asked questions which would puzzle the most profound philosopher to answer. For instance, they inquired, 'Who made the world and everything therein?'

"I replied, 'God.'

" 'Where does he live?'

" 'In the sky.'

" 'What does he sit on?' "

Poston didn't preserve his answer to that one. Instead he went on to report a discussion re kinship which he had once had with a brave. "When I was Superintendent of Indian Affairs, I selected a stalwart Pima named Luis, who was proud of his acquirements in the English language and gave him a uniform, sword and epaulettes about the size of a saucer, to stand guard in front of my headquarters. One day when I came out and found Luis walking with an ununiformed Pima, with their arms around each other's waists, according to their custom, I inquired, 'Luis, who is that?'

" 'That is my brother-in-law.'

" 'Did you marry his sister?'

" 'No.'

" 'Did he marry your sister?'

" 'No.'

" 'Then how is he your brother-in-law?'

" 'We swapped wives.' "

A few men of print became versed in the lore of the Indians living in their respective regions and made valuable recordings. One of these was Samuel Clarke of the Portland *Oregonian* and Salem *Statesman.*

Mistakenly, for Hippocrene just wasn't his brand, Sam encased his findings in verse. As such it was poor stuff, but some of the material was fascinating; and so thought a New York editor who somehow got hold of a collection of poems which Clarke had published in Salem in 1872. It thus happened that the February 1874 issue of *Harper's New Monthly Magazine* ran several of Sam's pieces under the title *Legends of the Cascades.*

The best of these was *The Legend of the Tillamook,* based on an Indian tradition of the discovery of America by people of superior civilization, sailing from west of the Pacific instead of east of the Atlantic. In this case, though, the ship from overseas had been wrecked in place of sailing back to Asia with word of the New World. There had been no follow-up, accordingly, of a discovery made in a craft whose cargo in chief was beeswax.

In that lay the primary substantiation of the Indian tale. The bee was such a newcomer to America that it didn't reach parts of the West until well into the nineteenth century. Yet white pioneers kept turning up ancient deposits of beeswax along Tillamook Bay, where the Indians swore that the ship from beyond the sunset had cracked up.

There was more to the story than that, because there was a survivor of the mysterious sailing vessel—believed, from its description, to have been a Chinese junk—who was a man of organizational parts. Marooned among savages, he not only came to be hailed as their chief, but used his following to put himself at the head of the multi-tribal empire he proceeded to build with the aid of a superior navy. Of these apparently sail-powered warcraft, Clarke noted that

> From broad Columbia down to Coos
> They swooped as if by eagles flown,
> And still they say that no canoes
> Like these have ever since been known.

The man from west of the West not only made himself monarch of an all-conquering confederacy; he imposed his religion—assumed from descriptions of its rites to have been Buddhist—upon Oregon's natives. There was something more concrete than tradition to lean on here, for there was a sacred grove, sworn to as the site of some has-been holy structure, which the Indians still tiptoed around in the 1870s.

Even more unexpected than Clarke's Oregon find is the wholly native lore which Junius Wharton put between the covers of a pamphlet in 1889. The same fellow who authored the first history of Denver, Junius was then operating in Phoenix, Arizona.

Wharton's inability to get along with fellow Coloradoans has been mentioned. Whether or not he had decided that he wasn't temperamentally suited for newspaper work by the time he reached the desert, he does not seem to have been engaged in it while there. But he made at least one friend—a Pima old enough to have learned tribal lore before confidence in it was vitiated via contact with conquering Christians—and from him he obtained the material he incorporated in *The Sun God, An Indian Edda*.

Unlike Clarke's book of poems, this work did not come to the attention of any Eastern editor. It seems, indeed, to have been as ignored by Wharton's contemporaries as it has since been by literary historians. Yet it is on all counts a work deserving to be known.

Again, unlike Sam Clarke, Junius was an able poet. Always competent and sometimes packing plenty of lyric punch, he used some 650 lines of verse to make a clear presentation of the complex of beliefs expounded by the ancient Pima medicine man.

> And then they told the wondrous deeds
> Of Zaptor Zee and Zinktor Zun
> Who gave earth life to serve all needs
> At signal from the God of Sun.

The substance of *The Sun God* is a cosmology, and a more sophisticated one than any attributed to America's other tribes. Wharton properly subtitled it "Indian Edda," because it resembles the Norse ones in telling how the world will be destroyed as well as how it came into being.

Not geocentric, Pima cosmology held that the world was at once a perishable and replaceable unit, which had become habitable after a mass of molten matter, flung into space by the sun, developed a crust by cooling. While it remains fiery at the core, it will survive; but it will be destroyed when it loses its vitalizing central heating system. For it will be sucked back into the flaming center of the universe for renewal of the qualities it will have lost through cooling.

Such was the history not only of all worlds but of the two sub-deities in charge of each. The one who happened to be in command of this current world was Zaptor Zee, the also mentioned Zaptor Zun acting as his executive officer. Both dwelt in the earth's molten core, rejoicing in the heat that defined their period of continuity.

When they and their world will be called home for rehabilitation, human life won't cease to be, for the Sun God will vitalize the replacement. As for immortality, the life force was the only one recognized by the old-time Pimas. Consistent with their other beliefs, they held that souls left dead bodies as sparks, which flew to merge with the fiery center from which vitality originally came.

Along with such matters, *The Sun God* summarized Pima history. Of this it is sufficient to say that the tribe had one novel notion. In place of blaming all failures and loss of impetus on the white man, these Indians traced decline from happier days to a distant period when their civilization was wrecked by invading demons—a memory, no doubt, of the overrunning of an agricultural people by nomads.

There is one more thing to say of this remarkable work. It is illuminated by notes which show Junius to have been a scholar with a broad general background.

To leave writers about redskins only, in favor of those who dealt at large with both races, frontier journalists wrote histories of most of the Western states. Clement Lounsberry, of the *Bismark Tribune,* chronicled North Dakota, for instance; Julius Sterling Morton, of the Nebraska City *News,* wrote the story of his state; and the frequently noticed Sam Davis that of Nevada.

Among other records kept were reports of explorations. Author of a standard account of the Santa Fe Trail—known because it was published in New York—Henry Inman, of the Larned, Kansas *Enterprise,* had previously written of another wilderness thoroughfare. His work called *The Great Salt Lake Trail* was an 1889 Topeka imprint. Then there was a book belonging to the same general class by John H. Marion of the *Arizona Miner.* In 1870 John accompanied a military party which was making a reconnaissance of little-visited sections of Apache land. Upon his return he published at Prescott *Notes of Travel through Arizona, Being an Account of a trip made by General* [George] *Stoneman and others.*

There were, besides, accounts of individual experiences. The great period of remembering frontier things past didn't come along until the twentieth century. Sooners existed, though, and Horace Bell, of the Los Angeles *Porcupine,* produced his always entertaining, if not so pervasively reliable, *Reminiscences of A Ranger* as early as 1881.

But newspapermen sometimes ghosted for old timers before the frontier had run its course; and a handsome piece of work of this kind was published at Salt Lake City in 1893. Bearing the deceptive title of *The First Baby in Camp,* the pamphlet covers some of the experiences of a retired stagecoach driver named William Bennett.

At one time, too, he was a crack driver for Wells, Fargo Express, speeding between the railhead at Reno and Nevada's Virginia City. There was by good chance a rivalry between Bennett's outfit and the Pacific Express Company, which led to breakneck races and frenzied betting by backers of both entries. And it was into this situation that George Francis Train unwittingly intruded.

The tale of Horace Greeley's ride to Virginia with a stagecoach driver named Hank Monk has often been repeated, but Train's far-livelier ride with Bill Bennett has been generally ignored. In his day George Francis was every bit as well known as Horace, having a flair for publicity as well as a knack for doing and saying the unusual. But he was particularly noted as a globe trotter, having circled the world in the then fabulous time of sixty-seven days under the aegis of the Tacoma, Washington *Evening Telegraph.*

Still he hadn't seen anything until he got off the train at Reno, just as Bill was getting set to uphold the honor of Wells, Fargo again. What then transpired purports to be written by Bennett himself, but internal evidence shows that it was actually penned by a former Virginia City newspaperman, who had ridden with Bill in such races. Whoever he was, he remembered his experience well enough to picture what it must have been like for a tenderfoot. And sometimes he got so carried away by zest for his subject that he forgot about prose and guffawed in verse.

As the Reno train was late, the famous man couldn't wait for the stagecoach. But, having made arrangements in advance, he hustled up to where Bill was raring to get off his marks.

"'My name is George Francis Train. I am to lecture at Virginia City tonight and Mr. Latham telegraphed me that I could ride with you.'

"'But I can't. Damn if I'm going to let that pony beat me on account of George Francis Train or anybody else.'

"'But I'm billed to——'

"'All right. Jump aboard quick! Let 'em go!'

"And with a slap, dash and fierce jerk as the express bag was tossed on the buckboard, away they went amid cheering yells. . . . Over the bridge across the Truckee they bounced and out onto the Virginia City road, George Train holding fast to his seat and his breath at the same time.

> There was no time to think or joke
> On such a trip as that;
> Train, do not let your hold get broke
> And watch out for your hat.

"As they flew down the first slope . . . south of the bridge, Train's hat danced off, notwithstanding the warning already given him, and Bennett impatiently drew up a moment and George recovered his hat.

"'That's all right this time,' says Bennett, 'but next time your hat stays behind.'

"Poor Train was to be pitied; the flying gravel and sharp dodging seemed to be more than he could bear. Bennett wore a veil extending from the rim of his hat down over his face to protect it from the sharp pebbles and gravel spitefully thrown back from the heels of the flying mustangs, while George Francis dodged and was blinded by the severe infliction until Bennett compassionately tore off a piece of his face protector and gave it to him.

> He pitied the sorrows of poor old Train
> But he had to get there on time. . . .

"Near Huffabie's Station a small bridge over a muddy little creek was obstructed by a ten mule team which was coming. Bennett promptly dodged the bridge and jumped the stream, the mud and water from wheels and heels spattering them finely.

" 'Don't let go of anything. Hang on and don't be afraid!' said Bennett.

"George Francis's eager attention to the general outlook was too fully occupied for reply."

Six changes of horses were made on a trip of twenty-two miles, "each change occupying merely a few seconds. . . . In fact the buckboard would merely have come to a standstill before Bennett, grabbing the lines thrown to him, sang out, 'let 'em go'; and away they did go like a comet. . . .

"The somewhat slower rush up the steep Geiger grade gave Train a chance to collect his bewildered ideas," but "about that time . . . they went tearing and plunging more furiously than ever along the level and downward grades approaching Virginia City.

"Near the Sierra Mining Works, another one of those obstacles, in the form of a big hay team heavily laden, stood in the middle of the road, blockading the way completely, and Bennett, knowing no such word as fail, at once plunged his fiery team over the grade down through the sage brush and rocks and around up onto the road again, right side up and nobody hurt. Train's hair fairly stood on end. He set his teeth together, his eyes glared and his tongue was paralyzed.

> This was indeed an episode
> That would fore'er his memory load,
> And Bennett's name would linger till
> Death had made him cold and still."

When they at length dashed into Virginia City, Train was gratified to find what he took for a mass reception committee, but which turned out to be fans there to see how the race came out. It was a Wells, Fargo day, as Bennett and his series of teams took the measure of the Pacific Express Company rider and his relays of ponies. The winning time for covering twenty-two miles of unimproved road in a light wagon, bouncing over horrendous up-and-down grades, was one hour and ten minutes. But it could have been worse for George Francis; he wasn't with Bennett the day Bill set the course record of fifty-eight minutes flat.

18

A LITERARY DUKE'S MIXTURE

TO THE EXTENT that it has been assessed at all, Western literature has largely been measured in terms of the works about it published in the East. Although lists of pioneer imprints have been compiled with respect to most of the states considered in this chronicle, investigation has all but stopped there. The full depth and range of pioneer publications are therefore unknowns, but an attempt to give some idea of what the men of print published locally will be made in the ensuing two chapters.

Novels weren't commonly published on the frontier, because the demand for fiction in the ballooning cities of the Atlantic seaboard—the West never knew such boom towns as the immigrant hordes produced in the East—was running ahead of supply. It's hardly too much to say that anybody, game to stick with any sort of a story for the requisite number of pages, could find somebody to publish it in New York, Philadelphia, or Boston during most of the nineteenth century. Wherefore, and the record shows that this was a practice, Western fiction writers could entrust their manuscripts to eastward-bound friends, with the justified confidence that publication would result.

In spite of that dispensation, a few novels worth noting were published on the frontier. A hope that more may turn up springs from the history of the earliest so far discovered. It was not issued in San Francisco nor any of the towns which came to be recognized as pioneer publishing centers. Rather it was the production, the year being 1852, of the raw mining camp of Marysville, California.

Entewa, the Mountain Bird, a Romance of California founded on fact, was published by the job shop of the Marysville *Herald.*

Probably a writer for that sheet, its author was J. R. Poynter, M.D.; but knowledge about him stops there.

At present a lone copy has been located, the finder being that prince of Western imprint collectors, the late Thomas W. Streeter. Unfortunately the book is currently tied up in his estate, and is accordingly not available for examination either directly or via microfilm. Through the courtesy of Mrs. Streeter, however, it is possible to give some idea of the work's format and contents.

A paperback, *Entewa, the Mountain Bird* runs to 119 pages. Concerning it, Thomas Streeter made the following notation: "This is not only the first novel printed in California, but the scene is laid in the gold regions in 1849; and it is a first-class story with the villain of the piece a bandit whose crimes were ascribed to the Indians."

A novel with the curious fate of long being accepted as history was printed for the first of many times two years after *Entewa* made its obscure appearance. John Rollin Ridge was a Sacramento journalist who capitalized on popular interest in the career of a Mexican bandit by undertaking to provide him with a romantic past. Using the pseudonym Yellowbird, Ridge published *The Life and Adventures of Joaquin Murrieta* in San Francisco. As the newspapers of that city had previously found nothing to tell the public about a character who was the talk of 1854, they hailed Yellowbird's invention as straight biography.

Having nothing else to go on either, historians next found factuality in a work which out-Dumased Dumas. It wasn't seriously challenged, indeed, for about a full century, at which point the knowledgeable Joseph Henry Jackson made it clear that the very subject was apocryphal. What Jackson's researches taught him, in a word, was that Joaquin de Murrieta was a composite bandit —a name used by newspapermen of the 1850s as the perpetrator of all the crimes committed by dozens of faceless Mexican rogues.

It is pleasing to report that the sound work of an able critic did no harm to the popularity of Ridge's novel. Still in print—and of how many novels published in the East in Yellowbird's day can that be said?—it shows no signs of lapsing from it. From the first *The Life and Adventures of Joaquin Murrieta* was read because people love stories about wronged aristocrats who help the downtrodden while getting square with their enemies. But even such tried fare has to be served up with zip in order to last, and as John Rollin succeeded in tingling spines, his work has endured.

The history of another novel by a Westerner contradicts the statement that Eastern publishing houses would accept anything in the way of fiction. That wasn't the experience of Edgar Watson Howe, who'd moved from the Golden, Colorado *Globe* to the Atchison, Kansas one. But then Howe had produced a serious piece of realism in a day when the book market was not rife with such items.

Turned down by all the leading publishing houses, Edgar Howe began printing *The Story of a Country Town* in the job shop of the Atchison *Globe*. He set the type himself, managing a page a day while carrying on as editor and publisher of his paper.

Differing from most of his colleagues, Howe was a pessimist. The town he let others see through his eyes was no queen city in the making; it was a graceless trull that he exposed to view in 1883. As Howe wasn't a natural storyteller and had no ear for dialogue, his work seemed likely to be an Atchison stay-at-home. In it, though, was Edgar's powerfully realized concept of an isolated community after it had lost all the forward motion and creative effort which energize pioneering. As critics grasped as much, a publisher wasn't long in taking an interest in a book they praised. Rejected in manuscript, *The Story of a Country Town* was reprinted on the Atlantic seaboard in place of being originally issued there.

What was true of lengthy fiction held good for smaller efforts. Those who could peddle their wares in preferred markets did so; and the famed hands of the West—Mark Twain, Bret Harte, and Ambrose Bierce—published their short-story collections elsewhere.

Yet two able men did not follow suit. One of these was a Sacramento and mining-camp newspaperman called Alonzo Delano and the other was the frequently introduced Sam Davis. At Sacramento in 1856 Alonzo published his assortment of prose pieces under the title of *Old Block's Sketch Book*. And twenty-nine years later Sam put his *Short Stories* through the press at San Francisco.

Each of these volumes is remarkable on the score of including a delightful number dealing with known figures in the realm of pioneer journalism. Because of its calendar priority, *Old Block's* will be noticed first.

Brief as it is, *The Phantom Court* is a worthy addition to the tales of Never-Never Land experiences, of which Lucian's *Icaromenippus* was a charter member and Carroll's *Alice* books the supreme realization. Beating Alice to the punch by nine years, Old Block had a marvelous dream which he owed, as she presumably did not, to overdrafts of lager beer.

Borne away by a demonic cat that later doubles as a bailiff, Block winds up in a court peopled by fellow figures of Sacramento's fourth estate. Presiding as judge was Ferdinand Ewer, formerly of the *Transcript* but then editor of the *Pioneer*, the San Francisco literary magazine to which Block was a prized contributor. Also present were A. C. Edmonds, editor of the *Star of the Pacific;* Richard Rust, of the *Democratic State Journal;* James Allen, of the *State Tribune;* Edwin Waite, of the *Union;* and Yellowbird, or John Rollin Ridge, of the *Bee.* Running a rival show and presiding as bartender was John Phoenix, or Lieutenant George Horatio Derby, who was another *Pioneer* contrib. On his setup was emblazoned:

Phoenix bitters—One bit a glass.

Squibob, proprietor.

Testifying are John Bee, or former Governor John Bigler; Yankee Sullivan, once the world's heavyweight prize-ring champ; and David (not yet U.S. Senator, but in there pitching) Broderick. For a change of pace, Lola Montez flits on and off the scene. Meanwhile, the cat takes no nonsense from anybody, which requires some doing, as there is plenty on hand, served up with a nice touch.

In *The Typographical Howitzer* Sam Davis recounted a little-known episode in the joint lives of Mark Twain and Dan De

Quille. It seems that before joining the *Territorial Enterprise* they had trekked north of San Francisco, taking with them the printing outfit with which they intended to start a paper in Mendocino County. En route they met a party of immigrants from Lower California, towing a cannon which they had needed for protection against Indians in Mexico but which they felt they could now dispense with. They were therefore glad to sell it to Mark, together with a couple of kegs of powder, for fifty dollars.

Although Dan wasn't sure the money was spent wisely, Twain reassured him. "When we start our paper we must fire a salute." If that was a sentimental consideration, Mark also had a practical one. "If a man comes in for a retraction, we can blow him into the next county."

By the powder blast, he meant. Not having foreseen any need for cannon shot, Twain had bought none.

Yet when he and Dan were camping in the Mendocino wilds that night, warpath redskins surrounded them. Hoping to scare the Indians by the roar of the explosion, Mark crammed powder into the howitzer. But just before the big gun was fired, Dan stuffed the muzzle with something which brought cries of anguish from the savages.

"What in hell did you put in it?" Twain asked.

"A column of solid nonpareil and a couple of sticks of your spring poetry."

"The poetry did the business, Dan. Get one of your geological articles ready for the next charge, and I guess it'll let the red devils out for this campaign. . . ."

The two men of print got even rougher than that before the battle was over; but this chronicle will turn from that carnage to give some account of Western contributions to the stage. If Old Block published his *A Live Woman in the Mines* in New York, other playwrights had their works printed locally.

The earliest was one based on Yellowbird's novel about Murrieta in 1858; but as its author was a loblolly, there's no reason to name him or his work. Charles Henry Webb's *Our Friend from Victoria*, which 1865 saw published in San Francisco, is more pleasant to contemplate. Cited in a foregoing chapter as editor of the *Californian,* Webb had a wit that was agile, if not awe-inspiring; and by anyone versed in the jokes and social infighting of the Coast at that period, his farce can yet be found worth scanning. Its real value, though, lies in the light it casts on the theatrical fare enjoyed by the scribblers then rounding into shape for national recognition by the Golden Gate. Mark Twain, Bret Harte, Prentice Mulford, and Charles Warren Stoddard must all have taken special delight in a show, featuring Western slants, which was written by the drum major of their own pen and bottle band.

Another play with a Mark Twain association was *The Psycho-scope, a Sensational Drama in Five Acts,* by Joseph T. Goodman and Rollin M. Daggett. Published in Virginia City in 1871, its scene was New York rather than any part of the West. But one of its main characters is a reporter—the "local" in fact that Mark was when working for the *Territorial Enterprise*—and he supplies a lively and no doubt accurate summary of the professional attitude toward news voiced in the city room of the West's most famous paper.

SCENE II—A Street

Enter Tripp with a note-book in hand

Tripp (looking at his watch) Past two o'clock. Hot and sultry with the suggestion of a storm. (looks up) No, it will not storm. It never does when I want it to. What a blessing a hurricane would be, with thunder like a cannonade to frighten horses, rain to flood streets, and cellars, lightning to tear church steeples to splinters! There would be meat in such a feast as that! I have traveled like a locomotive since nine this morning, and could crowd everything I have discovered in the shape of news into the length of this pencil . . . (opens his notebook). RUNAWAY ON FULTON STREET. Now if some fellow had not caught the horses, they would have darted through a drug store window, I know they would. . . . Some people have an insanity for stopping runaway horses in the streets, and generally rendering themselves obnoxious to report-ers. The news of the death of such men is always gratifying to me. . . . *Attempted suicide in Blee[c]ker Street.* Good for half a column if discreetly handled. *Large dog bit a small boy in Grubb's Alley.* Something in this. I can frighten the parents by following the item by an essay on hydrophobia. *Bursting of a soda fountain on Broadway.* No danger of consequence but a chance to indulge a bit of humor. *An elopement in Fifth Avenue.* I will keep this until tomorrow and give it sensational headings. . . . *Row in Central Park . . . An excited Cripple Woman*—Well, I can make something of a showing after all (closing notebook). Ah, here comes Captain McNabb. I may be able to pump a paragraph or two out of him.

As the authors obviously had fun writing *The Psychoscope*, the reader is cut in for a share. It was billed, as has been noted, as a "Sensational Drama." A different type of excitement was aimed at, and to some extent brought off, by Hiram H. McClane, whose *The Capture of the Alamo* was published at San Antonio in 1886.

In a forenote to his five-act, blank-verse tragedy, McClane described himself as author of *Irene Viesca; a Tale of the Magee Expedition in the Gauchapin War in Texas in 1812–13.* He also stated that his grandfather, and the presumptive source of his information, was a veteran of said filibustering try. If anywhere still extant, Hiram's novel has not been located by this chronicler. But the very name of the work is of peculiar interest here, as the finale of what McClane called the Gauchapin War was the engagement on the Medina River in which Aaron Mower—the West's first typesetter—is believed to have lost his life.

As for McClane himself, nothing seems to be known except that he was probably a newspaperman who wrote *The Capture of the Alamo* in connection with a semi-centennial celebration of the greatest event in San Antonio's history. As he was not a poet, his lines seldom get off the ground. Yet his concept was interesting, and he keeps his play from being stridently melodramatic by using the earthy comments of Davy Crockett as a sort of chorus.

McClane was dead right as to how to finish his piece, too. Another man might have had the final stand made by some well-worded hero blatting lines about Thermopylae and the like. But Hiram gave the big scene to Crockett, who went down growling

and showing his teeth, with never a word to spare for anything
but defiance voiced in frontier terms. Nor is it a well-ordered
series of brags that he grinds out while swinging the butt of his
rifle at the men who have him cornered. It is rather just such a
jumble of notions as might have rambled through the brain of an
old cock when on his last legs.

> Bring on yer lioners and tigers,
> Yer catermounts and alligators,
> For I'm half hoss and half alligator myself I ar;
> Bring on yer sea hoss, yer red hoss, and yer land terrapin,
> Yer white bar, yer black bar and yer grizler bar
> Yer big fish, yer little fish and yer whales,
> Yer boer-constrictors, yer snappin' turtles and yer tad poles,
> Yer black-and-tans, yer grey hounds and yer terriers,
> Yer bob-tail cats, yer long-tail cats and yer ring-tail roarers.
> For I'm the he-coon of the valleys
> And the she-coon of the ridges!
> I'm the old eriginal zip-coon,
> And that other coon er sottin' on er rail,
> And I'm that same old coon
> What allus was a coon
> And that never got a lickin' till yet. . . .

Belles-lettres got an occasional nod from the aforementioned
James Gally. A regular contributor to the *Territorial Enterprise*
under the name of Single-line, James also wrote for the *Overland
Monthly* and the *Argonaut*. Among his never collected works was
an article published in that last magazine, titled *Snakes*. Orna-
mented with learned allusions, it does not overlook the most famous one in the history of romance.

"Everybody can certainly have read of or seen the engravings
of the serpents in the ancient coronets of the Nile. Everybody has
read or heard of Mrs. Ptolemy and the asp; which is a very
ancient story, a very salacious story, and therefore pawed all over
by the poets. I care little about Mrs. Ptolemy, but I am interested
in the asp, hence I give the true story as follows:

> She put him in her bosom,
> Then pinched his little tail.
> The reptile gave a wiggle
> And the sorceress a wail,

And then she cried, 'O Anthony!'
And turned exceeding pale—
But the serpent died instanter
While the harlot went to jail."

The result of researches on a more formidable scale, a *History of Medicine and Surgery from the Earliest Times* was published in Portland in 1884. Its writer was William L. Adams, earlier noticed as the author of the verse political satire called *Treason, Stratagems and Spoils*.

Charles Warren Stoddard's studies of South Sea life and his work on Hawaiian lepers were published in the East. That is where Prentice Mulford issued a report of his life and musings while in California, too. Yet a former *Overland Monthly* associate, whose book was to prove one of the most provocative works ever written by an American, published *Progress and Poverty* in San Francisco.

Henry George took an active part in the publishing, too, for he had reacted as had Edgar Howe, with respect to the rejection of *The Story of a Country Town*. Cold-shouldered by editors in the East, Henry enlisted the services of a couple of fellow printers and set type for his book himself in 1879. Hailed or hated, his work stirred up so much controversy that once again an Atlantic seaboard publisher had to swallow in print what he had turned down in manuscript.

Now George couldn't have written *Progress and Poverty*, if he hadn't been a Westerner. The differences in the destinies of the haves and haven'ts had bothered him when a sailor in India. Yet California was a perfect laboratory in which to look specimens over. Starting from the scratch of a country where bygones meant nothing, all the early comers theoretically had a chance to live on the right side of the railroad tracks. But that isn't what had taken place, especially in San Francisco, where Henry lived. By the middle 1870s there was a cluster of moneybags perched on Nob Hill, while down below were slums culminating in the civic atrocity known as the Barbary Coast.

In less than three decades, in brief, California had come up with an imbalance the like of the one that India had taken 3000 years to develop. It was something for a cash-minded philosopher to mull over, and George not only faced the problem but offered answers that are still being discussed, if not acted on, by political economists today.

"Taxes which lack the element of certainty tell most fearfully upon morals," he pointed out. "Our revenue laws as a body might well be entitled 'Acts to promote the corruption of public officials to suppress honesty and encourage public fraud.'. . . . This is their true character, and they succeed admirably." And he had an idea which was a rider to that. "A corrupt democratic government must finally corrupt the people, and when a people become corrupt, there is no resurrection. The life is gone, only the carcass remains; and it is left for the plowshare of fate to bring it out of sight."

The other great work of non-fiction printed in the West during the pioneer era was the book Ned McGowan wrote at the close of his year as a fugitive from injustice. Although he could not safely return to San Francisco in 1857, he arranged for the publication of his work in that stronghold of his enemies, where he also had faithful friends. Among these was a printer named Jeremiah Sullivan. From his press was issued *The Narrative of Edward Mc-Gowan, Including a Full Account of the Author's Adventures and Perils While Persecuted by the San Francisco Committee of Vigilance of 1856.*

There is nothing in literature quite comparable to this human document. For, along with the many other qualities he marshaled, Ned was a poet. Unlike many such, he could write prose with blood in it, too; and as he had a poet's ability to nail sensations down on paper, the result was a masterpiece of autobiography.

The title of his work mentioned "adventures and perils," of which he endured an amazing profusion. Here was a man who within the compass of a few days of civic hysteria was reduced from a prosperous and politically prominent attorney to the quarry of a lynch mob. He was a quarry, moreover, that couldn't break and run for it; he was trapped in a city of which all the land and sea exits were watched. Largely composed of an organized army, the vigilantes had established patrols which were active on a twenty-four-hour basis. Having thus blocked retreat, Ned's hunters commenced the systematic ransacking of the city for him.

McGowan's narrative tells what it was like to lurk in hiding alone for weeks, while knowing that thousands—some of them occasionally seen and heard by him—were relentlessly seeking to stamp out his life. It also tells what it was like to escape via the nerve-twisting means of walking past his hunters in disguise.

"The starlight that glistened back from the sabres of my enemies was not more quick and sudden in its coming and going than the changes of my thoughts from hope to fear and back again from fear to hope as, marking every incident around me, I walked unquestioned and unheeded through the meshes of the net my persecutors had thrown around me."

But Ned hadn't left trouble behind by slipping out of San Francisco. Inspired by that city's vigilantes, a mob in Santa Barbara came very close to doing him in. The odds against his escape were at that time so great that nobody could understand how he had managed it; and it was only when Ned published his *Narrative* that the mystery was resolved.

McGowan's deliverer was a noted sportsman turned outlaw, who undertook to horn in while Ned and two friends were haplessly listening to the shouts of approaching lynchers. "At this moment, when I was giving up all for lost, a horseman came dashing toward me at full speed, mounted on a beautiful animal, magnificently caparisoned. . . . It was Jack Power. Bandit and Destroying Angel though he may be, he was my guardian angel then, and may Heaven, which sent him to succor me, be merciful to him in his hour of need. . . .

" 'Judge,' said he, 'there is no time to lose. Will you trust yourself to me? I will protect you as far as I am able.'

"Parkinson and Dennison didn't want me to leave them, but I knew Power's desperate courage well and would have chosen him out of the whole state for a partner in a desperate fight. . . . In less than three minutes Dennison was arrested, but I had vanished.

"Jack ran with me about twenty yards up a street at right angles with the one in which he found us, passed me through the window of a house, rolled me up in about forty yards of carpeting he had found lying on the floor, told the woman of the house, in Spanish, what he had done . . . and then rushed out and joined the pursuit after me, louder than the loudest. . . . It was all done in less time than it has taken me to tell it. I had in an instant, as it were, been snatched from certain death.

"As I afterward learned, there were at least a hundred men in pursuit, some mounted and some on foot, armed with guns, pistols and swords. . . . The din was terrible, and the tramping of hoofs and yells of the mob as the chase swept pell-mell, up one street and down another . . . now roaring past the very house in which I was lying and next dying away in the distance. They ransacked Santa Barbara but came not to me. *Jack Power was leading them.*"

An important feature of Ned's *Narrative* is the array of newspaper reports with which it is documented. Through these the reader is able to follow the chase, as understood by the pursuers as well as the pursued. It's a bonnie book, and only because of the obloquy that dogged McGowan beyond the grave has it so far failed of being recognized as the ornament of American literature which it is in spades.

Another fugitive had better literary luck than Ned. Before Fred Hart was chased from the sanctum of the *Territorial Enterprise,* he was in better control of one at Austin, Nevada. *The Reese River Reveille* was his paper there, and on doings in connection with it Fred based *The Sazerac Lying Club.* Published in San Francisco in 1878, it has been freely drawn upon by modern anthologists and was tapped for a quote in an earlier chapter here.

Fred's work might be described as a sort of Western version of Christopher North's *Noctes Ambrosianae,* with Sazerac brandy playing the role in Nevada that Glenlivet whiskey did in Scotland. To this chronicler the annals of the club seem better in concept than in execution, but the book is interesting as a picture of a mining camp's social life and the part that oral narratives played in it. In common with the *Decameron, The Sazerac Lying Club* is essentially a string of yarns told by a coterie of individual spinners. But the tall tale is a bubble that has to be artfully blown; and not all the club's members knew the difference between using just the right amount of breath and giving the extra puffs that collapse the structure and make it a parody of itself.

The pioneer West had one fine parodist in the person of Bret Harte. Many of his take-offs were included in his *Condensed Novels and Other Papers,* published at San Francisco in 1867. But as that title does not make clear, he was skilled at burlesques in verse; witness a spoof of Longfellow's hexameters contributed to the *Territorial Enterprise,* when Bret made an 1866 visit to Virginia City.

In *The Stage Driver's Story,* a jehu of the stamp of Bill Bennett tells of a remarkable trip to the Comstock, complicated by the loss of wheels. After relating that he had lost two of them, the driver tells of how he fared on the very slope that later paralyzed George Francis Train.

As some huge boulder, unloosed from its rocky shelf on the mountain,
Drives before it the hare and the timorous ground squirrel, far leaping,
So down the Geiger Grade rushed the Pioneer Coach, and before it
Leaped the wild horses, and shrieked in advance of the danger impending.

But to be brief in my tale; again ere we came to the level,
Slipped from its axle a wheel, so that—to be plain in my statement——
A matter of twelve hundred yards or more, as the distance may be,
We traveled upon *one* until we drove up to the station.

That is my story, sir; a trifle, indeed, I assure you;
Much more, perchance, might be said, but I hold him of all men most lightly
Who swerves from the truth in his tale. No, thank you—well, since you are pressing,
Perhaps I don't care if I do—you may give me the same. Jim—no sugar.

Remaining to be dealt with in this chaper are two views of an American way of life at which the nation's literature seldom looks. Although untold millions of the country's male citizens belong to other than college fraternal orders, the creative writers of the United States have tended to pass the phenomenon by. Or at best they have made fun of institutions of whose inner workings they haven't been qualified by experience to give an accurate glimpse.

Outside of the pioneer West, that is. One for, and the other against, two of its authors made it clear that they knew what they were talking about when treating Freemasonry and the like.

The one who honored such a brotherhood was Richard R. Rees of Leavenworth, Kansas. In 1873 he there published *The Eleusinian Mysteries, a Drama Beginning with the Creation and Terminating with the Great Fire in London, A.D. 1666, and the Death of Sir Christopher Wren, in Four Acts; Comprising Eight Periods of Time.*

While that is a lot to stage in what was a pageant rather than a play, *The Eleusinian Mysteries* isn't as goofy as the subtitle makes it sound. Judge Rees, who seems to have been a frequent contributor to local papers, if perhaps not officially connected with any, had a logically worked-out idea. As for the title of his work, what it meant to him was expounded in a passage he labeled *Introductory.*

"It is believed with reason, that the ancient mysteries are all resolvable in one; that their varieties are but the different names and forms assumed in different countries, and at different times, acknowledging a common parentage in India's mystic rite, the undisputed mother of societies wherein was first conceived and taught the doctrines of the resurrection. Much as the Christian, the Mohammedan, or the Jew may have denounced the Brahman faith, it is from that school they all imbibe the faith in resurrection."

A free thinker, the judge was no more than giving Aryan beliefs the seniority which many scholars accorded them before there was any general understanding of how much earlier the civilizations of Sumer and Egypt were. But after saying as much in prose, Rees makes the numerous deities he introduces sound off in verse.

Here, for instance, is how Vishnu describes his functions:

> By my command the fields are redolent,
> The air is filled with music of the birds,
> The lowing herds give animation to the scene
> And to the dancing fishes are prescribed
> A thousand glistening hues.

If Osiris and Isis speak for Egypt, the Far East has a lone delegate:

Act I, Scene 3—The Chinese Empire. Brama, Vishnu, Siva and Buddha:
Buddha: Great Brama, God of all creative power,

> The representative of China and Japan, I come in deep
> Humility of heart to learn the origin of man,
> His progress and his destiny,
> That I may hence disseminate and to the creatures of
> Thy providence dispense the blessings of a hope
> Of immortality and bliss.

Yet what all the superior beings are working at, under Brahma's guidance, is to raise humanity to the point where it will be independent of Heaven's apron strings. That state of grace gets reached when the deities of Greece and Rome are at length heard from and Bacchus, of all unexpected personages, makes the following motion:

> Let men, not gods, from this time forth,
> Direct the helm of state, and of our mystic rite.
> I bid the earth farewell. To other realms the Gods
> Must now retire, and man, unaided by our counsels,
> Hence must guide the world.

Now the rite Bacchus talks about is the Masonic one. Shown as evolved through many centuries, the traditions of a fraternal order are thus recognized as a complete guiding philosophy, and a fico for any church. Now for Christopher Wren: As the great modern master builder, he symbolized the arrival at a level which succeeding Masons could be counted on to maintain.

So much for the passionate yea-saying of Judge Richard Rees of Leavenworth, Kansas. Judge Francis Henry, of Olympia, Washington, had divergent views. In fact, if he had ever shown Rees the *Lodge Odes* Frank published in 1868, Dick would have shot him.

In that event, Henry would probably have died laughing, for he was as much a man of mirth as was Rees a serious cousin. Reverence was not a part of the Olympian judge's make-up, and neither was delicacy. For he proved as much when running his

poems through the job shop of the Washington *Standard,* a paper
with which he can be visualized as having some connection.

The odes are aimed at a "sour faced" lot who "Ran a Lodge
they call the Templars," whose ritual and songs Henry proceeds
to satirize. Undoubtedly a renegade lodge member, he knew what
went on in the enemy's camp or he wouldn't have been able to cut
at his foes successfully; and he wanted to hit them where it hurt,
as well as to give joy to certain named cronies.

His method was to form a mock lodge and endow its rites with
just such immemorial standing and supernatural worth as Rees
had seriously predicated when writing of the Masons.

> Far back in the primitive ages,
> When all of creation was new,
> An order arose from the darkness
> And was christened U.F. of F. U.

Although Frank never said what the third initial and the following symbol stood for, he made it abundantly clear.

> 'Twas in an eastern garden
> Our ancient writers say,
> The founder of our order
> Did take the first degree;
> Did in his simple blindness
> The cursed apple bite
> Because with wicked kindness
> A woman did invite.

Even more explicit was a verse dealing with the last bugle blast;
and an archangel's insouciance as to however importantly or pleas-
urably engaged any mortal might be when he called a halt with
his trumpet. Nothing could better describe that impertinent instrument than the initials prefixed by Frank.

> The stars must fade, the sun decay
> And time itself must pass away,
> But we, but we, we won't knock under;
> We'll gather on that final morn
> When Gabriel toots his F. U. horn,
> For we, for we, we won't knock under.

But there was an earthly trumpet, too, which was a signal for
the brotherhood to assemble, and, in telling of it, Henry parodied
The Star-Spangled Banner.

> Though faint was that bugle when first it was blown
> Far back in the twilight of early creation,
> Like echoes that swell as the winds sweep them on,
> Its blasts shall be carried from nation to nation
> Till Friendship below
> Through all bosoms shall flow
> And each shall do as he'd have other to do,
> And then all mankind, being loyal and true
> Shall make the earth ring with the song of "F.U."

In addition to taking lodge rituals and aspirations for a thorough
ride, Frank dealt with a Western phenomenon which has been
little noticed by others. In reaction to the heavy drinking which
was normal to most parts of the frontier while dominantly stag,
the region came to be afflicted with temperance movements which
were so successful that many parts of the ex-Wild West were
bone dry decades before Prohibition desiccated the effetest parts
of the Effete East.

Apparently there was a move to dry up Olympia as early as
1868, for *The Lodge Odes of the Independent Order U.F.F.U.*
are followed by a group of songs which both gird at the proponents
of temperance and charge them with hypocrisy. With reference to
leaders of the movement Frank wrote:

> Old Cowchips, who is chief of these
> Would skin a flea to get the grease,
> Away, away up yonder.
> He never learned Old Whiskey's merits,
> And yet his brain is turned with spirits
> Away, away up yonder.
>
> Some stay home both night and day
> And guzzle smuggled "Hudson Bay"
>
> Some are intellectual asses
> Who shave their heads and comb their faces
>
> Such men are our solid thinkers,
> Stay at home and damn all drinkers.
> Away, away up yonder.

But Frank and other opposers of Old Cowchips had a haven; a speak-easy, as it would seem:

> Old man Wood's a clever feller,
> He keeps office in a cellar,
>   Away, away down under.
> He shuts up late and opens early
> To sell a beverage made of barley,
>   Away, away down under.
> Away down in the cellar,
>   Away, away down under,
> The F.U. band still takes their stand
>   To slug and drink at Wood's
> Away, away down underground at Wood's.

19

THE WINGED BRONCO

AS IN OTHER parts and times, the poets among the Western men of print found the smallest commercial welcome for their wares. It thus came about that some remarkably capable ones published their work only in such newspapers as they edited, or issued them as job-shop pamphlets which have since attracted little notice or none.

The one pioneer poet who did get general recognition owed most of his acclaim to his genius for public relations. If Joaquin Miller isn't quite as negligible as some modern appraisers make him out, he was nearer to nothing than he ever got to mastery. Where he would dearly have loved to thunder and shout, the best he could do was to breathe an occasional plaintive note of respectable quality. He had more force to put behind growing a beard than in writing verse, and his pretensions to being a rugged bard of the great outdoors were vested in the phony mountaineer getup in which he was wont to parade city streets.

Some nineteenth-century enthusiasts tried to press poetic laurels on Charles Warren Stoddard and on a Sacramento editor named Edward A. Pollock. But these, as has since been generally recognized, owned even less talent than Miller had.

Not a Western novelty, purveyors of topical verse sometimes drew a veneration that couldn't outlast popular chat about their subjects. An example was Eugene F. Ware; his pen name Ironquill. The verses he contributed to the Fort Scott, Kansas *Monitor* and at length issued in book form gained him a wide reputation that didn't survive the coevals who shared his outlook.

Although he called his first volume of poems *A Little Book of Western Verse*, Eugene Field did not publish it or any succeeding collection on the frontier. As for Bret Harte, his best metrical work was achieved in his parodies of other makers.

So, all in all, it can safely be urged that only one well-known pioneer poet published any considerable body of still readable lines in the West. That was Ambrose Bierce, whose lively collection, titled *Black Beetles in Amber,* was issued in San Francisco in 1892.

As intimated, nevertheless, there were Western editors and printers whose poems never gained the general audience they deserved. Still, one of them had at least a considerable local following, and that was the bard whose verses re the launching of a battleship have previously been quoted.

The fate of Samuel Simpson was antipodal to that of Joaquin Miller, except for the fact that they both came to the same section of the frontier when young. Sam had passion and a good deal of poetic equipment; Joaquin not much of either. Disliked where he was reared, Miller had honors heaped on him everywhere else. The state's ranking souse as well as its laureate, Simpson was revered on his own stamping ground until the last hiccough; but outside of Oregon his work was without fans.

In part that was due to Sam's indifference to acclaim. He was as modest as Joaquin was prone to self-advertisement. "I have not even a copy of my poems," he replied, when once asked why he didn't publish a book of them. "There are so many half-way poets deluging the world with so-called poetry that I am disgusted, and do not wish to add to the burdens of the long suffering public."

The collection of his verse which was posthumously issued doesn't fall within the scope of this chronicle, either with respect to its date or point of publication. But some of the included items show that Sam wasn't fair to himself. For instance, there was one called *Beautiful Willamette* (accent falling on the middle syllable), though titled *Ad Willametam* when originally published in the Albany *Democrat* in 1868.

The poem with which it inevitably invites comparison is Sidney Lanier's famous *Song of the Chattahoochee.* To point out that Lanier didn't publish his poem until 1883 is not to suggest that Sidney was influenced by Sam; for it's a virtual certainty that the renowned Southern poet could never have seen the verses which Simpson contributed to an obscure Western newspaper. But the

two river poems suggest each other, nor is the often anthologized
piece out of the class of Sam's little-known lines:

> From the Cascades' frozen gorges,
> Leaping like a child at play,
> Winding widening through the valley,
> Bright Willamette glides away;
>   Onward ever,
>   Lovely river,
> Softly calling to the sea,
>   Time that scars us,
>   Maim and mars us,
> Leaves no track or trench on thee.
>
> Spring's green witchery is weaving
>   Braid and border for thy side;
> Grace forever haunts thy journey,
>   Beauty dimples on thy tide;
> Through the purple gates of morning
>   Now thy roseate ripples dance;
> Golden, then, when day, departing,
>   On thy waters trails his lance.
>   Waltzing, flashing
>   Tinkling, splashing,
>   Limpid, volatile and free——
>   Always hurried
>   To be buried
> In the bitter, moon-mad sea.
>
> In thy crystal deeps inverted
>   Swings a picture of the sky,
> Like those wavering hopes of Aidenn,
>   Dimly in our dreams that lie;
> Clouded often, drowned in turmoil
>   Faint and lovely, far away——
> Wreathing sunshine on the morrow,
>   Breathing fragrance round today.
>   Love would wander
>   Here and ponder,
> Hither poetry would dream;
>   Life's old questions,
>   Sad suggestions,
> Whence and whither? throng thy stream. . . .

It was earlier, stated in the course of discussing his *Narrative,* that Ned McGowan was a poet. To fill holes in the *Phoenix* and the *Ubiquitous*—the Sacramento papers he published in 1857 and 1858—he printed a body of poems that would have gained him recognition, had they been written by anybody but the man posted as a criminal by the powerful Vigilance Committee of San Francisco, and the historians they paid to parrot them.

A remarkable thing about Ned's verse was the variety of his technical equipment. Although he generally used the heroic couplet, when maintaining that vigilante was another spelling of bastard, he didn't elsewhere metrically repeat himself. How wide his range was won't be discovered unless a systematic search turns up a considerable body of his work. On the basis of the known titles, however, it can be guessed that he had a measure to fit every nuance of mood. That is at the opposite end of the professional scale from the commoner practice of picking a form—the sonnet, say—and pouring a wide variety of matters into it. Probably in Ned's case the measure started buzzing in his bonnet as soon as he began realizing an idea. At any rate, form and substance are always good McGowan team mates, as in the case of his lines called *Hope.*

> How many there are who sing and dream
> Of happier seasons coming;
> And ever in fancy, to catch a beam
> Of a Golden Era, roaming.
> The world may grow old—and young again——
> And the hope of a better shall still remain.
>
> Hope comes with life at its dawning hour,
> Hope sports with the infant creeper;
> Hope cheers the youth with her magic power
> And when, too, the gray haired weeper
> Has closed in the grave his weary round
> He plants the tree of hope on the mound. . . .

From such pensiveness, Ned could switch to the ballad with a fine swing which told of how his enemies once put to sea in quest of him. In writing it, he was careful to include the claims to superior virtue which the vigilantes leaned on, nor did he over-

look the fact that their strong-arm men were recruited from saloon moochers.

> In San Francisco town a Vigilance Committee
>   Composed of the "best and purest" in the city,
> Spent other people's cash and made great commotion,
> To catch old Uncle Ned, they sailed on the ocean—
>   Thirty of these braves,—all Lunch Eaters, too,
> Were selected from among this bold Vigilante crew.
>   To catch old Uncle Ned
>   It was more than they could do,
>   For he knew how to dodge
>   That assassinating crew. . . .

Then again McGowan could toss off a gay drinking song; but,
to appreciate the one that follows, it must be understood that for
him, as for many earlier poets, "oi" and "i" were one sound.

> In sparkling wine our glasses join
>   They make the nectared drink divine
> Since mirth and laughter rule the hour,
> While roses plucked from friendship's bower
>   Around our moistened temples twine
>   And add fresh fragrance to the wine.

A first-rate elegy, crisp epigrams, lilting lyric lines, savage invective—Ned showed himself capable of all these and more. Few,
if any American poets, have evinced such versatility, and certainly
no Western one has done so.

Publishing his work in California's capital, and arranging for the
distribution of his paper in its metropolis, McGowan at least had
a shot at an audience that might have waved him on to national
recognition. But Matt W. Alderson issued his verse where it would
have been surprising if it had found its way to the notice of knowledgeable critics.

Twice mentioned previously, in connection with Montana papers, Alderson was with the Butte *Miner* in 1887. In that year
Butte used up the last of its silver and became a copper camp
only; and, like all such, it was owned by a company which didn't
specialize in hiring literate men to burrow in the earth and fetch
the copper topside.

In 1887 there were about 6800 residents of a town which can be seen as boasting more cathouses than cultural circles. But it was then and there that Matt published the only group of poems so far traced to his hand.

Reared on the frontier, Alderson knew the odds against him, and he made such a well-conceived move to beat them that the *Miner's* job shop sold the first thousand copies of his pamphlet and ran off a second edition. Why it became a best seller in Butte can be gathered from its name. This was *How She Felt in Her First Corset and Other Poems.*

The title piece sings of a frolic held in the cow town of Belgrade, Montana; and it established the motif by relating that the dance was attended by young bucks game "to ride anything that wore hair." As the girls of the vicinity also thought in horsy terms, the heroine of the poem likened herself to a bronco not yet resigned to the saddle and cinch.

> There was one blushing damsel, just budding sixteen
> Whose waist by a corset ne'er circled had been,
> But whose mother insisted that on such a night
> One should find a place there and the lacing be tight.
> "What's the matter?" was asked by some one at her side,
> "I feel just like bucking," the maiden replied.

If that hit Montana where it then lived, the companion items could scarcely have done so, for they were amatory poems which offered nothing to snicker at. And the two longest ones were written in blank verse, a form in which Alderson was as casually at ease as most who undertake to use it are not.

> . . . But come to think, this love is all I have;
> No titled rank is mine, no Astor's wealth;
> And one, you know, can't live on love alone,
> Ah no! But better starve for want of bread
> Than want of love; for when we starve for bread
> And hunger gnaws with all its well-known force,
> A day and all desire for food grows weak
> And in its stead one craves but rest and sleep. . . .
> But starve for love, and when doth come relief?
> The weary soul still lives or drags along
> As prisoner doomed for life goes to his work. . . .

> Living, Ah yes! But devil never cursed
> His vilest victim with a death so dread;
> Standing as stands an engine on the track,
> Perfectly built in all its mighty parts,
> Its boiler and its furnace amply fed,
> Yet powerless. . . .

Those lines are part of *A Love Letter and Its Answer*, "A Montanian to His Sweetheart," a Western version of Marlowe's "Come live with me and be my love," and "The Answer she Gives Him" rings of the mocking reply which Raleigh put in the mouth of the adored shepherdess. As Matt wrote the retort as well as the plea that provoked it, they serve to demonstrate both the writer's native romanticism and his awareness of how little such coin will buy him in a hard scrabble world. The forms he chose were admirable for their purposes. For after the poet makes his petition, the shepherdess, Montana style, responds in four-beat couplets whose tinniness is exactly antithetic to his graceful blank verse.

> Your note to me, of recent date,
> Where you are so importunate,
> Has been received, and I have read
> With greatest care what you have said.
> I am quite pleased that you can see
> So much to praise in one like me,
> And only wish that I could say
> Nice things in such a pretty way.
> But tell me! Do you really think
> That love is better than "the chink?"

Another poem of Alderson's, blank verse being again the form, is called *Political Economy*. In it he treats the human life cycle under four divisions headed "Production," "Exchange," "Consumption," and "Distribution." He had the first qualification of a poet, in other words, which is an eye by which he can enable others to see things in a new light.

Matt was either thirty-one or thirty-two when he published the twenty-eight pages of verse titled *How She Felt in Her First Corset and Other Poems*. If he lived much longer, he must have written more verse, and perhaps some scholar will eventually perform the service of exhuming it.

Perhaps, too, additional lines by Joseph B. Gossage will some day come to light. In the meantime all that can be said is that he produced a work which is an even more astonishing production than Junius Wharton's *The Sun God*. That would have been dealt with in this chapter, incidentally, had it not been allotted to another because of its subject matter; for it is certainly a poetic as well as an anthropological achievement.

But to go on with Gossage: he styled himself a miner on the title page of the one metrical work so far ascribed to him. Doubtless he had come to Dakota Territory's Black Hills as a prospector, too. But he was a printer, and in 1878, or a year after his arrival, he started the Rapid City *Journal*, a weekly which graduated to a daily eight years later.

In 1888 the connected job shop issued a pamphlet for which the type was unquestionably set by himself. Its title *The Quest of St. Brendan*, it was prefaced by this modest disclaimer:

"A test run of pay-dirt taken mainly from the claims of others by a prospector. As no assays have been made and he knows nothing of its value, he has prepaid the mill charges so that nobody may lose anything. He is somewhat in doubt as to whether he should make the shipment at all, as he has barely done more than to sack such ore as he found already mined upon the claim when he relocated it."

Thereafter Joe Gossage of Rapid City proceeded to give, in about a thousand lines of sound blank verse, his own highly individual verse rendition of an eleventh-century Latin prose narrative called *Navigatio Sancti Brendani*. As of 1888, by the by, it had appeared in no English translation, although there had been a French and a German one by then.

But never mind how Joe got hold of the story of a mariner—"Brendan the Voyager," as he was known to hagiology—who was supposed to have sailed to the New World a half a millennium before Leif the Lucky got around to doing so. His adventures sparked the only European epic cycle which majors in the Western Hemisphere. It is with its theme, in fact, that histories of American literature should properly begin.

Taking in prose as well as verse, there have been Norse, Flemish, Italian, French, German, and Middle English versions, as well as those written in all the Celtic languages and, of course, Latin. But the only significant contribution in English as now commonly understood was achieved by a Western man of print, born on the sub-frontier of Wapello County, Iowa.

What with the strange places visited and remarkable beings encountered, Brendan's voyage is not an easy one for a poet to compass, but nothing stumped Gossage's blank verse. Although he didn't choose to include its dour opposite number, he thus dealt with the famous friendly whale of the *Navigatio:*

> Then the angel revealed
> This isle was not that which the shepherd had told
> But the back of a fish, the largest that swims,
> Jasconius by name, and ever it tries
> In a ring to unite its head with its tail;
> But by reason of length no room could it find
> In all ocean's expanse. . . .

Having probably roved other parts of the frontier before making port in the Black Hills, Joe makes telling use of Western imagery.

> For a moment the cloud would be lifted on high,
> And pale, icy peaks to a rosy bright hue
> Would warm to the light; but recede or sank
> As the desert's mirage, when to them they sailed.

He remembered Western scenery when telling of a spirit on its way to Heaven, too:

> Then unweighted by clay, with an angel for guide,
> His soul, mounting high, its journey began.
> Above the dark sea, beyond the pale moon,
> It passed by the stars as they whirled in their joy,
> And systems of worlds innumerable saw.
> Constellations sublime in order appeared,
> Orion, Pleiades, and thousands unnamed
> Were seen, were at hand, and left far behind
> While higher they rose on the wings of swift thought
> Till, rejoicing in light, the battlements high
> Of the Heavenly Lord burst fair on their view
> As some mighty Sierra that rises snow-clad
> His summit adorning in lilac's pale hue.

Rapid City in Joe's day was even smaller than was Butte in Matt Alderson's. How many appreciators of his great accomplishment were co-resident with Gossage is something that can't be tabulated but can be guessed from the fact that only one copy is now known to exist.

Yet Sam Simpson wasn't the only poet who wasn't starved of recognition by his associates. In hard-boiled Virginia City two bards basked in all the adulation they could have asked for.

Who they were and how they were heaped with laurels were matters reported in the reminiscences of Sam Davis, at one time of Virginia City and its *Enterprise*. "Who would suppose that with all the hurly-burly of money-making there would have been such poetry or sentiment?" he began by asking. "But the [Comstock] Lodge maintained two verse makers and rhyme weavers of the highest order. One was Joe Goodman and the other Rollin Daggett. On all other propositions these two men were like brothers, but when it came to poetry they were like two pugilists in a ring. About once a week a poem written by Daggett or Goodman would appear in the Territorial Enterprise. . . . Each of the bards had an army of followers, and the Enterprise office had its warring factions. Steve Gillis [Mark Twain's code duello second that shot the head off the sage hen] was a pronounced Daggett man, while Denis McCarthy was an unswerving partisan of Goodman.

"It was . . . a sight to see Steve, well filled with Joe Mallon's whiskey, delivering a barroom lecture on the excellence of Daggett's verse. 'This is the real stuff!' he would shout, waving the Enterprise in the air. . . . 'Hear this everybody,' and in a voice like a ton of coal rattling down the cellar stairs he would roll out the strong passages . . . and point out their beauties to the admiring crowd.

"'No use talking, boys, no one in this country can trot in double harness with this man. . . . Joe Goodman is no slouch of a writer, but he can't stay the distance with speed like this.' Then the crowd would empty foaming tankards of beer to Daggett, the Comstock bard and the glory of the town."

But next his rival would pop a poem into the *Enterprise*, giving

McCarthy a chance to hold forth. "Denis had a rich melodious voice," Sam Davis remembered, "and he would lean back and roll out the lines which had flowed from Goodman's pen. 'Talk about poetry! This is the only true music ever written on the Ledge. . . . I tell you it's the divine fire from Olympus. Where is the man who says Daggett can write poetry. . . . Did you ever see him tackle spenserian verse? No, it's too high for him. But Joe can sit there just as straight as if he were keeping books and roll the verses out just as cozy as I could write the Lord's Prayer. . . .'"

Neither Daggett nor Goodman appear to have made any effort to collect their respective lines, and the broken files of the *Enterprise* forbid an assessment of the works pressed so warmly on the poetry lovers gathered in Joe Mallon's saloon. But one poem which Joe Goodman published elsewhere is pertinent, because it harked back to the time and place where his verse was rejoiced in.

> In youth when I did love, did love
>> (To quote the sexton's honest ditty)
> I lived six thousand feet above
>> Sea level, in Virginia City.
> The site was bleak, the houses small,
>> The narrow streets unpaved and slanting,
> But now it seems to me of all
>> The spots on earth the most enchanting.
>
> Let Art with all its cunning strive,
>> Let Nature lavish all its splendor
> One touch of sentiment will give
>> A charm more beautiful and tender;
> And so that town, how'ere uncouth,
>> To others who have chanced to go there,
> Enshrines the ashes of my youth
>> And there is fairyland or nowhere.
>
> Who tends its marts, who treads its ways
>> Are mysteries beyond my guessing;
> To me the forms of other days
>> Are still about its centers pressing
> I know that loving lips are cold
>> And true hearts stilled, ah, more's the pity!
> But in my fancy they yet hold
>> Their empire in Virginia City. . . .

The California broadside adorned with these lines was not
dated, but the concluding stanza makes it clear that they were
written after word was passed that the end was in sight for the
Comstock. This was realized with finality in 1893, when the *Territorial Enterprise* ceased to report the daily happenings in the
most fabulous queen city of them all.

JOURNALISTS IN OTHER GUISES

THIS CHRONICLE WOULD not be well rounded if it failed to notice how variously talented—and/or given to unusual experiences—many Western men of print were when away from their presses. Some of them also displayed a gift for landing non-run-of-the-mill jobs.

Later of papers in Wyoming, Texas, and Oregon, Asa Shinn Mercer put in a stint as president of Washington's university, and as the territory's immigration commissioner. In that capacity he pulled a stunt in 1866 which harked back to the Casket Girls and other ruses for populating colonial America. What Asa did was head East with money enough to recruit and transport a bevy of New England lasses. On the Atlantic seaboard the understanding was that they were needed by Washington as schoolteachers. In the Pacific Northwest, however, it devolved upon them to mate with stag pioneers and raise a crop of pupils for instructresses of the future to wrangle.

Stepping out of the sanctum of the San Francisco *Herald* in 1853, William Walker formed a scheme for fusing a new country out of the Mexican states of Lower California and Sonora. Proclaiming himself president, after he and his following of filibusters had scored a few victories, he briefly ruled Lower California in fact—though Sonora in theory only—before a revolution ousted him.

In 1855 Walker made a better race of it, for after he had shot his way into the presidency of Nicaragua, he managed to hold on as chief of state for two years. And before he got himself executed, in the course of trying to take over Honduras, he had as one of his chief ministers a San Francisco and Sacramento newspaperman named Parker H. French.

After his poetic war with Joe Goodman had run its course, Rol-

lin Daggett was appointed United States Minister to Hawaii while
that archipelago was still a Kanaka kingdom. Nor were he and
Charles Poston—whose mission to the Emperor of China has already been referred to—the sole pioneer men of print to hobnob
with royalty.

Dave Day did, but, though acting in common with others, he
was singular in one respect. It can be affirmed with confidence
that he was the only Colorado newspaperman who both acted as
Indian agent for Southern Utah and called on Queen Victoria in
her palace in Southern England. Presumptively the Empress of
Prissiness was not a reader of the *Solid Muldoon;* or, if she was,
she had overlooked this piece of reporting by her guest from overseas:

"A novel suit will be tried before Justice Cobb on Saturday. A
former landlord sues one of the 'scarlet daughters of prosperity'
for a month's rent and she brings in a contra bill for wear and
tear."

While an Indian agent in Arizona in 1877, the Tombstone *Epitaph's* John Clum organized the Apache police force which
rounded up Geronimo and his band for the first time in that chieftain's career. A she redskin came near ruining his coup, though,
as John made clear in the course of an account of it.

"There are always a few belligerent squaws who insist upon
intruding whenever a 'war-talk' is impending, and one of these
athletic ladies had stationed herself . . . close by our chief of police. With a wild yell she sprang upon Beauford and clung to his
neck and arms in such a manner as to draw down his rifle, making
a superb 'tackle' and 'interference.' I had been keeping my two
eyes on Geronimo, but with the echo of that genuine Apache yell,
I turned just in time to appreciate Beauford's expression of profound disgust when he discovered he had been captured by a
squaw. Then he swung that great right arm to which the lady was
clinging and she landed ingloriously on the parade ground—and
at a respectful distance. Really, a bit of comedy injected into a
most serious situation."

Joe Ellis Johnson's relation with Indians was, typically, a genial
one. Three years before he began publishing the Omaha *Arrow,*

he organized what appears to have been the first "Wild West Show."

In 1851 Johnson conceived that people in the East would flock to watch savage war rituals and the like. But he was shrewd enough to see that the dance tempo of untutored Indians was much too slow to jibe with civilized notions of what barbaric frenzy was like. So with Joe to coach them, some Omaha braves learned to dig jazz and step lively. Their mentor wasn't satisfied with their flat prairie habitat, though, so he moved them west and perched them on dramatic heights.

That done he brought his team to the Atlantic seaboard, where he scheduled exhibitions in all the big burgs and quite a few of the smaller ones. He was the show's publicity man as well as its manager, naturally. Although there were earlier blasts on his horn, one dated January 2, 1852, will suffice to describe what he was staging.

"Nine O-ma-ha Savages, just arrived from their Rocky Mountain Home . . . will give a specimen of their Wild, Exciting, Rude and Popular Entertainments.

"The Exhibition Consists of their Wild and Unique, War, Wedding, Harvest, Hunting, Scalping, Worship Dances and Songs.

"Many of their Native Curiosities and Instruments will be exhibited, with explanations of their Manners, Customs, Modes of Life, Weddings, Buffalo Hunts, etc.

J. E. Johnson, Agent."

Stanley Huntley of the Bismarck, Dakota Territory *Tribune* actually became titular chief of the Teton Sioux, in combination with Dull Knife's band of Cheyennes. The head of the alliance, Dull Knife had adopted Stan—because the editor had doctored an ankle which had been troubling the chief—and given him the name of Wau-pey-wau-bar, or Holy Leaf. A genuine son inherited leadership from Dull Knife, but when Young Antelope died, tribal custom passed the mantle to the old chief's fosterling.

By that time Huntley was prominent enough politically to be on joshing terms with Chester A. Arthur. That particular President of the United States seemed doomed to get wacky letters

from Western men of print. The one Chester received from Bill
Nye, when the *Boomerang's* editor resigned as postmaster of
Laramie, was quoted some chapters ago. In 1885 Arthur got one
from Holy Leaf Huntley, asking "whether your nation and mine
are to live on terms of friendly equality or whether you want
strife and carnage." The head chief of the Teton Sioux furthermore asked the President for "cast off war material, plug hats
and light literature now on file with the state department as a
guarantee of good will."

Not feeling able to discuss his problems with high officials, Will
Porter got himself posted as "wanted." As the *Rolling Stone* had
folded up, he was on the Houston *Post* when the law made a
pass at him in 1896 because of an error in the books of the Austin
bank he'd once worked for. Its directors never accused him of
wrongdoing, but long after Will had gone on to other jobs and
places, some federal countinghouse inspector decided to file
charges, as a warning to other bookkeepers in a region where the
minutiae of banking hadn't been taken too seriously.

Had Porter reached for an attorney, he would have been freed,
for he hadn't done anything to raise the hackles of ought but a
two-for-a-picayune bureaucratic snoop. Yet if he'd been exoner-
ated, he would have doubtless kept his pleasant job as a columnist for a prospering daily, and America would have been
literarily short changed. It wasn't, because Will put his ears back
and scooted not only out of the state but the country.

For many months he knocked around the Central American
banana republics. Others that slipped on something were among
the exiles he joined forces with, chief among them being Al Jennings, the celebrated book-writing train robber.

But Al wasn't a man of letters yet, and Will himself was still
not ambitious of authoring anything but more Texas newspaper
columns. Unable to do so, he might have gone to seed—easy to
do when there's not enough work to space the drinks—but word
of the fatal illness of his wife caused his return to the States and
confrontation with the music there.

Having fled, he was by that token adjudged guilty and shagged
off to a doghouse of Uncle Sam's in Columbus, Ohio. If the price

was high, there was a return for it, however. For he went in as
Will Porter and came out O. Henry.

Some of the victims of the practical jokes that Eugene Field
perpetrated, in newspaper offices and out, thought he was a like-
lier candidate for jail than ever Will Porter had been, or Al Jennings either. But that same rough japester, and creator of such
saloon wall literature as *The Piddling Pup,* was one of the most
scholarly authors America ever produced.

The Englishing of poems written in Latin and a wide range
of other languages was one of his delights. He was likewise a
book collector, who knew what was inside all the volumes in the
fine library he assembled. His last piece of writing was, indeed,
a work called *The Love Affairs of a Bibliomaniac.*

Field wasn't as at home in prose as he was in verse. But in
addition to being a locker full of pleasantly dispensed learning
and offhand autobiography, the book includes illustrative poems.

At one time, as Gene swore, he was so enraptured with the
works of François Villon that he decided to turn outlaw in order
to have at least something in common with the object of his
veneration. But there was a flaw in this scheme: Field wasn't able
to find any modern rogues who were as literarily savvy as Villon's
companions of the Coquillard had been in the Paris of the fif-
teenth century. So, because latter-day desperadoes bored him,
his plan to become one fell through. Yet as he still couldn't get
over the difference separating his fortunes from those of a happy-
go-lucky thug, he wrote as follows:

If I were François Villon, and François Villon I,
What would it matter to me how the time might drag or fly?
He would in sweaty anguish toil the days and nights away,
And still not keep the prowling, growling, howling wolf at bay!

But with my valiant bottle, and my frouzy brevet-bride
And my score of loyal cut-throats standing guard for me outside,
What worry of tomorrow would provoke a casual sigh,
If I were François Villon, and François Villon I?

If I were François Villon and François Villon I,
To yonder gloomy boulevard at midnight I would hie;
"Stop, stranger! and deliver your possessions, ere you feel
The mettle of my bludgeon or the temper of my steel!"

He should give me gold and diamonds, his snuff-box and his cane——
"Now back, my boon companions, to our brothel with our gain!"
And back within that brothel, how the bottles they would fly,
If I were François Villon, and François Villon I.

He in his meager, shabby home, *I* in my roaring den——
He with his babes around him, *I* with my hunted men!
His virtue be his bulwark—my genius should be mine!
"Go, fetch my pen, sweet Margot, and a jorum of your wine!" . . .

Certain pioneer editors were inventors of things more concrete than such fancies. It has been pointed out that Gail Borden, of the San Felipe and Columbia *Telegraph and Texas Register,* was one with the deviser of condensed milk. But before he perfected that money-maker, Gail tried to benefit mankind on a grander scale.

Living in Galveston, after he had sold the *Telegraph,* he was moved to deep thinking by an island city's problems. What he came up with in 1849 was an idea for a transportation gem which could carry Galvestonians into the sea, ferry them across the intervening strait, crawl up on the shore of the mainland, and breeze toward any chosen destination there. In concept it was cards and spades more admirable than Wind Wagon Smith's prairie blow-about. Preferring Latin to the Greek "amphibian," Gail called his nonesuch the "Terraqueous."

Luckily the Reverend William Mumford Baker was in Galveston at the time and included an account of the invention in *A Year Worth Living.* The Terraqueous resembled a large wagon, except for the mast up forward. To get it moving, a square sail was raised. When it left land for water, the wagon's wheels were somehow supposed to function as propellers.

Of the two voyages it made, the Terraqueous failed to get its screws wet on the first. A breeze bowled the wagon along so fast that women of the party screamed, and Gail had to put on the brakes. That caused the skipper to invite only stags for the next run.

Again the machine performed well on land, which was all Borden's guests had bargained for. So when Gail steered into the bay without a word of warning, one of those with him cut the cruise short by dropping the sail, and the frantic general scramble for the landward side of the vessel tipped it over.

When the rest made their way ashore, somebody asked, "Where is he?" [meaning Borden]. "Drowned, I most sincerely hope," was the reply of one soaked Galvestonian.

Staying with his ship in the best marine tradition, Gail finally crawled atop the capsized Terraqueous, the better to bawl out those who had had no faith in his device. "It can't sink," Baker quoted him as expostulating. "Part of the invention! What did you make such fools of yourselves for? . . ."

Just the same, he dropped his seagoing wagon at that point, thereby showing less devotion to the cause of advanced transportation than did Frederick Marriott, of the San Francisco *News Letter*. Now chiefly remembered as the man who gave Ambrose Bierce his alpha crack at journalism, Fred seems to have been the first to invent a heavier-than-air craft which actually flew for an appreciable distance under power supplied by its engines.

It was said of Marriott that, when he commenced publishing the *News Letter* in 1856, his purpose was to raise the capital to finance flying-machine experiments. After many trials and errors he emerged thirteen years later with a gadget in which he was confident enough to proffer a public demonstration.

What he had worked out was a gas-filled dirigible, thirty-seven feet long, and eleven as to diameter. Cigar-shaped, it had seven-foot wings, swept back like those of a swallow. The propellers on each wing were spun by a steam engine which weighed eighty-four pounds. To make it possible for such weight to defy gravity, 1360 cubic feet of hydrogen were fed into the body of what Marriott called his "Avitor."

Patented in 1869, the Avitor was on display at San Francisco's Shellmound Park on two summer days of that year. On the Fourth of July it stayed aloft long enough to fly about a mile, a distance covered in twelve minutes. As it had no pilot, it was guided by groundlings who controlled it by means of ropes.

Having been that far successful, Fred planned to build an Avitor that was 150 feet long and would carry a crew of four. He even projected a flight to the Atlantic coast, which he estimated that his machine could reach in four or five days. Needing more money than his newspaper could supply, in order to build on such a grand scale, he had meanwhile formed the Aerial Steam Navigation Company. He could find but few investors, though, and after his model was accidentally set ablaze, he didn't have the heart to continue.

Not an inventor, but a man willing to back one that seemed to know what he was about, Mark Twain was the angel of a man with a scheme for revolutionizing the printing industry. The fellow was James W. Paige, and the machine he was fiddling with was designed to set type automatically.

Having added experience as a book publisher to his knowledge of the newspaper field and training as a printer, Twain didn't have to be persuaded that his protégé had a potentially very profitable idea. But there were bugs to be taken out of the Paige typesetter before it was marketable. When Mark first began handing James cash, for instance, the inventor still hadn't worked out a way to justify lines, or make them flush at both ends with the margins of a page or a column.

James was a deliberate worker and progress was further slowed by the fact that his device was a highly complex one, with hundreds of parts which had to be reshaped every time he came up with an improvement. Although it was in 1881 that he first sought assistance from Twain, the calendar reading was 1889 by the time Paige had licked the justification problem. Meanwhile, other inventors had begun working toward the same goal, and one of these was Ottmar Mergenthaler. Ottmar was readying a device which he or somebody had dubbed the "Linotype."

Having faith in James, Mark counted on making any number of millions from the half interest Paige had agreed to concede; but the company they had formed needed big capital before it could begin manufacturing. It was then that Twain asked Joe Goodman—in solid with the tycoons who owed their wealth to the Comstock bonanza—to help him raise money.

Having sold the *Territorial Enterprise* while it was still a profitable concern, Goodman had moved to California, where he was improving his leisure by the study of archaeology. Eventually he was to become such a recognized expert on a certain phase of it, in fact, that a London publisher brought out his *The Archaic Maya Inscriptions* in 1897.

Responding to Mark's appeal, Joe did his best to rally bullion to the aid of his old employee, but financiers who might well have invested in the Paige typesetting machine, had it been in shape for marketing a few years earlier, had by then heard of the Linotype. After reports of engineers as to the comparative merits of the two machines were in, James Paige had something which was valuable only as scrap metal, and Mark Twain had nothing to show for the $190,000 he had squandered.

So in spite of himself the frontier's greatest man of print was not responsible for thrusting into composing rooms an invention which destroyed the printing and publishing era which had schooled him and directed the use he made of his talents in so many ways. For a machine which set type faster than hands could did more than force manual setters to forfeit their jobs.

Where typographers and writers had been inextricably associated, and so often been one and the same, the Linotype divided them into two camps. After Mergenthaler's triumph, the printer who applied to a newspaper did not expect to do other than work in a portion of the plant from which writers were barred. And the journalist could rise from cub to managing editor without knowing more of the mechanical end of publishing than that it was accomplished by arts he didn't have to master.

It took a little longer for the Linotype to become as generally used in the West as it swiftly came to be in the East; but by the end of the 1890s it had ousted former means of operation in all towns of any size. It thus chanced that the practices which had fostered and flavored pioneer publishing became vestigial in the same decade that saw the close of the West's frontier epoch as a whole.

ICHABOD: A POSTSCRIPT

THERE IS MORE to say about the downfall of pioneer journalism than that it lapsed when the frontier did. It might have persisted in some modified form, tailored to the new requirements of a changed area; but that is not what happened. It bequeathed nothing that the West of the immediately succeeding era wanted to keep.

The reasons can be partially found in the lack of regional impetus which followed the tremendous pioneer surge. In other sections of the United States, the passing of the frontier signaled economic development on a pervasive scale. In the West, that only took place in the Pacific Coast states and Eastern Texas, where sea traffic remained an energizing element. Elsewhere the region subsided into a static rural empire, enlivened only by the rule-proving exception of Denver.

The general feeling, in the quiet that followed the explosive frontier period, was close akin to the melancholy mood of reform which sometimes accompanies other hangovers. The unbooming West was bent on living down its rowdy beginnings. Among the results was the sweeping Prohibition movement, mentioned in connection with the protests of Francis Henry.

Among a populace so gone of spirit there was no home for newspapermen accustomed to dipping indiscriminately into ink and whiskey bottles. As for their individualistic approach to journalism, it was a dead drake.

Taking its place were telegraphic news services and editorial policies dictated by the business office. Invention was no longer invited either. Where former Western readers had delighted in locally based tall tales, later ones munched other fare. In paper after paper it was the regular practice to run on the front page installments of sticky romances, set in the East by the Eastern hacks who wrote them.

The surviving Western men of print tended to go East themselves, as Arthur McEwen did, and Ambrose Bierce as well. Those who stayed on the nation's sunset side were much of a piece with the Elizabethan playwrights whose fate it was to flounder in the theatreless England of Cromwell and his fellow rooks.

But the journalistic epoch of which they were holdovers has much to say to successors with spirit enough to listen. And now that the West has left the post-pioneer doldrums behind, and is again becoming vital in other ways, there may be a renewal of interest in what was bequeathed by the men who furnished it with a unique cultural floor.

If financially theirs was seldom a success story, cake doesn't have to have frosting on it to be worth eating. They were the voices of an unparalleled period, when the act of reaching for prizes was the prerogative of not just the usual minor percentage, but of the majority of those in the field. In spite of the fact that the booms generally went bust, there was excitement for all while one lasted, and the hope of another when that fizzled.

Living that way themselves, and more aware of the era's essence than most of their fellow citizens, the men of print reveled in a commodity known only to hard-living chance takers. And that is swank. Sparked by it, they could even strut and laugh at the moment of failure.

Proof of that is to be found in the curtain lines with which they mocked both shabby odds and their doubtfully paying subscribers. One such farewell—composed by either Eugene J. Trippet or D. M. Brannan, when they were forced to fold the Bristol, Nevada *Times* in 1882—will serve as the tailpiece of this chronicle. The devil celebrated was, of course, the printer's one.

"Bury us deep under the fragrant sagebrush. Let the festive hog and the rollicking chipmunk sing sweet lullaby to our departed memory. The many hued lizard will drop a sorrowing weep upon the lonely mound. Don't stay the pensive donkey from braying a tender obituary notice over our 'dead' corpse. Let

sympathizing coyotes gather about our grave. Let them yelp a
mournful dirge over what was but is not. Ta ta. Vale! Vale! Vale!

> Down we go cheerfully,
>   Nary a sigh;
> Sober, but beautifully!
>   Thus do we die.
> Yet we're not kicking
>   Though called rather soon;
> Plant our toes sticking
>   Straight up at the moon.
> We ran with the devil
>   And paid pretty dear;
> Rewarding our evil,
>   They planted us here."

BIBLIOGRAPHY

Adams, William L. HISTORY OF MEDICINE AND SURGERY FROM THE EARLIEST TIMES. Portland, Ore., 1884.
—— TREASON, STRATAGEMS AND SPOILS. Portland, Ore., 1852.
Alderson, Matt W. BOZEMAN, *a guide to its places of recreation and a synopsis of its natural resources.* Bozeman, Mont., 1883.
—— HOW SHE FELT IN HER FIRST CORSET AND OTHER POEMS. Butte, Mont., 1887.
Allen, Albert H. DAKOTA IMPRINTS, 1858–1889. New York, 1947.
Allen, Albert H. and McMurtrie, Douglas C. EARLY PRINTING IN COLORADO. Denver, 1935.
Alter, J. Cecil EARLY UTAH JOURNALISM. Salt Lake City, Utah, 1938.
Armstrong, Moses K. THE EARLY EMPIRE BUILDERS OF THE GREAT WEST. St. Paul, Minn., 1901.
Ashton, Wendell J. VOICE IN THE WEST. New York, 1950.
Ayer, N. W. N. W. AYER'S NEWSPAPER DIRECTORY. Philadelphia, 1873.
Beadle, John Hanson THE UNDEVELOPED WEST. Cincinnati, 1873.
—— WESTERN WILDS AND THE MEN WHO REDEEM THEM. Cincinnati, 1878.
Beebe, Lucius COMSTOCK COMMOTION. Palo Alto, Calif., 1948.
Belknap, George N. MC MURTRIE'S OREGON IMPRINTS, A FOURTH SUPPLEMENT. Oregon, Historical Quarterly, Vol. 64, Portland, Ore., 1963.
Bell, Horace REMINISCENCES OF A RANGER. Los Angeles, 1881.
Bennett, William P. THE FIRST BABY IN CAMP. Salt Lake City, Utah, 1893.
Bierce, Ambrose G. BLACK BEETLES IN AMBER. San Francisco, 1892.
Brann, William Cowper BRANN AND THE ICONOCLAST, *A Collection of the Writings of William Cowper Brann,* Waco, Tex., 1898–1903.
Browne, John Ross ADVENTURES IN THE APACHE COUNTRY. New York, 1868.
Bruce, John Roberts GAUDY CENTURY. New York, 1948.
Carver, Charles BRANN AND THE ICONOCLAST. Austin, Tex., 1957.
Chapin, W. E. SOME WYOMING EDITORS I HAVE KNOWN. *Annals of Wyoming, Vol. 18, No. 1.* Cheyenne, Wyo., 1946.
Clarke, Samuel A. SOUNDS BY THE WESTERN SEA. Salem, Ore., 1872.

Connor, Seymour V. (Ed.) A BIGGERS CHRONICLE. Lubbock, Tex., 1961.

Davis, Carlyle Channing OLDEN TIMES IN COLORADO. Los Angeles, 1916.

Davis, Robert H. and Maurice, Arthur B. THE CALIPH OF BAGDAD. New York, 1931.

Davis, Samuel Post THE HISTORY OF NEVADA. Los Angeles, 1913.

—— SHORT STORIES. San Francisco, 1885.

De Quille, Dan THE BIG BONANZA. Hartford, Conn., 1876.

—— HISTORY OF THE COMSTOCK LODE AND SILVER MINES. Virginia City, Nev., 1889.

—— WASHOE RAMBLES. Los Angeles, 1961.

Delano, Alonzo A LIVE WOMAN IN THE MINES. New York, 1857.

—— OLD BLOCK'S SKETCH BOOK. Sacramento, Calif., 1856.

Derby, George Horatio PHOENIXIANA: or Sketches and Burlesques. New York, 1856.

—— THE SQUIBOB PAPERS. New York, 1865.

Dimsdale, Thomas J. THE VIGILANTES OF MONTANA. Virginia City, Mont., 1866.

Drury, Wells AN EDITOR ON THE COMSTOCK LODE. Palo Alto, Calif., 1948.

Duckett, Margaret MARK TWAIN AND BRET HARTE. Norman, Okla., 1964.

Emrich, Duncan COMSTOCK BONANZA. New York, 1950.

Estell, James Madison SPEECH OF GEN. JAMES M. ESTELL DELIVERED IN THE HALL OF REPRESENTATIVES. Sacramento, Calif., 1857.

Evans, Elwood PUGET SOUND. Olympia, Wash., 1869.

—— WASHINGTON TERRITORY. Olympia, Wash., 1877.

Fatout, Paul MARK TWAIN IN VIRGINIA CITY. Bloomington, Ind., 1964.

Field, Eugene A LITTLE BOOK OF WESTERN VERSE. Chicago, 1889.

—— THE LOVE AFFAIRS OF A BIBLIOMANIAC. Chicago, 1889.

—— A SECOND BOOK OF VERSE. Chicago, 1892.

Folkes, John Gregg NEVADA'S NEWSPAPERS: A Bibliography. Carson City, Nev., 1964.

Fowler, Gene TIMBER LINE. New York, 1933.

Frantz, Joe B. GAIL BORDEN. Norman, Okla., 1951.

Freeman, Legh R. THE HISTORY OF THE FRONTIER-INDEX (THE "PRESS ON WHEELS"), THE OGDEN FREEMAN, THE INTERMOUNTAINS FREEMAN, AND THE UNION FREEMAN. Evanston, Ill., 1943.

George, Henry OUR LAND AND LAND POLICY. San Francisco, 1871.

—— PROGRESS AND POVERTY. San Francisco, 1879.

Gibson, George R. JOURNAL OF A SOLDIER UNDER KEARNY AND DONIPHAN. Glendale, Calif., 1937.

Goodman, Joseph T. and Daggett, Rollin M. THE PSYCHOSCOPE. Virginia City, Nev., 1871.

Gossage, Joseph B. THE QUEST OF ST. BRENDAN. Rapid City, S.D., 1888.

Graham, Hared B. HANDSET REMINISCENCES. Salt Lake City, Utah, 1915.

Greeley, Horace RECOLLECTIONS OF A BUSY LIFE. New York, 1868.

Greenwood, Robert (Ed.) CALIFORNIA IMPRINTS, 1837–1862, A Bibliography. Los Gatos, Calif., 1961.

Hargrett, Lester OKLAHOMA IMPRINTS, 1835–1890. New York, 1951.

Hart, Fred H. THE SAZERAC LYING CLUB. San Francisco, 1878.

Harte, Bret CONDENSED NOVELS AND OTHER PAPERS. San Francisco, 1867.

—— THE LOST GALLEON. San Francisco, 1867.

—— THE LUCK OF ROARING CAMP AND OTHER SKETCHES. New York, 1870.

Hawley, Lorene Anderson and Farley, Alan W. KANSAS IMPRINTS, 1854–1876. Topeka, Kan., 1958.

Heartman, Charles Frederick MC MURTRIE IMPRINTS. Hattiesburg, Miss., 1942.

—— SUPPLEMENT TO MC MURTRIE IMPRINTS. Biloxi, Miss., 1946.

Henry, Francis LODGE ODES. Olympia, Wash., 1868.

Henry, O. ROLLING STONES. New York, 1913.

Historical Records Survey INVENTORY OF AMERICAN IMPRINTS. Lansing, Mich., 1942.

Howe, Edgar Watson THE STORY OF A COUNTRY TOWN. Atchison, Kansas, 1883.

Howes, Cecil PISTOL PACKING PENCIL PUSHERS. *Kansas Historical Quarterly, May, 1944.* Topeka, Kan., 1944.

Hunter, John M. PEREGRINATIONS OF A PIONEER PRINTER. Grand Prairie, Tex., 1954.

Inman, Henry THE GREAT SALT LAKE TRAIL. Topeka, Kan., 1888.

Jennewein, J. Leonard BLACK HILLS BOOK TRAILS. Mitchell, S.D., 1961.

Johnson, Rufus D. JEJ, *Trail to Sundown.* Salt Lake City, Utah, 1961.

Kansas State Historical Society and Department of Archives HISTORY OF KANSAS NEWSPAPERS. Topeka, Kan., 1916.

Karolevitz, Robert F. NEWSPAPERING IN THE OLD WEST. Seattle, Wash., 1965.

Kemble, Edward C. A HISTORY OF CALIFORNIA NEWSPAPERS. Los Gatos, Calif., 1962.

Lee, James Melvin HISTORY OF AMERICAN JOURNALISM. Garden City, N.Y., 1923.

Lewis, Oscar   THE TOWN THAT DIED LAUGHING. Boston, 1955.
Lingenfelter, Richard E.   THE NEWSPAPERS OF NEVADA. San Francisco, 1965.
Lutrell, Estelle   NEWSPAPERS AND PERIODICALS OF ARIZONA, 1859–1911. Tucson, Ariz., 1950.
Lyons, Richard   THE FIRST POET IN NORTH DAKOTA. *North Dakota History, Vols. 24, No. 3.* Bismarck, N.D., 1957.
McClane, Hiram H.   THE CAPTURE OF THE ALAMO. San Antonio, 1886.
McGowan, Edward   NARRATIVE OF EDWARD MC GOWAN, INCLUDING A FULL ACCOUNT OF THE AUTHOR'S ADVENTURES AND PERILS WHILE PERSECUTED BY THE SAN FRANCISCO COMMITTEE OF VIGILANCE OF 1856. San Francisco, 1857.
McMurtrie, Douglas C.   EARLY OREGON IMPRINTS, 1847–1870. Eugene, Ore., 1950.
—   EARLY PRINTING IN WYOMING AND THE BLACK HILLS. Hattiesburg, Miss., 1943.
——   MONTANA IMPRINTS, 1865–1880. Chicago, 1937.
——   PIONEER PRINTING IN TEXAS. Austin, Tex., 1932.
McNeal, Thomas A.   WHEN KANSAS WAS YOUNG. New York, 1922.
Mack, Mona Effie   MARK TWAIN IN NEVADA. New York, 1947.
Mercer, Asa Shinn   THE BANDITTI OF THE PLAINS. Cheyenne, Wyo., 1894.
Miller, Joaquin   SONGS OF THE SIERRAS. London, 1871.
Miller, Joseph   ARIZONA, *The Last Frontier*. New York, 1956.
Morton, Julius Sterling and Watkins, Albert   HISTORY OF NEBRASKA FROM THE EARLIEST EXPLORATIONS OF THE TRANS-MISSISSIPPI REGION. Omaha, Neb., 1885.
Mott, Frank Luther   AMERICAN JOURNALISM. New York, 1962.
Mowry, Sylvester   ARIZONA AND SONORA. New York, 1864.
Mulford, Prentice   PRENTICE MULFORD'S STORY. New York, 1889.
Myers, John Myers   THE ALAMO. New York, 1948.
——   SAN FRANCISCO'S REIGN OF TERROR. Garden City, N.Y., 1966.
Nevada Historical Society   THE BACK NUMBER, Vol. 2, No. 3. Reno, Nev., 1959.
Nott, Henry Junius   NOVELETTES OF A TRAVELLER: or, *Odds and Ends from the Knapsack of Thomas Singularity, Journeyman Printer,* 2 vols. New York, 1834.
Nye, Edgar Watson   BALED HAY, A *Drier Book than Walt Whitman's Leaves o' Grass.* Chicago, 1884.
Older, Fremont   GROWING UP. San Francisco, 1931.
O'Meara, James   BRODERICK AND GWIN. San Francisco, 1931.
Perkin, Robert L.   THE FIRST HUNDRED YEARS. Garden City, N.Y., 1859.

Poston, Charles D. BUILDING A STATE IN APACHE LAND, Tempe, Ariz., 1963.

Powers, Alfred HISTORY OF OREGON LITERATURE. Portland, Ore., 1935.

Realf, Richard POEMS BY RICHARD REALF, POET, SOLDIER, WORKMAN. New York, 1898.

Rees, Richard R. THE ELEUSINIAN MYSTERIES, *a Drama Beginning with the Creation and Terminating with the Great Fire in London, A.D. 1666, and the Death of Sir Christopher Wren.* Leavenworth, Kan., 1873.

Rice, William B. THE LOS ANGELES STAR, *the Beginning of Journalism in Southern California.* Los Angeles, 1947.

Roby, Wentz ELEVEN WESTERN PRESSES. Los Gatos, Calif., 1961.

Rye, Edgar THE QUIRT AND THE SPUR. Chicago, 1909.

Schmitt, Jo Ann FIGHTING EDITORS. San Antonio, 1958.

Smith, Henry Nash MARK TWAIN OF THE ENTERPRISE. Berkeley, Calif., 1957.

Sorenson, Albert R. HISTORY OF OMAHA, *Or Walks and Talks among the Old Settlers.* Omaha, Neb., 1876.

Spell, Lota M. PIONEER PRINTER, *Samuel Bangs in Mexico and Texas.* Austin, Tex., 1963.

Strahorn, Robert E. THE HANDBOOK TO WYOMING AND GUIDE TO THE BLACK HILLS. Cheyenne, Wyo., 1877.

—— THE RESOURCES AND ATTRACTIONS OF IDAHO TERRITORY. Boise, Ida., 1881.

—— THE RESOURCES OF MONTANA. Helena, Mont., 1879.

—— TO THE ROCKIES AND BEYOND. Omaha, Neb., 1878.

—— WHERE ROLLS THE OREGON. Denver, 1882.

Stratton, Royal B. CAPTIVITY OF THE OATMAN GIRLS. San Francisco, 1857.

Streeter, Thomas W. BIBLIOGRAPHY OF TEXAS, 1795–1845, 5 vols. Cambridge, Mass., 1955.

Sweet, Alexander E. and Knox, J. Armoy SKETCHES FROM TEXAS SIFTINGS. New York, 1882.

—— THROUGH TEXAS ON A MEXICAN MUSTANG. London, 1884.

Taper, Bernard (Ed.) MARK TWAIN'S SAN FRANCISCO. New York, 1963.

Thompson, Slason THE LIFE OF EUGENE FIELD. New York, 1927.

Thornton, Jesse Quinn OREGON AND CALIFORNIA IN 1848. New York, 1849.

Turnbull, George S. THE HISTORY OF OREGON NEWSPAPERS. Portland, Ore., 1939.

Twain, Mark THE CELEBRATED JUMPING FROG OF CALAVERAS COUNTY AND OTHER SKETCHES. New York, 1867.

—— ROUGHING IT. Hartford, Conn., 1872.

—— SKETCHES OLD AND NEW. Hartford, Conn., 1875.

Twitchell, Ralph E. LEADING FACTS OF NEW MEXICO HISTORY, 5 vols. Cedar Rapids, Ia., 1912.

University of New Mexico Library A CHECK LIST OF NEW MEXICO NEWSPAPERS. Albuquerque, N.M., 1935.

Walker, Franklin D. SAN FRANCISCO'S LITERARY FRONTIER. New York, 1939.

—— A LITERARY HISTORY OF SOUTHERN CALIFORNIA. Berkeley, Calif., 1950.

Ware, Eugene F. RHYMES OF IRONQUILL. Topeka, Kan., 1885.

Webb, Charles Henry OUR FRIEND FROM VICTORIA. San Francisco, 1865.

Wharton, Julius E. HISTORY OF DENVER FROM ITS EARLIEST SETTLEMENT TO THE PRESENT TIME. Denver, 1866.

—— THE SUN GOD, an Indian Edda. Phoenix, Ariz., 1889.

Wilder, Daniel W. THE ANNALS OF KANSAS. Topeka, Kan., 1866.

Wright, H. Clay BURLESQUE STATESMANSHIP. Leavenworth, Kan., 1864.

Yellowbird (John Rollin Ridge) THE LIFE AND ADVENTURES OF JOAQUIN MURRIETA. San Francisco, 1854.

Young, John P. JOURNALISM IN CALIFORNIA. San Francisco, 1915.

INDEX

Adams, Enoch George, 134, 135
Adams, William L., 59, 60, 113–14, 142, 224
Alderson, Matt, 69, 70, 206, 238, 239, 240, 243; *Bozeman, a Guide to its places* . . . , 206
Allbright, Sam J., 67
Allen, James, 219
Ames, Judson, 81, 82, 137, 138
Anderson, Kirk, 105, 106
Anthony, Dan, 122
Arizona:
  Arizona Miner, Fort Whipple, 133
  Arizonian, Tubac, 117, 123
  Boomerang, Tombstone, 56, 145
  Citizen, Tucson, 85, 92, 114, 123
  Epitaph, Tombstone, 56, 71, 145
  Gazette, Phoenix, 10
  Journal-Miner, Prescott, 90
  Miner, Prescott, 65, 114, 123, 133, 137, 212
  News-Herald, Wickenburg, 76
  Prospector, Tombstone, 38, 62, 63, 65, 100
  Republican, Phoenix, 156
  Sentinel, Yuma, 45, 100
  Star, Tucson, 123, 124, 145
  Sun-Democrat, Flagstaff, 54, 55
Armstrong, Moses K., 144
Ashbridge, 22

Austin, Stephen, 22, 23, 24
Ayer's report, 51, 52, 53

Babbitt, Harry, 77, 78, 79, 81
Bagg, Stanley, 100
Baker, Joseph, 127, 128
Baker, William Mumford, 251, 252
Bangs, John Kendrick, 187
Bangs, Sam, 18, 19, 25, 27, 32, 39, 56, 68, 90, 129, 185
Barleycorn, John, 151
Barreiro, Antonio, 130
Barter, George Washington, 91
Baylor University, 106, 107
Beadle, John Hanson, 48, 49, 50, 51, 52, 55, 82, 101, 105
Bell, Horace, 212; *Reminiscences of a Ranger*, 212
Bennett, Addison, 61, 62, 64–65; *The Little Old Sod Shanty on the Claim*, 61, 64
Berry, William J., 45
Bierce, Ambrose, 88, 159, 182, 184, 218, 235, 252, 256
Bigelow, Horatio, 20, 21, 22
Biggers, Don, 4, 28, 56, 76
Blyman, Joseph, 121
Boomer Run, 58, 105
Borden, Gail, 127, 251, 252
Boyakin, Judson A., 45, 143
Bradley, J. H., 82
Brand, Charles W., 47
Brann, William Cowper, 88, 106, 107, 186, 187, 188
Brannan, D. M., 256

Brannan, Sam, 79, 113
Brook, Harry Ellington, 38, 58, 62, 65, 88
Brown, G. W., 115
Brown, John, 115
Brown and Son, 51
Browne, Charles Farrar, 43
Browne, John Ross, 157; *A Peep at Washoe*, 157; *Adventures in the Apache Country*, 157
Bullard, Henry Adams, 16, 18, 23
Bush, Asahel, 114, 142
Butler, Thomas (Long Tom), 189
Byers, William, 52, 97, 98, 206

California:
  Alta California, Eldorado, 80, 107, 182
  Argonaut, San Francisco, 184, 223
  Broad-Axe, Los Angeles, 112
  Bulletin, San Francisco, 35, 43
  Cactus, Los Angeles, 56
  California American, Sacramento, 119
  Californian, Monterey, 79, 131, 145
  Californian, San Francisco, 79, 80, 92, 113, 132, 145, 182, 190, 191
  California Star, San Francisco, 79, 80, 113, 131
  Call, San Francisco, 154, 180, 181
  Chronicle, San Francisco, 108, 181
  Chuck-Walla, Greenwater, 4, 84, 86, 174, 190
  Coso Mining News, Darwin, 70, 122
  Daily Mail, San Francisco, 74, 75, 76, 158, 159, 160, 161, 165, 168

Dramatic Chronicle, San Francisco, 181
Era (see *Golden Era*)
Evening Bulletin, San Francisco, 118, 119, 120
Examiner, San Francisco, 184
Expositor, Fresno, 44
Golden Era, San Francisco, 30, 44, 82, 154, 164, 167, 176, 177, 178, 179, 181, 182, 184
Green-Eyed Monster, Ivanpah, 29
Herald, Marysville, 216
Herald, San Diego, 82, 137, 138
Herald, San Francisco, 246
Independent, Los Angeles, 112
Irresistable, Los Angeles, 111
News, Los Angeles, 111
News, Panamint, 70, 122
News Letter, San Francisco, 45, 184, 252
Overland Monthly, San Francisco, 182, 183, 184, 208, 223, 224
Phoenix, Sacramento, 28, 35, 93, 109, 118, 119, 120, 121, 237
Pioneer, San Francisco, 175, 176
Plain Dealer, San Francisco, 120
Porcupine, Los Angeles, 212
Print, Calico, 68, 73
Republican, Los Angeles, 122
Signal, Ventura, 82
Standard, Bodie, 122
Star, Los Angeles, 5, 91, 112
Times, Los Angeles, 38, 62, 118, 119, 120
Tribune, Sacramento, 119, 149
Ubiquitous, Sacramento, 237
Union Democrat, Sonora, 42
Varieties, San Francisco, 120

California (cont'd)
Wasp, San Francisco, 38, 88, 184
Watch-Dog, Sacramento, 121
Yolo Democrat, Cacheville, 82
Casey, James, 118, 119
Casey, William, 118
Chatham, Jim, 109
Clarke, Matthew St. Clair, 12; Sketches and Eccentricities of Col. David Crockett . . . , 12
Clarke, Samuel, 209, 210; collections of poems, 209, 210
Clum, John, 56, 71, 145
Cochran, M. C., 99, 100
Cole, E. C., 141
Colorado:
Agriculturist and Stockman, Denver, 206
Cherry Creek Pioneer, Denver, 97, 98
Chieftain, Pueblo, 65, 68
Chronicle, Leadville, 34, 37, 56, 145, 150, 151
Daily Camera, Boulder, 89
Globe, Golden, 218
La Plata Miner, Silverton, 83
Miner, Central City, 3
News, Boulder, 4
Rocky Mountain News, Denver, 51, 70, 97, 98, 206
Solid Muldoon, Ouray, 9, 31, 91, 144, 189, 190, 247
Tribune, Denver, 81, 95, 154, 155, 156
Colton, Walter, 113, 131; Ship and Shore, 131
Cone, John P., 114
Cotton, Godwin B., 17, 18, 22, 23, 24, 32; Translation of the Laws, Orders . . . in Texas, 24

Cross, Edward Ephraim, 117
Curry, John R., 83

Daggett, Rollin M., 82, 162, 172, 176, 179, 243, 244, 246–47
Dakota Territory:
Dakota Republican, Vermillion, 54
Dakotian, Yankton, 144, 203
Democrat, Sioux Falls, 67, 68, 88, 108
Frontier Scout, Fort Rice, 133, 134, 138
Journal, Rapid City, 241
Pioneer, Black Hills, 62
Press, Yankton, 203
Times, Springfield, 53
Tribune, Bismarck, 211, 248
Union, Yankton, 144
Dalziel, Davison, 75, 76, 158, 160
Dana, Charles, 81
Daniels, Doc, 186, 187
Davis, Cad, 34, 56, 145, 150, 151, 153; Olden Times in Colorado, 151
Davis, Sam, 111, 121, 162, 184, 211, 218, 219, 243, 244
Day, Dave, 9, 31, 91, 144, 189, 190, 247
Delano, Alonzo, 218
Denver, James, 107
De Quille, Dan, pen name (William Wright), 162, 164, 166–70, 172, 173, 178, 179, 207, 219–20; Washoe Rambles, 167, 172, 178, 179; History of the Comstock Lode and Mines, 207
Derby, George Horatio, 137, 138, 219
De Wolfe, C. H., 204, 205
Dexter, Timothy, 27

Dickens, Charles, *Bleak House,* 30
Dimsdale, Thomas, 27, 207; *The Vigilantes of Montana,* 207
Donaldson, Thomas, 105, 143, 189; *Idaho's Yesterdays,* 105
Doten, Alf, 32, 52, 64, 75, 80, 99, 109, 163
Drury, Wells, 80, 109, 121, 163, 165; *An Editor of the Comstock,* 32
Dryer, Thomas J., 113
Dunbar, Oscar, 152

Eckert, T. W., 85
Edmonds, A. C., 219
Estell, James Madison, 119
Ewer, Ferdinand, 175–76, 219

Field, Eugene, 80–81, 95, 153, 154, 155, 156, 185, 200, 201, 234, 250; and Wickersham, 154, 155, 156; *Dutch Lullaby,* 156; *The Clink of the Ice,* 156
Fitch, Tom, 116, 163, 180
Fleming, John, 77, 79
Foard, J. Macdonough, 82, 176, 177, 179
Forbes, William J. "Semblens," 3, 4, 36, 42, 55, 63, 93, 163, 169, 198, 199
Frazee, Willmont, 29
Freeman, Legh, 40–41, 86, 102, 103, 104, 121, 132, 200
French, Parker H., 246

Gadsden Purchase, 14, 96
Gally, James, 184, 223
George, Henry, 182, 224, 225
Gilbert, Edward, 107, 108
Gillis, Steve, 172, 173, 243
Glasscock, Carl B., 4, 86
Goodman, Joe, 109, 116, 162–63,
164, 165, 167, 168, 169, 172, 180, 182, 193, 221, 243, 244, 246, 253
Goodwin, Charles C., 162
Gossage, Joseph B., 241, 242, 243
Graham, Jerry B., 59
Greeley, Horace, 8, 9
Gutenberg, 6, 7
Guttierez de Lara, 16, 17, 18, 19, 21

Hale, Henry, 123
Hale, Thomas, 123
Hall, Dick Wick, 76
Hall, Frank, 68
Harcourt, Herbert S., 122
Harnell, John, 106
Harris, C. N., 65, 121
Harris, Eli, 20, 21
Harris, J. L., 33
Harris, Thomas S., 70, 122
Harrison, Elias T. L., 175
Hart, Fred, 26, 29, 99, 162, 227
Harte, Bret, 181, 182, 183, 184, 218, 221, 228, 234; *The Luck of Roaring Camp,* 183; *Plain Language from Truthful James,* 183
Henry, Francis, 230, 231, 232, 255
Heslep, Augustus, 120, 121
Hey. *See* Hosmer
Hopkins, Ernest J., 159
Hosmer, Hezekiah L., 89
Howe, Edgar Watson, 218, 224
Huntley, Stanley, 248
Hyland, John P., 39

Idaho:
Statesman, Boise, 45, 63, 105, 143, 189
Vindicator, New Bogy, 53
Inman, Herman, 212; *The Great Salt Lake Trail,* 212

Ironquill, pen name. *See* Ware, E. F.
Irving, Washington, *History of New York,* 11, 12

James, Alfred, 163, 164
Jennings, Al, 249, 250
Jernegan, William, 82, 163, 164
Job work, 58–59
Johnson, Joseph Ellis (Joe), 28, 31, 56, 60, 61, 66, 67, 206, 247; *The Farmer's Oracle,* 28
Johnston, Albert Sidney, 105
Jones, Elbert, 113
Jones, Grant, 77
Jones, Orlando E., 55
Jordan, Aristotle, 144–45
Joyce, John A., 150, 151

Kalloch, Rev. Isaac S., 108
Kansas:
  Barber County Mail, Medicine Lodge, 99, 100
  Call, Pearlette, 62, 64, 140
  Chieftain, Garfield County, 140
  Citizen, Stafford, 83
  Conservative, Leavenworth, 122, 142
  Cresset, Medicine Lodge, 99
  Daily Republican, Short Creek, 109
  Enterprise, Larned, 212
  Enterprise, Maryville, 114
  Globe, Atchison, 218
  Grasshopper, Grasshopper Falls, 52
  Herald, Leavenworth, 122
  Herald of Freedom, 115
  Independent, Oskaloosa, 100, 101
  Ingalls Messenger, 114
  Iowa Point, 113
  Jacksonian, Cimarron, 114

  Journal, Leavenworth, 204
  Kansas Chief, White Cloud, 112, 113, 143
  Kansas Spirit, Lawrence, 108
  Mercury, Kingman, 85
  Monitor, Fort Scott, 234
  Nemeha Courier, Seneca, 114
  New Republic, Bunker Hill, 52
  Thomas County Cat, Colby, 66
  Times, Leavenworth, 142
  Traveler, Arkansas City, 85
  Weekly Herald, Leavenworth, 59, 60, 64
  Western News, Marion, 54
Kerr, Theodore L., 83
King, Henry, 59
King, James, 118, 119, 120
King, Tom, 118, 119, 120
Knox, John Armoy, 185
Kunze, Curt E., 4, 86

Laird, James, 172, 173
Lanier, Sidney, 235
Laughlin, W. A., 62
Lawrence, Joseph, 181
Longstreet, Augustus Baldwin, 12; *Georgia Scenes,* 12
Lounsberry, Clement, 211
Lynch, Philip, 193, 194, 196, 197

McCarthy, Denis, 163, 164, 165, 243, 244
McClane, Hiram H., 222
McCormick, Richard, 114, 132, 133, 145
McDonald, A. C., 123
McDonald, Mark, 74, 75
McEwen, Arthur, 74, 75, 76, 159, 160, 161, 163, 165, 173, 256
McGowan, Ned, 28, 35, 93, 107, 109, 119, 120, 121, 147, 148, 149, 225
McGuiness, William, 53
MacLaren, John, 19

McNeal, Tom, 99; *When Kansas Was Young*, 99
Marion, John H., 65, 114, 123, 212; *Arizona Miner*, 212; *Notes of Travel through Arizona*, 212
Marriott, Fred, 45, 252
Marshall, James, 79
Martin, J. S., 85, 90; *The Song of a Cowboy*, 90
Maryland:
Baltimore, *Nile's Weekly Register*, 20
Texas declaration of independence, part of, 20
Massachusetts:
Boston, *Atlantic Monthly*, 184
Mercer, Asa Shinn, 207, 246; *The Banditti of the Plains*, 207
Mercer, J. K., 123
Mergenthaler, Ottmar, 253, 254
Merrick, A. W. (Jack), 62, 97, 98
Mickle, Edward, 185, 186
Mickle, Harvey, 185, 186
Mier, Father J. S. T. de, 18
Miller, C. H., 28–29, 190
Miller, Joaquin, 234, 235
Miller, Sol, 112, 113, 143
Mina, Francisco Xavier, 18, 19, 20, 25
Minor, C. L., 100
Montana:
Atlantis, Glendale, 40, 41, 86, 200
Avant Courier, Bozeman, 206
Chronicle, Bozeman, 44
Daily Miner, Butte, 206
Miner, Butte, 69, 238, 239
Missoulian, Missoula, 53
Mountaineer, Missoula, 33
Post, Virginia City, 27, 207
Union-Freeman, Butte, 102

Weekly Republican, Virginia City, 89, 139
Moore, J. H., 53
"Morning Bath, The," 91, 92
Morton, Julius Sterling, 211
Mowbray, Melton, 191
Mower, Aaron, 15, 17, 18, 23, 222
Mowry, Sylvester, 117; *Arizona and Sonora*, 117
Mulford, Prentice, 181, 182, 183, 221, 224

Nebraska:
Arrow, Omaha, 60, 61, 247
Bee, Omaha, 206
Bugle, Council Bluffs, 61
Frontier Index, Fort Kearney, 102, 103, 104, 121, 132
Huntsman's Echo, Wood River, 28, 31, 56, 66, 67
News, Nebraska City, 211
Republican, Broken Bow, 55
Nesmith, James N., 115, 116
Nevada:
Appeal, Carson City, 111, 121
Big Bonanza, Virginia City, 164
Crescent, Reno, 78
Daily News, Gold Hill, 32, 33, 52, 75, 80, 109, 165, 193
Daily Times, Carson City, 70–71
Daily Trespass, Virginia City, 3
Daily Union, Virginia City, 55, 172
Evening Bulletin, Virginia City, 43
Humboldt Register, Unionville, 36, 42, 63, 93, 169, 198
Index, Carson City, 65, 121
Mangler, Wabuska, 111
News (see *Daily News*)
Oasis, Hawthorne, 55

Nevada (cont'd)
 Occidental, Virginia City, 180
 Reese River Reveille, Austin,
  26, 99
 Scorpion, Virginia City, 163
 Sentinel, Como, 39, 63–64
 Star, Aurora, 56
 Territorial Enterprise, Virginia
  City, 43, 52, 77, 78, 82, 99,
  109, 116, 163, 164, 165,
  166, 167, 168, 172, 180, 182,
  193, 194, 220, 221, 223,
  227, 228, 243, 244, 245,
  253
 Times, Bristol, 256
New Mexico:
 Amigo del Paiz, Albuquerque,
  96, 97
 El Crepusculo de la Libertad,
  Santa Fé, 13, 129
 Gazette, Las Vegas, 53
 Gleam, Gallup, 41
 News, Cimarron, 130
 Republican Review, Albuquer-
  que, 53
 Weekly Shaft, Rincón, 39
Newsboy's percentage, 69–70
New York:
 Harper's, 209
 Hearst, 75
 Sun, 74, 81
Niles, Edward, 70
Nott, Henry J., 5–6, 12; Novel-
  ettes of a Traveller: or Odds
  and Ends . . . , 5–6, 12
Nye, Bill, 28, 56, 57, 145, 185,
  187, 197, 249

Older, Fremont, 77, 78, 79, 159,
  160, 161
Oklahoma:
 Getup, Guthrie, 58
 Territorial Advocate, Beaver
  City, 145–46

War Chief, 104
O'Meara, James, 56
Oregon:
 Argus, Portland, 114
 Bee, Portland, 123
 Budget, Astoria, 151, 152
 Columbian, St. Helena, 134
 Democrat, Albany, 190, 235
 Gazette, Corvallis, 151
 Guard, Roseburg, 123
 Heppner Gazette, 38
 Journal, Canyon City, 26, 29,
  32
 Oregonian, Portland, 52, 113,
  142, 209
 Plaindealer, Roseburg, 123
 Register, Eugene City, 29, 190
 Spectator, Oregon City, 39, 72,
  73, 77, 79, 115
 Statesman, Salem, 114, 142,
  209
 Telegram, Portland, 123
Osborn, William J., 59, 60
Overshiner, John, 68, 73–74, 93

Paddock, Lucius C., 89
Paige, James W., 253, 254; type-
  setting machine, 254
Payne, David L., 104
Pennsylvania:
 North American, Philadelphia,
  131
 Public Ledger, Philadelphia,
  160
Perkins, Charles L., 63
Piracy, 30
Poe, The Haunted Palace, 27
Pollock, Edward A., 234
Poore, L. D. F., 53
Porter, William Trotter (Will),
  12, 40, 88, 144, 186, 187,
  199, 249, 250; The Big Bear
  of Arkansas, 12; Spirit of the

Porter, Will (cont'd)
    Times, 12; Plunkville Pa-
    triot (fictive), 144, 145
Post, Sam, 121
Poston, Charles D., 123, 124, 145,
    156, 157, 158, 208, 247;
    Building a State in Apache
    Land, 208
Poynter, J. R., 217

Ramage presses, 7, 8, 15, 16, 17,
    32, 130
Realf, Richard, 115
Redington, John W., 38
Rees, Richard R., 229, 230
Reitze, J. K., 42
Reynolds, James, 63, 143
Richards, Willard, 27
Ridge, John Rollin, pseudonym
    Yellowbird, 217, 218, 219,
    220, 221
Roberts, John, 100, 101
Roman, Anton, 182
Rust, Richard, 219
Rye, Edgar, 56, 89, 90; The
    Quirt and the Spur, 89

Satterlee, J. C., 122, 123
Schiffgen, M., 114
Semple, Robert, 79, 113, 131,
    145
Shaler, William, 16, 17, 18
Simpson, Sam, 151, 152, 153,
    235, 236, 243
Slack, E. A., 10
Smith, Mortimer J., 121
Sorenson, Albert R., 206, 207;
    Early History of Omaha,
    206
Stoddard, Charles Warren, 181,
    182, 221, 224, 234
Strahorn, Robert E., 206; The
    Resources of Montana Ter-
    ritory, 206; The Resources

    and Attractions of Idaho
    Territory, 206; To the
    Rockies and Beyond, 206;
    Where Rolls the Oregon,
    206
Stratton, Royal, 207; The Captiv-
    ity of the Oatman Girls,
    207
Streeter, Thomas W., 217
Sullivan, Jeremiah, 225
Sweet, Alexander E., 185

Tennessee:
    Clarion, Nashville, 20, 21
Texas:
    Banner, Brownwood, 185
    Billy Goat, Always Buttin' In,
        Rotan, 4, 76
    County Banner, Brownwood,
        33
    Courier, Ashbridge, 22
    El Mexicano, Natchitoches, 17,
        20
    Express, San Antonio, 51, 185
    Gaceta de Texas, Nacogdo-
        ches, 17, 20
    Galvestonian, Galveston, 25
    Gazette, Corpus Christi, 129
    Iconoclast, Waco, 88, 106, 107,
        186, 187, 188
    Josher, Colorado City, 28
    Mexican Advocate, Nacogdo-
        ches, 22
    Musquito, Houston, 27, 32, 39,
        41, 68, 90, 129
    New Era, Rockport, 89
    News, Albany, 56, 89
    News, Galveston, 185
    News Beacon, Beaumont, 52
    Our Bohemia, Fort Worth, 175
    Post, Houston, 199, 249
    Radiator, Graham, 89
    Rolling Stone, Austin, 40, 88,
        144, 186, 187, 199, 249

Texas (cont'd)
Sentinel, Brady, 35
Siftings, Austin, 185
Sunny South, Brownwood, 185, 186
Telegraph, San Felipe de Austin, 127, 128, 129, 251
Texas Gazette, San Felipe de Austin, 22, 24, 32
Texas Register, San Felipe de Austin, 127, 128, 251
Texas Republican, Nacogdoches, 20, 22
West Texas Republican, Blanco City, 53
Thomas, Alfred, 3
Thompson, Slason, 154, 155
Thompson, William, 123
Thornton, Jesse Quinn, 115, 116
Toledo y Dubois, José Alvarez de, 15, 16, 17, 18, 19, 21, 23
Train, George Francis and William Bennett, 212–15, 228
Trippet, Eugene J., 256
Tullidge, Edward Wheelock, 175
T'Vault, W. G., 39
Twain, Mark, 36, 92, 93, 116, 162, 166, 169, 170, 171, 172, 173, 180, 181, 190, 191, 193, 194, 218, 219, 220, 221, 243, 253, 254; Massacre in the Giant Forest . . . , 169; Roughing It, 180; The Celebrated Jumping Frog . . . , 182

Utah:
Deseret News, Salt Lake City, 27, 54, 68, 69, 73, 105
Freeman, Ogden, 121
Peep o'Day, Salt Lake City, 175
Reporter, Little Corinne, 48, 49, 50, 51, 52, 55, 101

Telegraph, Salt Lake City, 102
Tribune, Salt Lake City, 103, 104
Valley Tan, Salt Lake City, 105, 106

Vigilance Committee, 118, 119, 120, 121, 237, 238
Vigilante gang, 35
Villon, François, 250–51
Vitus, E. Clampus, 139

Waite, Edwin, 219
Walker, William, 246
Wall, Sam H., 122
Walton, William N., 82, 137
Ward, Artemus, 162
Ware, Eugene F. (Ironquill), 234
Washington:
Dispatch, Seattle, 51
Evening Telegraph, Tacoma, 122
Journal, Blain, 68
Leader, Molson, 54
News, Tacoma, 122
Register, Vancouver, 134
Standard, Olympia, 231
Washington Irving. See Irving
Washington presses, 10, 32
Wasson, John, 85, 92, 114, 123
Webb, Charles H., 181, 182, 220, 221; John Paul's Book, 181
Weightman, Richard, 96, 97
Wells Fargo Express ride, 212–15, 228
Weston, H. L., 39
Wharton, Junius, 4, 5, 206, 210, 211, 241; History of the City of Denver . . . , 206; The Sun God, An Indian Edda, 210–11
Wheeler, Simon, 191, 193
Whitehead, Charles, 122

Whitmore, J. A., 123, 124
Wilbarger, John Wesley, 207;
    Indian Depredations in Texas, 207
Williams, Jonathan, 164
Williamson, Robert, 23
Wollard, I. B., 164
Wright, H. Clay, 142
Wright, William. *See* De Quille, Dan
Wyoming:
    Boomerang, Laramie, 28, 145, 197, 249
    Doublejack, Dillon, 77

Independent, Laramie, 10
Leader, Cheyenne, 51
Northwest Livestock Journal, Cheyenne, 207
Sentinel, Laramie, 57
Sun, Cheyenne, 121
Sun, Laramie, 47
Wyoming Morning News, 57

Yellowbird. *See* Ridge, John Rollin
Young, Charles de, 108, 181
Young, Michel de, 181

Date Due